1096

A GASCON ROYALIST
IN REVOLUTIONARY PARIS

Claude Bazire
1764–1794.

A GASCON ROYALIST IN REVOLUTIONARY PARIS

THE BARON DE BATZ
1792—1795

FROM THE FRENCH OF

G. LENÔTRE

BY

MRS. RODOLPH STAWELL

ILLUSTRATED

London: WILLIAM HEINEMANN
New York: DODD MEAD AND COMPANY
1910

TO MY FATHER

A TRIBUTE OF RESPECT, GRATITUDE AND AFFECTION

PREFACE

"THERE are two kinds of history," said Balzac : "the official, lying kind that is usually taught, history *ad usum Delphini;* and the secret kind, wherein we must look for the true causes of events—the history of shameful things . . . ."

The portentous political struggle that staggered the world in 1793 and 1794 has furnished materials for a host of writers ; but for every honest reader it none the less remains inexplicable. It is still incomprehensible that all these men of the Revolution, who were born into the political world on the same day, and won their reputations side by side, and were closely united in opinion and interests, and had no chance of keeping their feet on the heap of ruins they had made, save by holding each other's hands tightly and leaning one upon the other—it is incomprehensible, I say, that these men should have suddenly, as though in the grip of some mad hallucination, begun to hate and suspect and denounce and kill one another, and should have gone to the scaffold with a degree of resignation that amounted to fatalism. They all disappeared in less than a year.

PREFACE

And no sooner was the struggle over than the historians set to work. From the common trench wherein all the great dead are sleeping each historian chooses out his favourite hero : digs him up and washes him, perfumes him, paints him, embalms him, presents him, wrapped in a flag, to the party politicians. The crowd applauds and expresses itself satisfied : but the less credulous, who can hardly recognise in these cold mummies the fiery passionate warriors of the Revolution, turn away from them, and say : " These are not they ; they were not made like this, all in one piece ; they had passions, and moments of anger, and weaknesses ; the lives of these men, during the most terrible crisis that ever racked humanity, could not have been so uniform, and regular, and reasonable : if they had a goal before them they rushed to it across a thousand obstacles, through a thousand dangers and intrigues. This story, we are told, is not their story : *there is something more.*"

All the men who played an active part in the Revolution, whether royalists or Jacobins, deserved something better than panegyric or detraction. Some day the historians will make up their minds to exclude politics from their writings ; to depict historical characters amid their proper surroundings, instead of isolating them on pedestals, above all the passions and prejudices and ferments of their day ; and to show them, side by side with the minor actors whose enthusiasms they reflected, whose hostility they feared, and whose weaknesses they humoured. When that day dawns, the writers of history will recognise that they should put away preconceived ideas before giving

PREFACE

a verdict ; that they should not use documents for the
purpose of scoring a point, accepting those they like and
rejecting those that are inconvenient ; but should accept
them all or consult none.

Then, instead of setting up a series of impassive statues
to be admired by posterity, the history of the Revolution
will show us that seething mass of humanity, that medley
of conflicting interests, that outburst of vital energy, that
fierce eruption of passions that constituted the sphere of
action of all those vague, aimless, unpractical bourgeois
from the provinces, and phrase-making lawyers, and unfrocked monks who played the leading parts. They were
all so new to political life that they soon became, in the
hurricane that tossed them hither and thither, of no more
account than so many puppets, whose wild, unconscious
movements are controlled by a mysterious hand, hidden
among the shadows.

Was it the Baron de Batz who held the threads of this
immense intrigue ?

If we may believe his contemporaries he was the hidden
impresario of the Revolution, the cause of every discord.
Those who succumbed in the fray invariably attributed
their downfall to the elusive leader of a vague conspiracy.
And, indeed, one has only to glance through the *Moniteurs*
of the dates between October, 1793, and July, 1794, to
see how large a place was filled, in the thoughts of the
political leaders, by this *Foreign Conspiracy*. To it was
attributed the failure of all the reforms that had been
made, and the inexplicable postponement of universal
happiness : it was made the reason for every act of perse-

ix

PREFACE

cution, and the pretext of every massacre. Élie Lacoste,
in his report of the 26th Prairial, clearly pointed to
de Batz as the enemy in whom all the forces of the reaction
were concentrated: "All the levers destined for the overthrow of the Republic," he said, "*were moved by this one
man*, who was prompted by the allied tyrants." Moreover,
the Assembly was unanimous on the subject: it was the
Foreign Conspiracy, the gold of Pitt and Coburg—the
Baron de Batz, in a word—that it blamed for all the dis-
turbances of the various factions: Chabot's, Danton's,
Hébert's, Ronsin's, Chaumette's, and the rest.

How can we account for the ignorance that prevails
with regard to this man, whom his contemporaries
believed to be so powerful? Nothing is known of the
Baron de Batz: his history occupies a few lines in the
biographical dictionaries: his *dossier* in the Archives tells
us no more. Would he be so entirely forgotten if he had
really held the fate of France in his hands throughout the
Terror, and had moulded events at his will? With whom
does the mistake lie? With his contemporaries, who
regarded him as the pivot of the whole Revolution, or
with posterity, who hitherto have been unaware that he
ever lived?

These are the questions that this book will try to
answer. We shall not attempt to deny that there is a
certain rashness in exhuming a man whose name has been
forgotten—or, rather, never known—and putting him forward as the chief actor in this drama, the story of which
has been so often told without one reference to him.
Immensely forcible deductions and arguments would be

PREFACE

needed to support a paradox of this kind. The reader who is good enough to follow our story will soon see that our ambition does not lie in this direction. We have made no deductions—we have put forward no arguments— we have merely brought together certain documents, which are none the less authentic for having hitherto been neglected. We will walk warily through the obscure story of the Baron de Batz, accepting no light to guide our steps save the light of authenticated fact. When this fails us we will not be ashamed to confess our uncertainty, since we have here no thesis to maintain. Our only motives are an ardent longing to know the truth, and a passionate desire to depict, as graphically as we may, the days of ceaseless agony and romantic intrigue that Paris lived through while the Convention reigned.

G. L.

CONTENTS

LIST OF ILLUSTRATIONS

xv

I

JEAN DE BATZ

WHEN Louis XVI, as he was hurried to his death, uttered his last memorable words : " I pray that my blood may not bring a judgment upon France ! " the Abbé Edgeworth de Firmont fell on his knees, half-dead with anguish, on the topmost step of the scaffold.

His strength had failed him ; and, flinging himself down, he sought to lose himself in prayer. When he raised his eyes he saw that the king was being bound to the plank : it sprang into place and the wooden collar descended : the victim once more raised his head and turned his eyes towards the priest. The huge steel triangle fell.

The youngest of the executioners[1] thrust his hand into the basket and seized the royal head by the hair. Then, holding it out at arm's length, he carried it round the scaffold and showed it to the people, while the platform streamed with blood. The Abbé would have been covered

---

[1] "He did not seem to be more than eighteen years of age : he walked all round the scaffold holding the head : he accompanied this monstrous ceremony with the most atrocious yells and the most unseemly gestures. A most melancholy silence reigned at first ; but soon there arose a few shouts of : *Vive la République !* Gradually more and more voices were raised, and in less than ten minutes this was the cry of the whole crowd, who repeated it a thousand times over, while every hat was in the air."—*Memoirs of the Abbé Edgeworth de Firmont.*

B

with it if he had not instinctively started back in horror a
the man drew near.

Some historians have described the mob's mad rush upon
the scaffold : others have followed the cart that carried the
body of the murdered king to the cemetery of the
Madeleine. We, however, will follow the agitated,
terrified priest who vanished in the crowd. The people,
closely packed as they were, instinctively made way for
him.[1]

Leaving the Place de la Révolution the Abbé de
Firmont crossed the bridge, plunged into the deserted
streets on the left bank of the river, and walked on at
random, without aim or object. At the end of an hour,
however, he recovered his self-control, and made his way to
the house of M. de Malesherbes, who on the previous day
had offered to give him shelter if a rising of the people,
such as was hoped for to the last, should prevent the royal
carriage from reaching the scaffold.

At the Hôtel Malesherbes the Abbé Firmont met, not
only the King's brave counsel himself, but also Louis
Bossuet, a young man who was entirely devoted to the
royal cause, and a boy of fifteen called Charles de
Lézardière. The priest, reducing his thoughts to order as
best he could, recounted the events of the morning ; and
then, since the horror of what he had seen made him shrink
from going home to sit alone with his tragic memories,
Charles suggested that they should go to the village of
Choisy, where his parents lived. The Abbé accepted the
offer,[2] and set off at about two o'clock in the afternoon

[1] " I was merely wearing a shabby overcoat, and was soon lost in
the immense crowd."—*Memoirs of the Abbé Edgeworth de Firmont.*

[2] The Abbé Edgeworth's first intention had been to return to
England as soon as his mission was over ; but during the night before
the execution the King had given him " some secret orders of great
importance," which obliged the Abbé to remain in France. The

accompanied by Louis Bossuet and Charles. The three took the Choisy road on foot, and arrived at their destination at nightfall.

There, in a house that stood a little apart from the rest, lived the family of Lézardière, which consisted of Baron Robert, his wife, and their three surviving sons. The eldest, a deacon at the Seminary of Saint-Sulpice, had been killed in the massacre at the Carmelite Monastery, in September, 1792.[1]

When the troubles first began in the West the Lézardières had been disturbed and threatened by the patriots, and even imprisoned for a few days.

They therefore left their château near La Roche sur Yon and settled in the suburbs of Paris, where they foresaw that their devotion might be more useful than in the country. They lived at Choisy under the bourgeois name of Robert. Jacques, the eldest, and Sylvestre, the second of the surviving sons, had helped to defend the Palace of the Tuileries when it was attacked by the people on the 10th August ; and the youngest, Charles, notwithstanding his youth, had enrolled himself in a little band of faithful adherents who had been holding themselves in readiness for anything that might occur, ever since the royal family had been imprisoned in the Temple. He was gifted with immense vitality, and being extremely quick and alert was useful as an agent to the royalists concealed in Paris.

safety of the Queen and her children was evidently concerned ; and this explains why the Abbé at once communicated with the Baron de Lézardière, one of the most active and devoted of the resolute royalists who had vowed to rescue the prisoners of the Temple.

[1] These are the names of Lézardière's four sons : 1. Jacques Augustin, priest, killed at the Carmes ; 2. Jacques Paul Toussaint ; 3. Sylvestre Joachim ; 4. Charles Eutrope Athanase Benjamin. The reader is referred to M. Chassin's chapter on the history of this family, during and after the Revolution, in his remarkable work : *La Préparation de la Guerre de Vendée.*

He made a practice of stealing into the various clubs, and was often to be seen in the public seats during the sittings of the Convention. It was through him that Malesherbes learnt, as soon as the voting was over, that the Assembly had granted to Louis XVI the right of choosing his own counsel; and the great lawyer was thus enabled, that very evening, to write his famous letter to the Convention, begging for the honourable task of defending the King whom he had served as a minister. And it was this same lad who, in obedience to a note that the King contrived to send him, discovered the Abbé de Firmont's retreat in the Rue du Bac, and made the arrangements for the last interview between the priest and the condemned man.[1]

Through all the hours of that 21st of January the Baronne de Lézardière, who had been an invalid ever since she lost her son in the massacre at the Carmelite monastery, was waiting alone, in a state of anxiety that can easily be imagined, for news from Paris. Her three sons and her husband had left her on the previous day, in the hope of taking part in the King's rescue; and the poor woman had been suffering tortures throughout the night.

At about five o'clock in the evening the Baron de Lézardière entered his wife's room with the Abbé de Firmont. There was no need for her to ask questions: her husband's sobs and the scared expression that was still on the face of the priest told her that the drama was ended. She was an ardent royalist, and this overwhelming blow was more than she could bear. She died.

She died on the 21st January, towards evening; and the priest who ministered to her was the same who, that very morning, had sustained and fortified the courage of

---

[1] *Biographie Vendéene*, by C. Mesland. Charles de Lézardière was assisted in this dangerous mission by a young man called Isidore Langlais. See the *Mémoires du Baron Hyde de Neuville.*

the King. She died of the agony she had suffered during the absence of those she loved, while she waited through the long hours, haunted by her memories of September, and expecting to hear at any moment that Paris was a prey to fire and sword, and that the last faithful royalists had been slaughtered.

For on one point their opinion was unanimous : an effort must be made to save the King. To attempt to tear the victim from the hands of his executioners might well seem a wild idea. None the less there was a man who conceived it; a man who, almost unaided, set this mad scheme on foot. This man was the Baron de Batz.

As soon as the hour of the execution was fixed he sent secret instructions to five hundred devoted royalists,[1] of whose names he had long had a list, to meet on the following day at a certain point of the King's route, and to provide themselves, at all risks, with weapons that could easily be hidden. The place of meeting was to be the corner of the Rue de la Lune, at the point where the Boulevard Bonne-Nouvelle, which had not yet been levelled, formed a considerable rise in the road.

We may still see, at this spot, the narrow, crooked corner-house at which the conspirators arranged to meet.

What did the Baron de Batz intend to do? To break through the line of troops, make a rush at the King's carriage, and disperse the escort of gendarmes? The folly of such an idea is incredible. And even supposing that it had been successfully carried out, what could he have done *afterwards?* By what means did he imagine he could contend with the hundred and thirty thousand men who guarded the town? Had he made arrangements for the

---

[1] "Four or five hundred young men," say the *Mémoires du Comte d'Allonville.* "A numerous band of devoted youths and men," says the Baron Hyde de Neuville.

King's flight into the country? Had he posted relays of horses on any of the roads? Did he hope that at the mere sight of his heroic attempt Paris would rise and suddenly take the part of the condemned man? Upon what chance, what unforeseen circumstance, what miracle did he rely?

All this is still a mystery: but it is quite evident that, since he made the adventurous attempt, he supposed it might possibly succeed. Taking his impetuous character into account we cannot doubt that he was quite prepared to sacrifice his own life, and those of his five hundred confederates: but that he would have risked the chance of the King being killed on the public road in the midst of riot and bloodshed is quite inconceivable.

The very fact that the scheme was wild beyond belief proves that the conspirators were sure of some powerful support.

It has been said—but the story cannot be verified—that the Baron de Lézardière, a few days earlier, had visited Dumouriez, who was then in Paris, and had received from him a solemn pledge that he would oppose, with all the strength of his great popularity, the execution of Louis XVI.[1] Unfortunately Dumouriez was "a man of *successive opinions.*" Hardly had the Baron de Lézardière left him before he started off into the country, and thus doomed to failure any attempt at a rising.

Be this as it may, de Batz passed the night of the 20th January in the feverish agitation of his final arrangements. He was assisted by two secretaries, two friends whose devotion was to the death: of whom one was Jean Louis Michel Devaux, a clerk in the National Treasury, while the other hid his name and style of Marquis de la Guiche under the pseudonym of Sévignon.

By seven o'clock on the morning of the 21st January de

[1] *Mémoires secrets du Comte d' Allonville.*

6

Batz was at his post. Devaux and la Guiche, in their haste to join him, had slipped through the line of troops that bordered the pavement, and had crossed the road, in spite of the positive orders to the contrary published by the Commune on the previous day. From the elevated post that he had taken up the adventurous conspirator anxiously scanned the throng that surged round him; and great was his dismay when he failed to detect, among the thousands of restless heads before him, a single friendly face. Every time that there was a movement in the crowd he thought a band of his fellow-conspirators must have arrived; and this hope, though quickly crushed, sprang into life again whenever the smallest incident occurred. For he did not know—how should he?—that at three o'clock that morning the greater number of his confederates had been awakened by the sound of knocking on their doors. To each man two gendarmes had appeared, with orders to keep him in sight, and prevent him by every possible means from leaving the house before mid-day.

The Baron de Batz, who had not spent the night at home, had escaped this untimely visitation. He did not know, therefore, why his friends were absent at the critical moment, and in his agitation cursed their cowardice, doubted their fidelity, and yielded to despair. When the time for action drew near he could see no more than four or five of the conspirators scattered among the crowd. And already, from the distant Temple, came the sinister sound of the beating of drums; while a kind of shivering sigh passed through the crowd—not the sigh of satisfied impatience to which people give vent when they are tired of waiting for a long-desired sight, but rather a suppressed murmur, a prolonged wail. Every head was turned, every eye was fixed upon the spot where the sad procession was about to appear.

7

A GASCON ROYALIST

The tall figures of the National Gendarmerie were the first to become visible through the fog—motionless figures on restless, impatient little horses—riding slowly by in well-ordered lines, filling the whole roadway with their ranks. Next to them came, in serried columns, the grenadiers of the National Guard, marching heavily in measured steps, with their white belts crossed upon their breasts, their three-cornered hats and horse-hair plumes, and their great pouches hanging beside them. They were followed by the artillery : the guns were dragged past, two and two, upon the shaking, jolting waggons, with a noise that sounded sinister amid the far-spreading solemn silence of the mute crowd. Then came the drums that heralded the carriage ; and finally the carriage itself, surrounded by soldiers, moved slowly on with its windows closed and clouded with moisture—impenetrable by curious eyes.

"Here, friends, here !—all who wish to save their King ! "

These words rang out in a resonant voice. Stirred by an instinct of terror the crowd opened, and the Baron de Batz was seen making desperate efforts to break through the line of soldiers that guarded the road. He flung up his arms, and waved his hat, as he cried :

" *À nous ! À nous !* Let us save the King ! "

All was over in a flash : there was a movement in the crowd ; the ranks of the people, dispersed for a moment, closed up again ; the line of troops was not even broken, and de Batz was seen with his arms still upraised as he disappeared—sinking in the tumult as a drowning man sinks in the sea. The carriage, whose progress this incident had not checked for a moment, went on its way to the inevitable end.[1]

---

[1] The Parisian populace, on the 21st January, was filled with such terror by the sight of the King being dragged to the scaffold that this

JEAN DE BATZ

It is said that two of the conspirators, at the summons of their leader, attempted to make a rush on the procession ; that they were instantly repulsed, and fled into

whole incident, which had more than ten thousand witnesses, seems to have passed unnoticed. We believe that not a single journal of the time alludes to it, a fact that has given rise to many denials of its authenticity. Dr. Robinet, in an interesting article on Danton (*L'Eclair* of February 26th, 1895) wrote : ". . . a vague, mysterious tradition that arose after the cataclysm of 1794, and emanated, after the reaction of Thermidor, from some unknown confessional : invented by the same people and from the same motives as all the other *tales concerning the rescue of the King on the 21st January, and of the Queen and Dauphin from the Temple, in August and September 1793, and other exploits no less fantastic*, of which the reactionaries and intriguers, clerics and laymen, had the sad and profitable monopoly for so many years, with the object of standing well at Court and swelling the lists of their services, of filling their journals and their pockets, and of winning the favour of fair ladies by covering all the great republican names with opprobrium and ridicule."

There is nothing, on the contrary, that is less *vague*, less *mysterious*, less *fantastic* than the bare fact of the attempt we have just described. If the details have never been known it is for the very reason that those who devoted themselves to this lost cause never thought of boasting of their heroism in order to *stand well at Court and fill their pockets*. If such inconvenient witnesses as Baron Hyde de Neuville and the Comte d'Allonville be disregarded, not to mention twenty others, it is impossible to refuse belief to official documents such as the examination of Devaux, who was with de Batz on the 21st January—which examination we quote in its entirety in Chapter VI. Was Devaux trying to *win the favour of fair ladies?* We think not, as his head was cut off immediately afterwards. Finally, there is one more document that removes all possible doubt, both of the terror that reigned that day and of the brave exploit of the Baron de Batz. This is an autograph memorandum by Sénar, the famous spy employed by the Committees. It was found among Eckard's papers and is now in the collection of M. Foulon de Vaulx.

"A FEW NOTES ON THE 21ST JANUARY. What I have been able to gather is that the Committees were informed that Paris was opposed to the King's death, that various movements were on foot, that the young men had risen, that there was talk of a party collecting near the Porte Saint Denis and above it, that the event would not take place quietly, that, to prevent any mishap by strong measures, it was decided to put the King in a carriage with firmly-closed doors, to have, inside

9

the Rue de la Lune, and being pursued by some soldiers were killed on the steps of the church of Nôtre Dame de Bonne Nouvelle, where they tried to take refuge but found the doors fastened. The story may be true;

the carriage, two or three men armed with muskets and bayonets, and round it a body of the most determined, on foot and horseback, with plenty of guns.

"Orders were issued for all the young men to proceed, according to their places of residence, to a certain spot, or a certain church, on pain of being regarded as conspirators and their fathers made responsible for them, and there was to be a call-over, and lists made of those who were present, or not, at the appointed place.

"There was an order for the men on duty to arm themselves with muskets or pikes and to be at the appointed spot before daylight; no one else was to be seen in the streets till after the execution; there were to be two lines of armed men reaching from the Temple to the Place de la Révolution, and no one was to cross the street between them on pain of being considered a conspirator.

"Once the men were at their posts they were to be absolutely silent and motionless. As soon as the carriage was seen in the distance the order *Eyes front!* was to be given to each corps forming the lines, so that the coming of the procession might not produce an unsteadiness favourable to a movement on the King's behalf. Four men, however, broke through several times, as we know, crying: '*À nous, Français:* shall we let the King be shamefully killed?' and other words of a like nature, and brandishing their swords. When they returned, calling their comrades to them, a horseman went to summon one of the troops that were in reserve at various distances, and it was seen hurrying towards the spot. No one made the least attempt to join the four, nor yet to stop them as they passed back through the line. Two of them were hacked to death as they tried to get into a house; the two others escaped. One of these, whose face was remembered by the *juré* Châtelet, was recognised by him and pointed out to Fouquier, who was ordered to send a report of his examination to the Committees. He was guillotined. The Baron de Batz, who instigated the whole attempt to save the King, and was the first to call out: '*Allons, allons!*' was not recognised at once. When he was known, and found to be inaccessible, he was outlawed, and a price put on his head. What prevented the success of the attempt was a rumour that the Committees had spies in all the ranks, that enormous rewards were offered to those who should denounce the conspirators, and that any movement would be punished by death. Everyone thought he would be arrested or killed by his neighbour if he moved. No one moved."

10

but the incident caused so little sensation that no eye-witness has recorded it.

As for de Batz, he vanished as completely as if the earth had opened beneath him.

Such is one of the rare exploits in which he is known to have taken part; the only one, indeed, of which we have any positive information to-day. He does not re-appear in history, in any active part, until three-and-a half years later, in the events of Vendémiaire, year IV. In the interval, however, we hear of him from time to time; we can guess at his connection with a thousand different matters; we know that he is plotting, that he is pursued, that he has a great number of confederates at his beck and call—but, as a matter of fact, we know nothing for certain of his life.

If we go to the National Record Office, and ask for the documents in the *dossier* of the Baron de Batz,[1] we shall find nothing; a few scraps covered with figures, two rather clever sketches, his tailor's bill and a bill for silk stockings; that is all. In the Archives of the War Office there is the same paucity of documents; but here a few extracts from promotion lists have been kept, and some memoranda dating from the restoration and containing the following passages:

"M. de Batz, until 1800, gave unceasing proofs of his attachment to the cause of the Bourbons. He was constantly employed in dangerous missions in France, but, though condemned to death and outlawed several times, he always had the good fortune and the ingenuity to escape."

And again: "He was the leader of Cortey's band, which nearly succeeded in rescuing the Queen and the royal family

[1] Series T, No. 699.

11

from the Temple ; on this account he was condemned to death, and outlawed, and a price was put upon his head. He originated the insurrection known as the Affair of the Parisian Sections ; he, with Chartier, led the principal column, which marched upon the Convention but forsook him when the first shot was fired : was again condemned to death ; escaped, though surrounded by gendarmes."[1]

What manner of man, we may ask, was this extraordinary individual who successfully evaded all the terrors of the pitiless laws of the Revolution ? By means of what talisman did he win his conquests over every obstacle ? What were these *dangerous missions*, and how did his actions influence the course of events ? These are the questions that we have tried to answer. We do not pretend that our work—carried on at first in utter darkness, and afterwards in an uncertain and fitful light—has completely illuminated the strange figure of the Baron de Batz. We have merely attempted, by putting together a number of facts that we have collected here and there, to supply the *dossier* that is lacking to our archives : we will leave it to others, more fortunate and more able than ourselves, to do the rest : we are content to have sketched the outline of the enterprising conspirator of whom, hitherto, so little has been known that it was possible for M. Édouard Fleury—to take but one example—in his otherwise accurate and well-authenticated *Histoire de Saint-Just*, to refer to him, without contradiction, as the *little German baron, de Batz*.

De Batz was by no means a German. He was born at Goutz[2] in 1761, and belonged to a noble and very ancient Gascon family.[3]

---

[1] Archives of the Ministry of War.

[2] Now in the department of the Landes.

[3] Here is his certificate of birth : "Dec. 6th, 1761, born at Goutz and baptised on the following day, Jean, legitimate son of Messire Bertrand

JEAN DE BATZ

At the age of twelve[1] he joined the Queen's Dragoons as a volunteer, and was made an ensign on December 8th, 1776. He was then fifteen years old! It was, we may add, with the help of a youthful gasconade that he won this promotion. In the letter in which he asks for his epaulet he asserts—in October, 1776—that he is *over twenty*.[2] The duties he desired to fulfil, however, were honorary.

The first reports we read of him as an officer, which are signed by his colonel, the Chevalier de Coigny, are fairly surprising.

> "*17th September*, 1784.
>
> "I never saw M. de Batz with the regiment, and Monseigneur had given me instructions to imprison him, if he should ever come."

His fellow-officers, however, do not seem to have been more assiduous than himself, for on the same page we read:

> "While I was in command of the Queen's Regiment M. de Briqueville joined once, in 1780, contracted a number of debts and never returned. I had Monseigneur's orders to imprison him if he ever came back."

de Batz, Baron d'Armanthieu, and of Dame Marie Delaboge. Godfather, Messire Jean d'Arros; Godmother, D^{lle} Quitterie de Chambre, widow of the late Messire Jean de Batz, whose signatures are below: D'Arros, Chambre, de Batz, de Laboge, present. De Chambre, present. Lacoste, assistant priest. M. le Curé, absent."

[1] This may seem extraordinary, and so it is. But the documents are indisputable. We have just seen the birth-certificate of the Baron de Batz, dated 1761. On Aug. 18th, 1776, the Comte de Flamarens wrote: "M. le Comte de Flamarens, brigadier of the King's army, colonel of the Queen's Dragoons, begs M. le Comte de Saint-Germain to be good enough to give a second-lieutenant's commission to M. de Batz, *who joined the said regiment four years ago. He is a good officer, has considerable talent, and is zealous in his profession.*" (From the Archives of the Ministry of War.)

[2] Archives of the Ministry of War.

13

"M. Ermangar de Bournonville obtained a half-pay lieutenancy in the Queen's Regiment, but he never appeared."

"M. de Kergus.—I never heard of him."

No doubt de Batz thought that with such a record as this, and with a colonel so careful of discipline, he had no chance of making his mark; and in 1784, with the King's permission, he entered the Spanish army. Three years later he returned to France, and obtained the rank of colonel on half-pay.

It was thus that the Revolution found him. Being chosen by the nobles of his province as their deputy to the States General he began, in 1789, the political career that was fated to be so active and so mysterious.

We will not linger over his early labours: it is enough for us to learn that, even in the first days of the Constituent Assembly, he showed himself to be an able financier and proved his technical knowledge of matters connected with the budget.[1] Having emigrated early in 1792 he served in the Princes' army as aide-de-camp to the Prince of Nassau.[2] But the inertia that reigned in the camp of the *Émigrés* failed to satisfy his craving for action; he soon regretted having left France; for, as he followed the course of public events with passionate interest, he came to understand that he would have more opportunities of showing his devotion at the Tuileries than at Coblenz.

When he heard of the rising of June 20th, 1792, he could bear it no longer, and in spite of the severity of the laws

[1] He energetically opposed the reforms of the Finance Committee. On the 3rd July, 1790, he drew up a report on the national debt; in September of the same year he voted against the issue of assignats, which he likened to the notes of Law's bank, etc. Later on Saint-Just showed that he had promoted the system of the *maximum*.

[2] Archives of the Ministry of War.—List of the services of M. de Batz.

against *Émigrés* he returned to Paris. He arrived there on the 1st July, on which date Louis XVI noted in his account-book :

" Return and perfect behaviour of M. de Batz, to whom I owe 512,000 *livres*."

It was at once evident to him that the march of events in the immediate future would be very swift, and that he was destined to take an active part in them. The partisans of the Court still dreamed of temporising, and hoped to disarm the Revolution by dint of forbearance and concession ; but the Baron de Batz saw clearly that the time had come to lay scruples aside, and to fight the enemies of the Monarchy with their own weapons. At the outset, to secure more liberty of action, he rid himself of a property he possessed in the outskirts of Paris. He lodged in the Rue de Ménars, at number seven, on the same floor as an actress from the Théâtre Italien, Citoyenne Burette, known as Babin Grandmaison.[1] She became his mistress ; and it was to her brother, the postmaster at Beauvais, that de Batz on the 28th July, sold—or, rather, pretended to sell—his property at Charonne, for which he had given 36,000 *livres* in 1787.[2] The sum mentioned in the agreement was 10,000 francs, but as a matter of fact the money was never paid. His object was to save the property from being confiscated, and in this he was successful. After the 10th August the *ci-devant* nobles

---

[1] "She came of an honest commercial family. Being an orphan she was given a home by a relation in easy circumstances, from whom she received a careful education, which was her whole fortune. A talent for singing, of the highest order, combined with a great deal of sense, steadiness, and economy to provide her with a modest competence at an early age. She brought her artistic career to an end, and at the same time developed a passionate taste for seclusion." (*La Journée des Soixante*, p. 44). In 1792 La Grandmaison's age was twenty-five.

[2] Archives of the Public Charity Office.

were relentlessly hunted down and persecuted, and the department of Paris appointed a commission "to institute inquiries, and make an inventory of the goods of the *Émigrés.*"[1] The house at Charonne, being entered on the list as the property of the Baron de Batz, was inspected by the commissioners and placed by them under seal; but Grandmaison produced his contract, and showed that he had lately become the actual owner of the house. It was thus that de Batz secured a safe retreat, whither he could retire at will, and conspire comfortably without fear of interruption.

Without definitely taking up his abode at Charonne he made it the centre of his operations. It was there that he organised his plans for the 21st of January. That scheme, as we know, came to nothing; but the failure of his attempt did not discourage the loyal ardour of the Baron de Batz. The King being dead it remained for the baron to save the Queen; and in the early days of February, 1793, he turned all his energies in the direction of the Temple.

The sorrows of the royal prisoner had already prompted a number of heroic acts of devotion. We have all heard how the Chevalier de Jarjayes, in conjunction with the municipal commissioners Toulan and Lepitre, devised a scheme for the escape of Marie Antoinette from the Temple—a scheme to which she refused to agree, being unwilling to desert her children and sister-in-law. It was necessary, then, to save the four prisoners at once, and this fact made the matter doubly difficult.

[1] National Archives, F[7] 3688[2]. These commissioners were not scrupulous. In December, 1792, the Mayor of Belleville accused of dishonesty those who had officiated in de Batz's house at Charonne. They had appropriated various objects on the grounds that, "since they were not paid, they had to get something out of the affair."

JEAN DE BATZ

After the 21st January an English lady named Mrs. Atkins, who had lived in France until 1790, conceived the brave project of bribing her way into the Temple prison, exchanging garments with the Queen, and making herself a prisoner in her Majesty's place. With this object she came from London to Paris, and succeeded in gaining admittance to the prison. Being unable to persuade Marie Antoinette to escape alone she at least made it possible to correspond secretly with the prisoner, by giving her two bottles of invisible ink, and providing several agents, who had agreed to help her, with a supply of the same liquid. These precautions taken she put her fortune at the disposal of the faithful royalists who were determined to save the Queen, and returned to England.[1] In the few existing documents that relate to the schemes of Mrs. Atkins the name of the Baron de Batz never appears ;[2] but none the less it is difficult to believe that

---

[1] Mrs. Atkins lived in Lille in 1790, and it was there she knew the Comte de Frotté. When her husband died she returned to England, in 1792, and kept up very close relations with the *Émigrés.* "This rare woman," says Frotté in his *Mémoires inédits,* quoted by M. de la Licotière, "risked her life and part of her fortune in the effort to rescue the Queen from the Temple, which she contrived to enter by dint of bribery. She proposed that the Queen should don her disguise, and leave the prison instead of her. The Queen refused because she could not save her children as well as herself. The lady then left her, charged with commissions, and returned to England to collect fresh funds, after providing a means of corresponding secretly with the Queen."

After the death of Marie Antoinette, Mrs. Atkins did not relax in her devotion to the royal family. She showed as much hatred of the Empire as devotion to the Bourbons. It is believed that she died in France, about 1827. On the subject of Mrs. Atkins see *L. de Frotté, et les Insurrections Normandes,* by M. de la Licotière, and especially a *brochure* by the Rev. Father Delaporte, S.J., *Centenaire de Marie Antoinette, documents inédits.*

[2] In a letter from Peltier to Mrs. Atkins, however, we read : " I hear that *the baron* is no longer at the house in the Rue Coq-Héron, where I said he lived."

there was no understanding between them. Be that as it may de Batz set to work. The audacity of his plan was unparalleled. It consisted in securing accomplices in sufficient numbers to compose, on a given day, the entire guard of the prison. Under pretext of inspecting the neighbourhood of the Temple a patrol was to march out of the enclosure, with the three princesses in their midst, dressed in military uniforms, and with them the little prince, whom no one would notice.

Who and what were the men, we may ask, whom M. de Batz had at his disposal, to make it conceivable that such a mad scheme as this could be carried out? We shall never know.[1] The names that we are in a position to give are those of his principal agents, his officers, so to speak : those of the private soldiers of the conspiracy are lost in oblivion. He could count on the absolute devotion of Devaux, the man whom we saw at his side on the 21st January; of the Marquis de la Guiche, who hid his identity under the name of Sévignon ; and of the two Lézardière brothers, who called themselves Robert and Desardy. In addition to these it was necessary to have a safe ally in the National Guard, and he secured the support of a grocer named Cortey, who commanded the guards in the Section Lepéletier. This was an important recruit, for Cortey was called upon, from time to time, to command the guard that was in charge of the Temple. And indeed this grocer, concerning whom we have little information, became, as we shall see, one of the baron's most trustworthy and faithful agents. Another of them was Pottier de Lille, who, in his capacity of secretary to

---

[1] The fellow-conspirators of the Baron de Batz were even, for the most part, unknown to each other. " We knew," wrote Hyde de Neuville, that communications were being carried on with our unhappy princes ; but we did not know all the agents, for it was a sacred duty to throw a veil of mystery round deeds of courage that might cost so dear."

the revolutionary committee of this same Section Lepéletier, was able to supply all the conspirators with any
number of passes and guarantees of safety. We shall meet
him again. A young man of independent means named
Balthazar Roussel, who was twenty-six years of age, was
also in the plot. He lived in the Rue Sainte-Anne, and
owned a country-house near Brie-Comte-Robert, in which
the conspirators hoped they might be able to hide the
prisoners of the Temple immediately after their escape.
Biret-Tissot, the baron's confidential servant, acted as
courier to the conspiracy. The Angevin banker Benoît
was its man of business, and acted as intermediary
between De Batz and the stock-brokers Jauge, and Boyd
and Kerr.

It is a remarkable fact that everyone who approached
this audacious Gascon, everyone who, so to speak, entered
his circle of attraction, instantly submitted to his influence.
They were all utterly subjugated, and became his humble
servants at once. He seems to have had some nameless
moral force at his disposal, which enabled him to attract
and keep the devotion of these people : one might almost
think that there emanated from him some fluid that
intoxicated them all, even the least impressionable, to such a
degree that they were faithful ever after—faithful to
the death—to this man whom they had made their master.

To practical folk this explanation will not appeal. Let
them find another, to account for certain facts that are
really incomprehensible. For instance, it is said that the
municipal commissioner Michonis joined the plot, though
Michonis always denied having known De Batz.[1] Did the
baron buy him ?[2]

[1] National Archives, W. 389.

[2] I have been reproached, in connection with my account of the
Carnation Affair, with being too severe on Michonis, whose attempt
to save the Queen, say my critics, was prompted by sheer devotion and

c 2

That is possible, after all. It may be that the secret of the magnetic fluid by which so many friends were attracted to the conspirator lay in the guineas of Mrs. Atkins.

The magistrate Burlandeux seems to me to have been one of those who were not indifferent to this kind of temptation. De Batz was denounced to him as an agent of the foreign powers ; but the lawyer, far from having the *suspect* arrested, " wormed himself into his house with a view to winning his confidence."[1] De Batz told him of his scheme for rescuing the Queen : Burlandeux made no objection, and continued to frequent the house at Charonne. He was always on the point of revealing the plot, but never made up his mind to it. He even spoke of it to Citizen Lafosse, head of the Bureau for Declarations to the Police, and to Citizen Leblanc, head of the Central Bureau, and asked them " what was the correct way of making so important a declaration to the Committee of Public Safety ? " To which Lafosse and Leblanc answered, after

not by self interest. I admit that many witnesses support this view. Hyde de Neuville wrote : " I can still see the devoted Michonis, whose good and generous soul was plainly visible in his frank and honest countenance. Beneath his appearance of candour he hid a great deal of shrewdness and cleverness, which helped him several times to escape the consequences of his devotion. He was an ardent partisan of the Republic when he met the august prisoners for the first time. All the suspicions of the royal family with which public opinion had been infected disappeared one by one from his mind, which was full of rectitude. He had an enthusiastic adoration for the Queen."

It is possible : after a hundred years it is difficult to discover whether a person of secondary importance, such as Michonis, were acting from conviction or for the sake of money : but candidly, until there is some proof to the contrary, we do not think we are being unjust in numbering Michonis among those who, like Burlandeux, Lafosse, Leblanc, Maillard, Vergne, and Sénar himself, were helping the Baron de Batz from motives of self-interest. They were all police officials ; they had all accepted posts which ill accorded with the *rectitude* and *honesty* mentioned above.

[1] Interrogatory of Burlandeux. Archives of the Prefecture of Police.

mature consideration, that "the best way was to write a letter, put it in an envelope, and take it to the Committee." The matter rested there. Neither Burlandeux, nor Lafosse, nor Leblanc, breathed a word of what they knew.

Now one day, when Cortey and his men outside the building, and Michonis within it, were on guard at the Temple, De Batz entered the prison in the evening, dressed in disguise. A few preliminary arrangements were rapidly made: thirty devoted men, on whom the brave royalist could rely, occupied all the posts in the tower and on the stairs, and composed the patrol. Michonis, for his part, had made an agreement with his colleagues that he should mount guard alone in the princesses' room: the other commissioners were playing cards in the Council Room. The royal family were warned, and were all awaiting the preconcerted signal to don their borrowed clothes.

The escape was to take place after midnight. It was eleven o'clock, and all seemed to be going as well as possible. In the streets that skirted the enclosure of the Temple trustworthy men were waiting, until the patrol should emerge to take charge of the Queen and escort her out of Paris. Baron Hyde de Neuville, who chanced to be among the conspirators, has left a very vivid and graphic account of the hours of waiting.

"I was at Michonis' house; he was on duty at the Temple, and I only found his wife: she seemed to me to be agitated. 'Michonis,' she said to me, 'has been expecting you since yesterday evening, and was sure you would come. He begged me to tell you to be at the corner of the Rue Charlot and the Rue du Temple[1] at about eleven o'clock

[1] The Rue Charlot ran by the side of the Temple walls, but did not then, any more than it does now, form an angle with the Rue du Temple. It was evidently at the corner of the Rue Charlot and the Rue de Bretagne that Hyde de Neuville waited.

to-night, and to walk up and down there, avoiding the patrols until you see one that you will recognise at once. They are hoping that they may be able to carry off the affair to-night, and a little help may be useful.'

" This devoted woman was obviously very uneasy about the dangers that her husband's zeal might lead him into; but I saw plainly that she had done nothing to dissuade him from his noble undertaking.

" I passed that evening in a state of agitation that prevented me from giving my mind to anything. Before the appointed hour I was in the Rue Charlot with a pistol in each pocket, and was all the more anxious that I was ignorant of the methods, and consequently of the probability of success, of the plot in which I unexpectedly found myself taking an active part. I was careful, without going too far, to walk some way along the streets in question, lest the few passers-by should observe my persistent haunting of the same spot; I thought I noticed two or three separate individuals who repeatedly crossed my path; and this circumstance could not but be alarming, since they might well be there to spy upon my actions; but I ended by being sure that an object similar to mine had brought them thither. Each of them, doubtless, came to the same conclusion; for though we said nothing, we all at last left off avoiding one another.

" In the meantime my ears were constantly strained in the direction of the Temple, to catch the slightest sound. No words can express the anxiety of the hours that passed thus—hours of which every minute robbed me of a hope. It was only when the first gleams of dawn appeared that I lost heart and went away. I could not make up my mind to go home, and continued to pace the streets of Paris till it was late enough to go to Michonis' house. Thither I went at last, and found his wife still

22

more agitated than on the previous day. She was not surprised, however, that her husband had not returned, as he would in any case have been kept by his duty at the Temple. I almost consoled her by telling her that the night had passed without incident.

"We were both thinking that no attempt could have been made that day to carry out the plot, when Jobert arrived and told us that Michonis had been summoned efore the Commune that very night."

And indeed a fatal catastrophe had occurred. At the moment when Cortey's patrol was preparing to leave the tower there was a sound of violent knocking on the great door of the Temple. There was nothing to be done but to open it. Simon the cobbler, who won his stripes that day, announced himself as the Commune's delegate, and ordered Michonis to relinquish his post on the spot and proceed to the head-quarters of the Committees. The secret had been betrayed in an anonymous letter, addressed, it is said, to Simon himself. The cobbler hurried to the prison, and first assured himself that the prisoners were there; then rushed out into the enclosure and hunted every corner for the Baron de Batz.

De Batz had disappeared.[1]

[1] See, on the subject of the affair at the Temple, *Mémoires sur Louis XVI.*, by Eckard, and *Le dernier roi légitime de France*, by Henri Provins.

We find, in an unpublished memorandum by Sénar all that the Committees knew of this bold attempt. "The Committees," he says, "received information of various kinds, both true and false. This is what they heard as to the attempts of Batz, which were the boldest and the best organised:

"He gained admittance to the Temple on the first occasion in order to make observatious, and this was how he did it. One of Péletier's captains, called Cortey, was in the confidence of Chrétien, the Committee's man in this section. Cortey was one of the few to whom the guarding of the tower was entrusted, and he picked his men.

"Batz was to have been admitted the second time with thirty men

A GASCON ROYALIST

Both Commune and Committee kept silence on the subject of this abortive attempt; Michonis did not lose his post; and when Simon appeared at the Hôtel de Ville on the following day expecting to be praised, he was treated as the victim of a nightmare. What was the object of all this forbearance? Was it, as the Committee declared afterwards, *to avoid suggesting such methods publicly?*[1] I do not think so. The secret of the Government's silence on this occasion lies in a fact that we believe has hitherto escaped observation. The Convention was intending to propose an exchange of prisoners with Austria. France would have given up the royal family; and the Emperor, in exchange, would have handed over the deputies who were arrested at the time of Dumouriez' flight.

This seems very strange; but nothing could be more authentic. There is among the National Archives a report addressed on the 2nd of May, 1793, by Metternich to Count von Trauttmansdorf, to which the following note is appended as a postscript:

" I have this moment learnt that the National Convention has sent a proposition to Marshal von Coburg to liberate the royal family, on condition that the members who meant to make their fortunes out of it and were already well paid. They were to guard the turret with the staircase in it. Michonis, who was in league with Batz, had had himself posted upstairs. At midnight the sentries were to be Batz's men, and the royal family were to leave their rooms after the three doors on the staircase were in the hands of their friends: if necessary anyone who opposed them was to be killed, and the royal family were to go out with the patrol, disguised in great-coats. The main gate always opened for Cortey's patrols round the Temple at night. This only served to allow Batz to escape. Otherwise they would all have perished, for a piece of vague information with regard to Michonis prompted the Commune to summon him at 11 o'clock that night, and Simon took his place, while the sentries were doubled."

[1] *See* letter to Fouquier-Tinville, Chap. VI.

of the Convention and M. Bournonville, who were arrested by Dumouriez, should also be set at liberty."

Later on Metternich wrote again :

" The proposition, which I told you had been made by the National Convention, to liberate the royal family. . . is an authentic fact, of the truth of which the Prince of Coburg assured me himself when I visited his head-quarters ; but as this proposition included the condition of an indefinite armistice, I suppose the Marshal did not think it was wise to acquiesce. And I have no right to express any opinion with regard to the silence that the Prince of Coburg has preserved towards the Court in this matter." [1]

It is a well-attested fact, then, that the revolutionary government was holding Marie Antoinette in reserve, and counted on using her as a means of obtaining a cessation of hostilities. That being the case it is easy to understand how important it was for them to put a stop to any idea that so precious a hostage could possibly be carried off, and why the Baron de Batz, Cortey, and the rest were left in peace.

The clear-sighted and disillusioned de Batz already foresaw the Queen's death. He put no faith in diplomacy, nor in the mercy of the revolutionary government : audacity and promptitude were his guiding principles, for he felt that to temporise with the Terror was to give up the struggle.

It was at this time that he conceived the most

[1] National Archives, K 164. The wrapper that envelopes these reports is thus inscribed : "Interesting papers, proving that in April and May, 1793, Austria had it in her power to save Louis XVI's family, and was more than negligent in the matter."

improbable scheme that any man in his position could
have imagined. To arrest the hurricane that was sweeping over France was not to be dreamt of; but might it
not be possible, by accelerating it, to hasten its end? If
the various parties who were struggling for power could be
infected with a feeling of mutual distrust these beasts of
prey, surely, would employ their devastating energies in
the destruction of each other. They made great profession of integrity; but it would be easy to corrupt and
disgrace them. The guillotine and the prisons were at
their service: they should be forced to use them, no longer
to destroy their enemies, but to destroy their friends. In
a word, the Convention should be sunk in such a slough of
mire and blood that at last the people, in their horror and
disgust, would resolve to sweep away all that was left of it
and demand, of their own accord, the restoration of the
Monarchy.

Such was the gigantic conception of the Baron de
Batz. From the day that the vast outlines of this
relentless scheme first took shape in his mind he refused to
listen to the voice of mercy or of conscience: the enemies
he had to combat had no scruples, and it was necessary to
fight them with their own weapons. To succeed in an
enterprise of this kind three things were needful: first,
money—and we shall show that de Batz had immense sums
at his disposal; secondly, courage—which he carried to
the point of foolhardiness; thirdly, a profound contempt
for those in power—and with this, too, he was well
endowed. Rightly or wrongly—it is not for us to say—
they seemed to him no better than ambitious cormorants
or bloodthirsty tyrants; he thought their honesty and
their convictions would easily be overcome; and it is only
fair to say, by way of excuse for this too severe and
sweeping judgment, that the specimens of the new *régime*

whom he had had the opportunity of studying were such as might well give him a poor idea of the men of the Revolution. For he had been receiving visits for some time past from two deputies to the Convention, Julien (of Toulouse) and Delaunay (of Angers). These two legislators knew perfectly well with whom they were concerned : they were not ignorant of the fact that de Batz was a conspirator, but it disturbed them very little.

Delaunay at that time was thirty-two years old : he was one of the most expert financiers among the members of the Convention. He consorted quite openly with de Batz,[1] to whom he confided all his financial schemes, and from whom he imbibed ideas in return. As he was probably brought to the house in the first place by his fellow-countryman Benoît, the Angevin banker whom we have already mentioned, he could have no doubts as to the counter-revolutionary sentiments of his host, to whom he appeared a valuable ally. This plausible intriguer was admitted to every public office, ransacked all the portfolios of the Committees, and was acquainted with all the secrets of the government. De Batz found him a mine of information.

As for Julien of Toulouse, he was the protestant minister who later on, together with Gobel, on the 7th November, 1793, solemnly denied his religious faith at the bar of the Convention, and, placing the credentials of his pastoral office on the president's table, begged that a bonfire might be made of them. This fact gives the measure of his principles ; and we may well believe that the fanatical royalist de Batz, when he saw such men as this at his table, enjoyed the bitter pleasure of satisfied malice. These men were specimens of the austere Con-

---

[1] Chabot's manuscript. National Archives, F⁷, 4637. Before the Tribunal Delaunay pretended he had only seen de Batz *on one occasion.*

ventionists, who never opened their mouths save to utter virtuous and patriotic sentiments, and loved to compare themselves to Brutus and Cato! It was de Batz the outlaw, de Batz the incorrigible conspirator, who was their host, their confidant, their adviser; their souls were laid bare before him; he knew the price of their consciences, and he passionately longed for the hour when he might unmask them, and show them to the world as they really were.

On that day Louis XVI would be indeed avenged!

De Batz, then, made use of these two men as one makes use of servants who are faithful, not from devotion, but because their interests are at stake. Did he confide his schemes to them? I think not. He only talked to them, I feel sure, of speculations to be embarked upon, and money to be made; and, finding obedience profitable, they asked no more of him. He questioned them, and laid stress on the great importance to their association of securing the alliance of some man of mark, one of the leaders of the Convention. What of Robespierre?—He was unapproachable, and moreover his integrity seemed to be genuine. What of Danton?—He was apparently disgusted with politics, and spent a good deal of his time at Arcis with his young bride, who monopolised all his energies. Who, then, should it be?

Delaunay and Julien thought the matter over; then, choosing out, from the most illustrious of their colleagues, those whom they thought the least likely to resist temptation, they said to de Batz:

"What do you think of trying Chabot or Bazire?"

II

THE ROMANCE OF AN UNFROCKED FRIAR

CHABOT was thirty-four years old.[1] Being of a fiery temperament and deplorably lax in morals, he promptly and eagerly availed himself of the opportunity to break his vows and cast off the capuchin habit that he had impatiently worn for fifteen years. This step had earned him great popularity even in the days of the Legislative Assembly, of which he was a member. The intoxication of success, and his pride in the varied information he had acquired during the enforced labours of the conventual life, had combined to develop him quickly and completely into a parliamentary speaker of the kind who is always ready to deal, with superficial ease, with the most diverse questions : war, finance, domestic policy, diplomacy, agriculture, or fine-arts. Being a *sans-culotte* of the most advanced sort—it is said that he invented the word—he made a point of appearing in the Assembly with his shirt unbuttoned, his legs half bare, and his head covered with the red cap of republicanism. To this affectation of cynicism he owed the most conspicuous part of his reputation—a reputation that he cherished to the point of paying some assassins to stab him, in order that the Jacobins might

---

[1] He was born in 1759 at Saint-Geniez, in Le Rouërgue. "Chabot was a short man. His thick-set, sinewy figure showed him to have a strong, vigorous constitution."—*Procès fameux*, by Désessarts.

accuse the Court of the crime, and parade his body round Paris to a cry that was then still new : *They are murdering our brothers!* Unfortunately his friend Grangeneuve, who had definitely promised to join the party in the capacity of second victim, prudently forgot to come for the death-blow that had been bespoken for him ; and Chabot escaped with a lonely two-hours' walk in the narrow Alley of the Dauphin, where he awaited the bravoes who never appeared.

As for his opinions, he proposed that every citizen should be armed, in order that each man might kill any counter-revolutionaries he chose ; he strongly approved of the idea of forming an association of tyrannicides, and wished to enlist in it himself ; and he regarded the September massacres as unimportant. It was impossible for the electors to refuse a seat in the Convention to so fervent a republican. He represented, in that assembly, the department of Loir-et-Cher, and continued his demagogic outpourings. Here he flourished, became of real importance, and made himself a position that nearly equalled that of Robespierre. This unfrocked Capuchin, however, this man without a conscience, this proved patriot, had one weak point : he loved—though he knew nothing of either—both luxury and women.[1]

De Batz, after quietly studying him, saw that this weakness was the vulnerable spot of the man, who had had no youth, and thought to crush his unsatisfied longings by a cynical exaggeration of slovenliness and violent language.

Julien and Delaunay having undertaken to introduce Chabot to de Batz they all lunched with him at

---

[1] "Chabot wrote to Robespierre that nature had endowed him with a fiery temperament ; that he was desperately attracted by women, and that this passion dominated his senses and his whole being quite irresistibly."—Désessarts, *Procès fameux.*

CHABOT.

Charonne,[1] where the baron, as we have said, owned a comfortable country house. Adjoining it was a charming pavilion, the remains of one that had been built by the Regent, for purposes of gallantry, at the end of the park of Bagnolet.

We can easily imagine the scene on this occasion. These tasteful surroundings were new to Chabot. The salon was adorned with pictures of mythological subjects, and a large bay window opened upon a smiling landscape ; Citoyenne Grandmaison did the honours with all the geniality and grace and charm of an actress ; the shady avenues of the park were full of memories of the luxurious and immoral Regency. Chabot was surrounded, and petted, and flattered by everyone. He spoke of " his virtuous mother, who made bread for herself with twice-ground bran, in order that she might give white bread to her children without diminishing her gifts to the poor " ;[2] he told of his scholastic successes, and how, " when he was only fourteen, he undertook three courses of mathematics at one time at the new school at Rodez— algebra, infinitesimal calculus, and the higher geometry " ;[2] he described how, being " flung by Providence into one of those schools where error and virtue are taught together, he learnt more from the cynicism of some of his comrades, and the austerity of others, and the ignorance of all, than he learnt from books,"[3] and how, when he had finished his novitiate, " he braved the fury of the fanatical priests and monks in order that the protestants'

[1] Chabot's narrative : National Archives, F[7], 4637. " Delaunay and Julien suggested that we should have a meal in the country with some girls. I was surprised at having dined with the Baron de Batz. . . . "

[2] *Francois Chabot, représentant du peuple, à ses concitoyens qui sont les juges de sa vie politique.* Chabot's Manuscript : National Archives, F[7], 4637.

[3] *Ibid.*

children might benefit from the lessons in mathematics that he gave to the children of the catholics."[1] His fellow-guests listened to him with approval and admiration. And I imagine that, when the evening found him once more in his humble lodging in the Rue Saint-Honoré,[2] with the servant-maid whom he had made his mistress, the ex-Capuchin meditated long upon his hard youth, and the meagre result of all his labours, and the enviable fate of those who enjoyed all the comforts of life without doing anything to deserve them.[3]

As for de Batz, he had appraised the renegade with the unfailing penetration that enabled him to take a man's measure as quickly as he organised an intrigue. He had discovered the vulnerable spot in this feigned auster-ity.

De Batz was not mistaken. If it be true that a body always falls in the direction in which it leans Chabot's integrity could not avoid falling, for it leaned in all directions.

At this point a new character comes upon the scenes : the Austrian banker Junius Frey. It is an undoubted fact that he was an agent of de Batz, and one of the most active ; but—as we shall abundantly prove—Frey was not one of the men whose devotion or principles prompted them to risk their heads rashly in deadly combat with the Convention. Not at all : this German Jew scented money in the affair, and that was enough for him. This plausible obsequious hypocrite, who affected dullness or arrogance according to the needs of the cause, played his minor part in the drama with undeniable, if somewhat coarse, talent.

[1] Chabot's Manuscript. National Archives, F[7], 4637.
[2] Facing the Rue de la Sourdière.
[3] *Histoire véritable* . . etc. Chabot's Manuscript. National Archives, F[7], 4637. Chabot, with unconscious cynicism, records details of his relations with this girl that cannot be repeated.

But after all, delicacy was not greatly needed. Chabot's degraded soul, apparently, was ripe for every kind of ignominy; for no other man, however great his simplicity, would have fallen into the extremely obvious trap that was set for him.

It was at the Jacobin Club that the ex-Capuchin had made the acquaintance of Junius Frey and his brother Emmanuel, who were introduced to him by Lavaux as two enthusiastic supporters of Equality. They possessed millions in their own country, said Lavaux, but it was so hateful to them to bend beneath the yoke of a tyrant that they had left Vienna, and had sacrificed their fortune that they might breathe the pure air of liberty in France.

With touching naïvety they related how, after realising some debts in Hamburg, they had gone to Strasburg, where their first care had been to have a medal struck " in honour of the triumph of the Jacobins over the Feuillants " ! They had forthwith dropped the honoured name of their fathers, and had adopted that of Frey, or *Free*. To this the elder of the two brothers had even prefixed the name of Junius, in honour of the Roman Republic, whose great memories he liked to invoke, for he had a smattering of education. These enthusiastic patriots, immediately on their arrival in Paris, had made friends with certain strong adherents of the Mountain, such as Bentabolle and Simon (of Strasburg), and had even entered into communication with the minister Lebrun. He, however, received them coldly, and they did not fail, in return, to call him an aristocrat.

Chabot made no secret of it : he was conscious from the first moment " of a great feeling of veneration for Junius Frey." This sentiment was considerably strengthened when he learnt that the two Austrian fugitives had undertaken the support of an old man, " chosen by their Section,

after they had acquired several *émigrés'* properties,"—
which was quite a new way of celebrating a happy event.
When the Republic was proclaimed their rapture was such
that they adopted a little French boy, promising to teach
him good principles.[1]

This ostentation of public-spiritedness, far from arousing suspicion, enlarged the Freys' social circle, and won
them many friends—and all the more because their hospital-
ities were lavish and their dinners sumptuous. They often
attended the meetings of the Assembly, where they sat on
the petitioners' bench and carried on long conversations
with the deputies. It was thus that Chabot gradually
grew to know them well.

The honeymoon of their friendship was all joy. Chabot
told them his story: the Freys related theirs. He thus
learnt that Junius, when entreated by Joseph II. to be his
prime minister, had flatly rejected the tyrant's advances;
and that this deadly enemy of superstition and aristocracy
had, moreover, renounced his rank as a German baron in
order to devote himself entirely to philosophy and the
happiness of his fellow-men. The Emperor Leopold, on
his accession, was rendered uneasy by the republican
theories that Junius professed, and bade him leave the

---

[1] After Robespierre's death there was found among his papers the
draft of a report on Batz's conspiracy, containing the following
interesting portrait of Junius Frey: "From the early days of the
Revolution there lived in Paris two monsters who were worthy to
serve the cause of tyrants, so profound was their hypocrisy. . . One
of them had supplemented his assumed name with that of the founder
of Roman liberty: he was laden with patriotic titles. . . . None of
the patriots whom he gathered round him ever found him save with
a pen in his hand, dreaming of the rights of humanity, or bending
over the works of Plutarch or Jean-Jacques. Junius, with his austere
appearance and revolutionary costume, corresponded perfectly with
one's ideal of so great a character: the philosophic cut of his hair, and
the *bonnet rouge* that adorned his philosophic head was a guarantee to
all the world of his unadulterated patriotism."

Empire; which he was delighted to do, since he preferred liberty to riches and honours. This eminent virtue made Chabot's heart glow. He did not wait to be pressed when the two brothers invited him home to supper with them in the Rue d'Anjou.

When the meal was over they regaled him by reading aloud a great philosophical work on equality : a dissertation addressed to the people of France, and intended to "give liberty to the Universe." Chabot, although "inconvenienced," he says, "by the stove and the tobacco-smoke," was filled with enthusiasm. He embraced his new friends, protested that he would live and die with them, swore that he would never leave them, and suggested buying a country house at Suresnes, where they might labour together, side by side, "and produce works that should hasten the happiness of the human race." Chabot, as we can guess, was horribly drunk, being unused to good cheer. Emmanuel Frey led him home. Such was the beginning of the friendship that was destined to destroy the miserable remains of Chabot's austere principles.

From that day forward Junius was his adviser, his guide, his leader. But who was it, we may ask, who took the part of prompter in this comedy? What was Frey's motive, if he were not incited by someone, in monopolising the repellent *sans-culotte* who had the ear of the Convention? As whose agent was this German acting? Who dictated to him—to this foreigner who spoke French with difficulty, was unfamiliar with Parisian customs, and had little knowledge of political intrigue—who dictated to him at the right moment the words and phrases that he was to repeat to Chabot, or pointed out the line of conduct that Chabot blindly followed? Who, if not de Batz? Indeed, hardly had the two German Jews of the Rue d'Anjou been brought to his notice before he saw how useful they might be made in all kinds of matters. Living in their house was the natural son of a great Austrian noble, Proly, who played the Jacobin so well that Lebrun, the Minister for Foreign Affairs, was deceived by his revolutionary protestations, and entrusted certain diplomatic missions to him. To put it briefly, Proly had been a spy. He secretly frequented the drawing-rooms of aristocrats, and was a regular visitor in the gambling-houses of the Palais Royal, especially that of Mesdames de Sainte-Amaranthe and the so-called Marquis de Champgrand. Champgrand was a member of the strange, frivolous, sceptical, pleasure-loving, and—we may add—deluded society that refused to regard the Revolution as anything but an ephemeral spoil-sport. It was through Champgrand that de Batz made Proly's acquaintance ; and, thanks to that intermediary, he entered into communication with Junius Frey, whom he intended to use as a battering-ram wherewith to destroy the whole edifice of the Revolution.

But what a host of enemies there were to be slain ! The Girondists, and Hébert's faction, and Danton's friends, and, at the very summit of the Mountain, the inaccessible Robespierre ! And all these men who made the Revolution seemed to have but a single aim, seemed to be standing shoulder to shoulder in defence of the avenues of power. No matter—the work must be done ! The Girondists were the first to be attacked ; but who should attack them ? Hébert, Léonard Bourdon, Desfieux, and Chabot : especially Chabot, who composed " for their undoing the long deposition, half truth, half fiction, whose cunningly distorted facts entangled them." [1] He confessed it himself. " The Freys," he says, " were not a little useful in enlightening me with regard to the faction of the

[1] Louis Blanc : *Histoire de la Révolution*, Book X, Chapter XIII.

Brissotins, who wished to save the tyrant. . . . They told me that insurrection was the only means of delivering us from the Brissotins, who had the word *loi* on their lips and the word *roi* in their hearts. . . . I begged them to write something on the unity and indivisibility of the Republic. At the end of twenty-four hours they presented me with the manuscript of *Les Aventures du Père Nicaise, ou l'Anti-fédéraliste*, a work that the government and the Committee of Public Safety distributed widely, as being the only one in existence that was capable of enlightening good citizens as to the aims of the Brissotin faction." [1]

By his own confession, then, it was Chabot, instigated by Junius, who caused the fall of the Girondists. Was Junius prompted by de Batz? Even if we suppose— which is incredible—that this German Jew throughout the affair had any aim beyond making money, it is impossible to believe that he, who knew very little French,[2] could have produced in twenty-four hours a pamphlet so able that *the government distributed it widely*. Surely an invisible hand pulled the strings of all these puppets : the hand of the man whose name appears from time to time in Chabot's notes, and whose money served to maintain the Freys' establishment ; the man whom we shall see driving Danton, and Fabre, and Chabot himself to the scaffold, and later on contributing to the crisis of Thermidor ; the man against whom the exasperated Convention, when at last they knew the source of all these attacks, let loose in vain all the hounds of the Committee of General Security. In this new fight between the lion and the gnat it was the

---

[1] *Histoire véritable.* Chabot's Manuscript. National Archives, F⁷, 4637.

[2] "I write French well, but I speak it badly," said Frey, with a view to explaining this improbability. Chabot's Manuscript: same *dossier*.

evasive insect, as in the fable, that finally triumphed over
the wild beast.

The story of Chabot is full of valuable instruction. We
see him being gradually swallowed up by the dangerous
quagmire on which he had set foot : it was imperative that
he should be absolutely at the mercy of the conspirators,
that he should be not merely their man, but their chattel.
His friend Junius Frey, who was never embarrassed by
scruples, undertook to smooth down the asperities of his
rugged and corroded nature.

It was through the pleasures of the table that Frey
began his work of corruption. In his house the food was
good and the drinking was deep ; and there was therefore
no lack of guests. Poor Chabot drew comparisons between
this excellent fare and the bread of bran that was kneaded
by the hands of his worthy mother ; and in his heart he
blessed the generous foreigners to whom he owed the
revelation of joys hitherto unknown. We must record
the good as well as the evil : Chabot was not without the
gratitude that is akin to cupboard-love. When, later on,
he was imprisoned in the Luxembourg he recalled the
luxurious meals of which he had enjoyed so large a share,
and praised the good cheer of his hosts, who incurred in
one year, for the satisfaction of their appetite alone,
" an expenditure of 40 or 50,000 francs." " Ask all the
men whom they entertained," he wrote ; " ask Bentabolle,
Richard, Fabre, Desjardins, &c., &c., Simon (of Strasburg),
Louis (of the Bas-Rhin) ! If the books of their caterer
be consulted it will be seen that their expenses were as
much as 2,000 or 3,000 francs a month, without counting
the surplus ! " To indulge in such repasts as these, at a
time when the people of Paris were mobbing bakers'
doors in the vain hope of securing a scrap of bread, was

evidently a proof of good citizenship in the eyes of this unfrocked friar, who was making up for all the Lents he had kept in the past. As soon as he had a place at the board his point of view became considerably modified.

Junius set to work at once to gauge his friend's honesty. He soon came to the bottom of it. Chabot had undertaken the defence, in the Jacobin Club, of certain privateering enterprises in which Frey had invested some money: and even before this he had introduced the Jew to the minister Deforgues, frankly in order that he might reveal " all he knew of the northern Powers, and of the Turkish government, which was to be persuaded to oppose Austria and Russia."

The Committee of Public Safety adopted the greater part of this diplomatic plan. The Executive Council granted "more than was asked" in the matter of the privateers ; and, in short, Frey was laid under an obligation to the *sans-culotte*.

We might pause here to comment on the ease with which the terrible Committee of Public Safety was persuaded to espouse the ideas and interests of a German Jew ; but this would be a digression.

A few days later Chabot, on arriving at Frey's house for dinner, found the latter considerably disturbed. From the confidences that Chabot has bequeathed to us we can easily reconstruct the scene that was enacted between the two cronies.

" You have a housekeeper, my friend ? " asked Junius sadly.

To this question Chabot gave no answer but a modest blush. It devolves upon us to reveal that he had indeed a housekeeper, who did her work so well that she became mistress of more than his house. Judging from certain details that Chabot does not scruple to divulge we feel assured that he could not have bestowed his affections more unworthily.

"You have a housekeeper?" repeated the austere Junius severely. "You must get rid of her without delay, for she is a worthless minx, and is very likely to compromise you."[1]

A minx! Chabot had good reasons for thinking so; but none the less he questioned his friend, whose brow again grew dark.

"Chabot," he said gravely, "it is impossible for the name of a patriot such as yourself to be tarnished by any breath of suspicion: if it were otherwise I should be the first to sacrifice you on the altar of your Country! The fact of the matter is this. Your housekeeper, having heard of your recent successful efforts on my behalf, came—without your knowledge, I know—to ask me for a present, a sort of commission. You must send that woman away as quickly as possible: she is not worthy to be the honest Chabot's servant."

The honest Chabot made a grimace and scratched his head.

"But, you see—" he stammered.

"Well?"

"You see—she declares—she has a claim upon me," said Chabot pathetically.

"All the more reason for getting rid of her. You can give her some money."

"But I have none."

"Well, is that not my concern? That is a matter of course. You can settle, yourself, what sum you think would be right."

[1] *Histoire véritable* . . . etc., and *François Chabot à ses concitoyens.* National Archives, F7, 4647.

THE ROMANCE OF A FRIAR

Then they sat down to dinner : Chabot, with tears in his eyes, likening his host, his benefactor, his hero, to the famous friends of mythology, to Nisus and Castor, while the Jew was rubbing his hands and laughing in his beard. Chabot's delicacy appeared to him by no means unconquerable. He plainly saw the possible usefulness of such a man, and he mentally calculated the additional profits that this powerful partner would bring him in all his future schemes for fleecing these imbecile Frenchmen.

What is really incomprehensible is that Chabot himself should have made these confidences without being asked for them, and should have regarded them as of the nature of a vindication ! Was it simplicity on his part, or irresponsibility? Be that as it may, his adventures were not over, and Junius Frey had many other traps in store for him. But it will be best, at this point, to quote Chabot's manuscript verbatim : for not only would the plot of the drama appear too farcical for truth if we had not the authentic document before us, but it would be a sin to delete anything from this touching idyll—except such things as cannot be written.

" A very intimate friend and distant relation of mine, called Glandy, was sent by his Commune at this time on a mission to the Convention, to ask for an indemnity for the war against the brigands of La Lozère. He came to stay in my rooms. I wished to give him the pleasure of seeing Versailles, which I had not seen myself, having only been there at night when I went to fetch the Swiss soldiers of Château-Vieux. I invited the Frey brothers, and the ladies who had taken care of my nephew during my absence. I had heard the Freys speak of their sister : I thought she was married. I begged them to bring her and her husband, and they burst out laughing. 'She is only sixteen,' they said, 'and we are the only men she has ever seen.' I

41

insisted all the more ; and persuaded them to let her join
the party. My friend Glandy monopolised her, and lost
his heart to her on this expedition. He begged me to take
him to see the Freys ; I did so ; we asked for the sister.
As a favour she was allowed to come in for dessert. She
played the pianoforte with so much taste and charm that
my friend and relation became madly in love. He begged
me to ask for her hand in his name. I told him we ought
first to find out whether they wanted to marry her, lest a
refusal that was really only on general grounds should
injure his chances elsewhere. I told him she had from
50,000 *écus* to 200,000 *livres*, judging from the fortune that
I knew, approximately, her brothers possessed. My friend
then told me that his fortune amounted to 200,000 *livres*
in cash or credit in his business. I asked Junius Frey if
he wished his sister to be married ; he told me he had
already thought of giving her to me. I did not answer.
I reported his answer to our lover, who insisted on my
making a definite proposal on his behalf. I did so. Here
is Frey's answer : ' I have been asked for my sister by
millionaires—he told me their names—whom I refused.
If the *ci-devant* Duc de Chartres were to ask for her
hand, and were a patriot, even then I should refuse it.
If you do not take her no one in France shall have her. I
have a regard for Glandy, both as your friend and as a
good fellow, but he shall not have my sister.' I was
bewildered : I pointed out to him that Glandy was on his
way to making a fortune in business, whereas all I had
was my Capuchin's pension, and that was very uncertain.
Frey then said to me : ' If you had more you would not
have my sister, because you would be a knave and a
counter-revolutionary. I will give her to you with
200,000 *livres*, as a reward for your good-citizenship.
But, should you ever prove false to the people, you would

have to give up my friendship and all hopes of the rest of my fortune—for if you marry my sister I shall forswear marriage, and you will be the only head of my family in France. My brother Emmanuel is not likely to have children.' I pointed out that my wife might die childless, and that if I had become used to the luxury of his house it would be hard for me to return to my own people, and spend my time in picking grapes. He told me I should have nothing to complain of in the marriage-settlements, and that a sum would be allotted to me in the case of my wife's death or divorce. 'I have some property at home,' I said; 'but I am keeping it for my mother and sister till the reform of the Civil Code.'— 'You must settle it on them,' he said; 'I do not want your property. My sister hates luxury and pleasure; she thinks of nothing but her music and her housekeeping.'— 'But,' I said to him, 'I do not wish to be in a different position to that of my parents,' which I described to him. He answered: 'They will be quite content with the settlements, and we shall all be like one family.' He showed me the settlements : I was astounded by them, and I admit the marriage alarmed me on account of the very advantages I gained by it. I asked for twenty-four hours to consult with my friends, whose advice was as follows : 'You are accused of philandering—your marriage would put an end to these slanders and rumours. One should not run after money, but one should take it when it comes.' I was asked for my answer; I begged for another day, and then answered in the affirmative. But I added that Léopoldine must be asked for her consent. 'I have it already,' replied her brother. 'To be happy myself I must be sure of your happiness and of that of my sister—both are necessary to me. If I did not believe you could make my sister happy, and would love her when you had talked to her, I should not give her to you ; and, if I were not aware that my sister loved your reputation already and would soon love yourself still more, I should not offer her to you. Be off now, and see her.' I went. I informed her of what had passed during the previous fortnight. She said she had already been told of it. I asked her what she thought of it. She answered that she would be delighted to be my wife. ' What ! ' I said, ' the wife of a Capuchin ? ' —'Yes—of a revolutionary Capuchin : I ask nothing better. In Germany the great ambition was to marry some great man in this country. Well ! after Robespierre, you are the greatest of Frenchmen. I wish to marry you, and I hope you will love me, for I am a well-meaning little thing. I am not vain ; I love work, and my brothers, and seclusion ; and I shall love you well.' Her eyes expressed more than her words. Then I said to her : ' I esteem you ; and your eyes give me no choice but to love you. Everything is settled upstairs with your brothers ; I have given my word on condition that you give your consent.'—' Well, everything is settled here too,' she replied. It was arranged that I should dine there on the following day and that we should sign the contract after dinner. A woman who was said to be in love with me and desirous of marrying me came to see me at Frey's house after dinner ; so Frey told me to go home, and said they would come and sign the contract at my lodgings. I went thither, and at half-past ten my two brothers-in-law and my wife came round to my rooms, where the contract was executed by Citizen Cortel." [1]

The thing was done. From that moment Chabot was a tool. Those who used him knew that if he resisted he

---

[1] *Histoire véritable du mariage de François Chabot avec Léopoldine Frey, en réponse à toutes les calomnies que l'on a répandues à ce sujet.* National Archives, F⁷, 4637.

could be forced to act; they had assured themselves beforehand that fear, with him, would be a stronger motive than any kind of scruple, and they had the means of inspiring fear : they had him in their power.

Moreover, if he had any scruples they were merely a matter of form. He was lunching one day with de Batz at Charonne, the other guests being Julien (of Toulouse) —who was accompanied by his mistress the Comtesse de Beaufort—Delaunay (of Angers), Bazire, the banker Benoît, and, it is said, the poet Laharpe. The conversation, skilfully guided by de Batz, turned upon the hardness of the times and the small advantage reaped by the Conventionists in return for their immense services to the nation.

" I do not know why it is," said Benoît to Chabot, " that people decline to make their fortunes in France. In England the members of the Government are bought openly."—" That is to say," whispered Delaunay to Bazire, " that a word spoken in the House is enough to produce a fall in the price of the financial companies' stock ! These men take advantage of the fall to buy, then produce a rise, and sell." [1]

" One wants funds for that," said Bazire dreamily.

Funds ? Nothing is easier than to obtain funds. Is not that what bankers are for—to advance funds ? is not the ex-Abbé d'Espagnac,[2] now an army contractor, a friend

---

[1] *Rapport d'Amar à la Convention*, 26th Ventôse, year II.

[2] In the history of the Revolution, where there are so few definite figures, none is more elusive and obscure than this Abbé Sahuguet d'Espagnac. He was a talented writer ; had speculated successfully in the days of Calonne's Ministry ; and had been exiled by the Court as a dangerous intriguer. When war was declared he gained admittance to the Jacobin Club, made friends among the revolutionaries, and succeeded in obtaining the contract for military transport. The expedition to Argonne brought him immense profits, and the State owed him several more millions towards the end of 1793.

of ours? The Republic owes him four millions; the Committees, when they are driven to it, give him all the money he asks for. He is the man to supply the funds!

It was thus that the trap was set for Chabot and Bazire. But indeed, before they consented to sit at the table of the Baron de Batz, their integrity must already have been in a very grievous state![1]

The Baron de Batz, while organising his great work of destruction, did not lose sight of his immediate object, the rescue of the Queen. We have dealt elsewhere with the attempt of the adventurous Rougeville, who succeeded in entering Marie Antoinette's cell and giving her a note that contained a plan of escape. Nothing has transpired to throw doubt on any of the details we gave of the extraordinary *Carnation Conspiracy*; but we now know with certainty that Rougeville was merely an instrument in the plot, of which the Baron de Batz was the soul.

The police-agent Burlandeux knew that de Batz—his own hands being tied after the abortive attempt at the Temple—had offered a million francs to any man who should save the Queen: so well did he know it that he greatly desired to win the million himself, even though he might feel it his duty, when the money should be safely in his pocket, to denounce de Batz as a "corrupter of officials!" De Batz, seeing that he was going to be imposed upon without any resulting advantage to the prisoner in the Conciergerie, behaved warily: and it was then that Rougeville appeared, confident that he could make his way into the Queen's presence. He too had dreams of the promised million, and we know that his need of it was

[1] "What, Chabot! . . . you knew these infamous people, and remained in the confederacy!"—*Amar's Report.*

pressing; but at least he was a royalist, called himself a gentleman, and had some idea of honour. So de Batz chose him, and, as a matter of fact, had no reason to repent so doing.

Rougeville himself has described how Marie Antoinette, after two interviews with him, left her cell on the appointed day, and had actually passed the two inner doors of the prison when the alarm was given. Time was when we did not put much faith in this story, since Rougeville's authority was not enough to make it credible; but it is now proved that he spoke the truth.

When, in 1796, the Baron de Batz was thinking of writing his memoirs, he wished to find out how far he had been helped—or hindered—by his fellow-conspirators. He applied to Sénar, the famous spy of the Committee of General Security, the man who had been behind the scenes of the Revolution, and was later on the author of a "great history of great crimes." This was Sénar's answer on the subject of the Queen's escape:

"In the Conciergerie some of the gendarmes had been won over: when the guard was relieved she missed the man who was wearing two coats one above the other, and was to have given her one of them and taken her out of the prison. Burlandeux on this occasion was faithful to de Batz: how many other men he denounced for his sake! He was waiting for the Queen, to take her to the place where de Batz was to be. That is all that the Committees were able to find out."[1]

Now these two statements, Rougeville's and Sénar's, coming from men of such opposite opinions, who had no

---

[1] Unpublished letter from Sénar, in the collection of M. Foulon de Vaulx.

connection with one another, and did not know that their narratives, after remaining in oblivion for a hundred years, would be set side by side and compared—these statements are practically tantamount to a proof: and it may henceforth be asserted that only the merest chance prevented the Queen's escape, after she had actually passed through the doors of her prison.

The Rougeville incident, however, had aroused the rapacity of Burlandeux. Since this Baron de Batz was so wealthy that he could offer a million francs to save a poor woman of no influence, might it not be possible for a man who knew his secret to *bleed* him a little? He made the attempt: but he had caught a Tartar. De Batz saw the danger, and, to nip it in the bud, went in person to denounce the unscrupulous police-agent to the conventionist Alquier, president of the Committee of General Security.

So remarkable an exhibition of coolness as this might well be thought improbable. It will not be amiss, therefore, to give the evidence of the Baron de Batz himself.

" Meanwhile I had no choice but to vanish, or to be the first to secure the ear of the Committee of General Security. I chose the latter course; but two days passed before I was able to speak to the President of the Committee. At last, however, I obtained an interview. I did not ask for what possible reason the department of public surveillance had decided to have me watched, but I complained of the fact, and offered to give an account of my actions. This assumption of frankness was salutary. A few days later I was summoned by this same president of the Committee of General Security. 'You are to be arrested this morning,' he said; ' the warrant is signed; the superintendent of police and his gendarmes are ready, and everything is prepared—but calm yourself, the warrant is forged. One of the spies of the Committee followed

Burlandeux, won the robber's confidence, and discovered everything. Burlandeux intended to fleece you. Having failed to catch you in the first traps he laid, he made out this sham warrant against you; the Committee's spy himself helped in its manufacture. The plan was to make a great show of entangling you, and then force you to pay for your liberty in proportion to the fright they had given you.' I also learnt that this was not the first attempt of the kind that the man Burlandeux had made. A few days earlier he had, by the same means, taken advantage of the fears of a certain merchant called Hoffman to wring a sum of 26,000 *livres* from him and his family. As for me, Burlandeux and his associates had at first fixed my price at 100,000, and then at 200,000 *livres*; and at last, growing braver on reflection, Burlandeux had said of me: ' He is rich: I will undertake to make him buy his head at 100,000 *écus*.' " [1]

Burlandeux was arrested that very day, and one does not know which was the more marvellous of the two: the royalist conspirator who went fearlessly to denounce the police-agent employed to watch him, or the president of the Committee of General Security who gave such strange information concerning the agents in his employ.[2]

[1] De Batz gives these valuable details in a brochure that is now unobtainable—*La Journée des soixante*. We will presently study this brochure, which M. Foulon de Vaulx has kindly allowed us to see. His copy and that of M. Victorien Sardou are the only ones now known to exist. By a chance that is sufficiently strange to be pointed out this little book is not in the National Library.

[2] If we doubted the evidence of the Baron de Batz we might support it by that of the official documents: for in the archives of the Prefecture of Police Burlandeux's arrest is mentioned under the date of Sept. 14, 1793, which agrees perfectly with the date of the *Affaire de l'Œillet*, Sept. 3. Burlandeux's wife was arrested with him, the charge in both cases being *bribery*. Moreover, Chabot wrote later on, when he was trying to save his head by dint of denouncing others: "In Sept. (1793), de Batz had offered a million to certain

In the meantime, in spite of all the ingenuity and money that had been expended, the plot had failed, the Queen had not escaped. The prisoner was more carefully guarded than before, and it was no longer possible to use direct means. The only conceivable way of saving Marie Antoinette was to force the Convention to cut its own throat. It was imperative to act quickly and boldly. The tool that lay ready to hand was Chabot; he must be used without delay.

The unfrocked friar, at this time, was living in the glamour of his approaching marriage and his imminent riches: to use his own expression, " he was bewildered." The Freys had bound themselves by the contract to provide their sister and her husband with "food and lodging for five years, and, in addition, with 4000 *livres* annually for necessaries and amusements."[1] At the end of that time they were to give the young couple a sum of 200,000 francs in assignats, or in *émigrés'* property. These terms—evidently devised for the undoing of Chabot—were very cleverly conceived. Here was an ex-Capuchin about to be lodged in his brother-in-laws' sumptuous house in the Rue d'Anjou-Saint-Honoré, and seated daily at the groaning board that had impressed him so profoundly. His comfort was assured: all that was wanting was money—for an income of 4000 francs is little enough for a man who wishes to make up for all his past Lents. But de Batz was watching. He entrusted to Delaunay the task of belling the cat, and with this object despatched him to Chabot. We can fix the date of this interview within the

citizens, whose names were not given, to rescue the Queen. He was denounced on this account. He was not arrested, and contrived to have his accusers arrested as being the sole originators of this criminal design, which, he declared, he had rejected with horror."—National Archives, F⁷, 4637.

[1] Chabot's Manuscript. National Archives, F⁷, 4637.

second fortnight of September, 1793; for Chabot himself remembered that it took place shortly after the reconstitution of the Committee of General Security, and the reconstitution took place on the 14th of September.

Delaunay spoke to Chabot in the entrance-hall of the Convention. It was at the foot of the statue of Liberty, the symbol of the young Republic trampling on all the baseness of the old régime, that the first fencing-match took place between these two representatives of the people who were preparing to trade with their commissions.

A few day previously Chabot had proposed to the Convention that the seals that had been affixed to the property of stockbrokers and bankers should be removed. He pointed out—prompted, doubtless, by Junius Frey, who was concerned in matters of finance—that these severe measures hampered the operations of commerce, and had even served as a pretext for several pretended bankruptcies.[1] This proposal gave an opening to Delaunay. He observed amicably to his colleague that he was too eager to take the part of the bankers.

"It was our intention," he added, "to ask for the removal of the seals; so much so that this was our sole object in proposing that they should be affixed. It was our friend de Batz who thought of this measure, and he is at this moment going into the question with Luillier.[2] If you had waited a few days longer the *Père Duchesne* would not have attacked you as it has. Your haste has cost us half a million between us."

Chabot was startled into a movement of surprise.

"Ah yes! there is no doubt," went on Delaunay, "that the *Père Duchesne* is a power; but I have a certain amount of influence in that quarter. In any case the matter can be

---

[1] *Moniteur*; sitting of the 9th Sept.
[2] *Procureur-syndic* of the Department of Paris.

put right. Cambon and Ramel are doing their best, and
Fabre d'Églantine is also hard at work : we too must put
our shoulders to the wheel. You would not think there was
any harm, would you, in working for our interests, while
caring at the same time for those of the Republic?
Danton, Lacroix, and several others have been doing
business with my friend Benoît, a safe man. Our names
do not appear at all : it is he who speculates to our
advantage, by gambling with the rise and fall of stock."[1]

Chabot, on receiving these confidences, did not know
what attitude to assume. He pretended afterwards that
he at once determined to *profess agreement with Delaunay's
views, in order to defeat him*. But this is the excuse that
all prevaricators and traitors put forward when they know
they are unmasked. Moreover the rest of the story will
show very plainly that Chabot's mind was full of quite other
things than indignation or stratagem. Delaunay continued :

" A new opportunity for an honest speculation is about
to occur. You know there has been a demand put forward
that foreigners' property shall be confiscated. Now this
word has a double meaning : property may be real or
movable. This ambiguity is very alarming to the bankers ;
so they are being told : ' If you want only real property
to be involved, you must pay a million francs—otherwise
everything will be confiscated and you will be ruined.'
One of the bills that de Batz is drawing up for Luillier
makes no mention of any but real property."[2]

De Batz! Chabot was haunted by this name. The
reports read in the Convention had been thought out in the
house at Charonne! This financial policy on the part of
the Mountain had been inspired by de Batz! What

[1] Chabot's Manuscript. National Archives, F7, 4637.

[2] These are Delaunay's own words as reported by Chabot himself.
National Archives, F7, 4637.

a revelation for an incorruptible politician like Chabot!
What an opportunity to cry once more : *O People, you
are being deceived !* This, however, he took care not to
do ; especially when, a few days later, he obtained
independent evidence that those who had vaunted the
influence of the Baron de Batz had by no means
exaggerated. The seals had been removed from the
premises of all the bankers except Boyd and Kerr—
English financiers who had settled in Paris, and possessed
a safe that contained government securities to the value of
more than four million francs. Chabot, at the request of
a friend whose name he does not give, proceeded to the
Committee of Public Safety in search of Luillier, to whom
he expressed his surprise that this exception had been
made. Luillier promised to attend to the matter ; but
did nothing. Chabot again urged him to act, and this
time visited him at his office. Luillier repeated his
promise to have the seals removed from Boyd and Kerr's
bank on the following day ; but he did not keep his word.
Chabot was amazed, on meeting the friend who had asked
him to interfere, when the latter said to him :

" Do not trouble about that affair any more. De Batz
has just spoken to Luillier about it. The matter is
settled, and the seals will be removed to-morrow." [1]

So it appeared that Chabot, the influential conventionist,
" the greatest Frenchman after Robespierre," had made
two vain attempts to move the *Procureur Général Syndic*
of the Department of Paris ; whereas the Baron de Batz
had but to express a wish, to give an order, and he was
promptly obeyed ! Did this man, then, rule the whole
Republic ? Here was food for thought. Chabot, I fancy,
hesitated no longer. His illusions were gone. He thought
himself very simple for failing to understand sooner that

[1] Chabot's Manuscript. National Archives, F⁷, 4637.

a democracy—in Mme. Roland's phrase—was *merely an auction of power, a sort of fair* ; and he faithfully promised himself to make up for lost time.

From that day forward we can follow, almost hourly, the movements of this castaway. We see him slip, we watch him struggling in the revolutionary ocean where the tempest is so fierce. He tries to cling to the wreck of his popularity ; he hopes that his disabled barque may not sink for a little while yet. But the fight is too unequal. The power that holds him has him in a firm grasp ; and he does not even suspect the enemy who is dragging him down.

Indeed he seems to have been very simple ! On the 30th of September, in the Jacobin Club, he made a touching speech on behalf of natural children—poor little creatures who have as much right as the others to the love and the property of their parents. The speech was coldly received. There, at the foot of the rostrum, was many a *sans-culotte* who knew the orator's private life in all its details, for Chabot loved to be considered a Don Juan. Among them was Dufourny, in whose contemptuous glance he could see the crushing accusation that was not brought against him until a month had passed : " Before your marriage was projected you had a mistress. She became a mother : what have you done for her ? Why did you desert her ? In marrying a foreigner you are disowning a Frenchwoman.[1] "

Chabot felt that his influence was on the wane. He was resolved on some movement that should secure him, at any rate, a safe retreat. If he were directly attacked he would say he was slandered, and would accuse Pitt and Coburg on the ground that they were jealous of his

---

[1] *Moniteur*, sitting of the 26th Brumaire in the Jacobin Club.

patriotism. On the 30th of September he made some trivial incident an occasion for the following speech in the Convention.

" Our enemies abroad would have found a capital recipe if they could contrive, by hiring slanderers, to destroy the people's confidence in their representatives."

Then, as this unfounded accusation seemed to cause surprise, he had recourse, for the development of his theme, to one of those fantastic revelations that he was always able to produce.

"There is in Paris," he went on, "a society of women which professes to be revolutionary, and intends to lay a petition before the Convention to expel all the *appellants*.[1] The object of this is to make divisions among you. These women have already harassed the really republican society of the Jacobins. The leader of these revolutionary women came to threaten me with the hatred of her whole sex if I would not yield to their representations. But, I declare solemnly, no woman shall ever make me march in advance of the Revolution, nor yet lag behind it." [2]

The *Moniteur* records the applause that greeted these words, but says nothing of the smiles. The approaching marriage of the Capuchin with a girl of sixteen was the common talk of Paris; he was known to be in love; indeed he did not hide the fact, but took pleasure in relating his good fortune. To make the thing more comic Chabot, three days later, solemnly announced his marriage to his comrades the Jacobins, from the platform of the club. He did so with much feeling.

"It seemed to me," he said, "that it was my duty to give an example of all the virtues! . . . I have been

---

[1] This was the name given to the moderates who, at the King's trial, had voted for an appeal to the people.

[2] *Moniteur*; sitting of Sept. 30, in the Convention,

accused of a weakness for women : I thought the best way
to put an end to that calumny was to take a wife—one for
whom my heart has long cried out."

And he proceeded, very indiscreetly, to tell the whole
tale of his love, and even to read his marriage-contract!
He was not sorry to let his comrades know that he was
marrying a young woman of substance : he obligingly
enlarged upon his own poverty : his whole fortune consisted
of some household furniture, bought in 1792 for 1,500 *livres*
but now worth 6,000 francs on account of the depreciation
of assignats. Having ended these confidences he begged
the society to select a deputation of their members to be
present at his marriage and at the civic banquet that would
follow it.

" I may inform you," he observed, " that no priest will
pollute my marriage ceremony, and that we shall employ
only the municipality. Will the deputation kindly be on
the spot by eight o'clock ? I wish everything to be over
by nine o'clock—(what ? the banquet too ?)—for I shall
not absent myself from the National Convention, and my
betrothed says she will cease to love me if my marriage
makes me neglect, even for one day, the Convention and
the Jacobin Club."

Poor Chabot evidently expected these noble words to be
greeted with thunders of applause. There was a freezing
silence. Dufourny rose and said, rather harshly, that the
society could not, as a body, attend a wedding and a
banquet. Some of the members, however, took pity on
the disconcerted bridegroom, and a discussion ensued.
It was finally decreed that a deputation should support
Chabot on the great day ; the prospect of a banquet,
however early in the morning, overcame their objections.

Ten days later Chabot, with a beaming face, returned
to the Hôtel Frey from the town-hall, with his wife upon

his arm. Were his old father of eighty-five, and his old mother of eighty years of age present at his wedding, I wonder? We have reason to believe they were in Paris at the time. They were born in the days of the *grand roi*, and being simple folk, unacquainted with the philosophers, were probably much attached to the beliefs and ideas of the old order of things. Strange indeed must their emotions have been, when they heard the son whom they had educated piously for the cloister giving their peasant name, under the eye of a municipal officer in a red cap, to a millionaire German-Jewess! Paternal affection, however, is singularly indulgent, and perhaps, in the great salon in the Rue d'Anjou, the old vine-grower of the Rouergue, seeing his " boy " greeted with acclamations by the band of Jacobins whom the banquet had attracted, may have naïvely appropriated a share of the ovation—may have straightened his back and said proudly in his heart : " He is my son ! "

In the very hour that the feast ended the Queen of France was taking her place on the prisoner's stool in the Revolutionary Tribunal. She had reached the summit of her Calvary.[1]

But, though Marie Antoinette died, the odious nickname that the *sans-culottes* gave her did not perish with her. In the evening of the ex-Capuchin's wedding-day Hébert perpetrated a witticism: he called Léopoldine Frey *Chabot's Austrian*. This sarcasm opened the campaign that was conducted so skilfully and secretly by the Baron de Batz.

[1] "Chabot braved public opinion by marrying a foreigner, and at what a moment ! *When Antoinette was before the Revolutionary Tribunal*, when the nation was at the *climax* of its execration of foreigners."

Dufourny's speech in the Jacobin Club. Sitting of 26th Brumaire (see the *Moniteur*).

III

THE HOUSE AT CHARONNE

WHILE Chabot, like a new Hercules in chains, was spinning at the feet of his Omphale from beyond the Rhine, certain events were taking place that we must record.

The citizens of each section elected, as we know, a revolutionary Committee composed of ardent patriots who possessed the entire confidence of their fellow-citizens. Since September 17th, 1793, these Committees had been endowed with the right of arresting *suspects*, a privilege hitherto reserved exclusively for the Conventionist Committee of General Security. Indeed, there was a close connection between this body and the Committees of the Sections—those terrible wheels of the revolutionary machine. Shopkeepers and artisans, jealous, timid, suspicious little *bourgeois*, who gloried in the exercise of the immense authority that had been deputed to them— such were the men who generally composed these Section Committees. And there were more than twenty-one thousand of them in France. "Twenty-one thousand arms bestowed on the government of the Terror!"[1]

Now in Paris itself there was one section whose sentiments had long been, if not royalist, at all events very moderate. This was the section of the Filles-Saint-

[1] Louis Blanc, Book XI. Chap. I,

Thomas.[1] Its national guards, before the 10th of August, had been in favour with the friends of the Court; and the inhabitants of the more advanced sections even declared that these guards had sold themselves to the Palace. On the day after the arrival of the Marseillais in Paris a skirmish had taken place in the Champs Élysées between them and the grenadiers of the Filles-Saint-Thomas. The latter were quickly routed, and it was declared that as they fled towards the palace the swing-bridge of the Tuileries Gardens was opened to let them pass, and closed at once to stop their enemies. The ladies of the Court were even accused of receiving the fugitives into the palace and lavishing the most tender care upon them.

This brawl of more than a year ago was quite forgotten, we may be sure, in September 1793; but it seems probable, none the less, that the section of the Filles-Saint-Thomas was still one of the least sympathetic with the Revolution.[2] When, after Saint-Fargeau's death, it became the Lepéletier Section, it was not counted among the most zealous.

This, no doubt, was why de Batz resolved to choose a house there.[3]

Every man had occasion to fear the vigilance, not only of the Committee of General Security, but of the Revolutionary Committee of his own section. De Batz had good reasons for believing himself safe from the Committee of

[1] The section took its name from the Convent of Dominican nuns in the Rue Vivienne, on the spot where the Exchange now stands. They had established themselves there in 1642, on the Feast of St. Thomas Aquinas, to whom their church was dedicated.

[2] "Three battalions, those of the Filles-Saint-Thomas, of the Petits-Pères, and of the Butte-des-Moulins, were inspired with a monarchical enthusiasm in no way inferior to that of the most devoted servants of the Crown."—*Aventures de Guerre*, Moreau de Jonnès.

[3] In 1787 he was living in the Quartier Saint-Eustache.—Archives of the Public Charity Office.

General Security : for if it had not made a firm resolve to shut its eyes to the movements of the conspirator the order to arrest him would have been given long ago. Alquier, who was the president of the Committee until September 14th, knew beyond possibility of doubt, as we have seen, that de Batz had promised a million francs to forward the Queen's escape. The connecting link between Alquier and de Batz seems to have been a woman named Janson, whom the baron employed in certain delicate missions and had sometimes sent to Chabot.[1]   Chabot, who admits the fact, also suspects that Lavicomterie, another member of the Committee of General Security, had " had communications, at all events indirectly, with de Batz." And even if we cannot accept Chabot's story unreservedly —though he wrote it at a time when it was greatly to his interest not to exaggerate—we cannot deny that Sénar at least, the too-famous secretary and reporter and factotum of the Committee of General Security, was altogether at the disposal of de Batz. This we can prove. On the 11th November, 1795, Sénar wrote, when sending some extracts from his memoirs to a man who had represented Redon in the Constituent Assembly, and begging him to forward them to the Baron de Batz : " *If I am not fortunate enough to see him* (de Batz) *I should at least like him to know that the man he obliged was not ungrateful.*" [2] Now Sénar, when he wrote thus, had been imprisoned in the Plessis since Thermidor : it was therefore when the terror was at its height that de Batz had *obliged* him.

[1] There is no *dossier* of the woman Janson among the archives.   We find in the *Moniteur* that a certain Hélène Janson, wife of one Duluc, a native of Maubeuge, calling herself an *ouvrière en modes*, was acquitted by the Revolutionary Tribunal on the 19th Nivôse, year II.   The very exceptional indulgence shown to this prisoner points to her having influential friends, and being the intriguing woman of whom Chabot speaks.

[2] Eckard. *Lettre à M. Alexis Dumesnil*, editor of the *Mémoires de Sénar*.

THE HOUSE AT CHARONNE

Being easy in his mind, therefore, as to the attitude of the Committee of General Security, his next care was to secure friends in the Committee of his section. Of the safe position that he won in his own neighbourhood we may judge from this fact: of all the names that we shall meet in this narrative, of all the men who were done to death later on as parties to the conspiracy of de Batz, the most important were, like himself, inhabitants of the Lepéletier Section. Roussel lived in the Rue Helvétius,[1] as did also the Abbé d'Alençon, the Abbé Briel, and Marino, an official in the police department, whom we shall find playing a part in our story. The Marquis de la Guiche lived in the Rue de Louvois; the retired actor Marignon in the Rue de Marivaux; Pottier de Lille and Admiral had rooms in the Rue Favart; Citoyenne Grand-maison, the woman Grivois, little Nicole Bouchard, and Birel-Tissot lived in the Rue de Ménars; Pain-d'Avoine in the Rue des Petits-Champs; and Chrétien himself—the fiery patriot, one of the most implacable jurymen of the Revolutionary Tribunal, and, it is said, a confederate of de Batz[2]—kept a coffee-house in the Place du Théâtre-Italien,[3] at the corner of the Rue Favart. Cortey had a grocer's shop at the corner of the Rue de la Loi[4] and the Rue des Filles-Saint-Thomas; while Sartines and the Sainte-Amaranthe ladies were in lodgings in the Rue Vivienne.

We must not attach too much importance to the fact—which may have been quite accidental—that the agents of de Batz were grouped together in this way. It is probable, however, that when he fixed on this quarter he had these people in his mind, and hoped gradually to secure the neutrality of the Section Committee, of which Pottier de

[1] Now Rue Sainte-Anne.
[2] H. Provins: *Le dernier roi légitime de France.*
[3] Now Place Boïeldieu. [4] Now Rue de Richelieu.

61

Lille was the secretary and Cortey the commandant of the National Guard.

But a grain of sand was enough to clog the machinery that had been so cleverly put together. This grain of sand took the form of a denunciation. Had it been addressed to the Committee of General Security it would probably have been merely entered in the books by Sénar; but it was sent to the Section Committee. It reached its destination on the 30th September, at midnight, and the two commissioners who were still on duty at that late hour, Vergne and Péron, were not, by an aggravation of ill-luck, friends of the Baron de Batz. The denunciation, which called attention to an association " of *suspects* and *émigrés*, who generally met at Cortey's house," was due to the labours of Maillard, the famous *Tape-dur* (or Thumphard) of the Abbaye, who, being already invalided by the illness that killed him shortly afterwards, was represented by Lafosse, head of the intelligence department of the Parisian police. What is really inexplicable to this day is that Élie Lacoste, nine months later, wrote in his report to the Convention : " Batz and his agents were denounced long ago to Maillard, who has died since. *He knew everything and said nothing about it.*" As for Lafosse, he was guillotined as an accomplice of the Baron de Batz.

To what conclusion can we come ? That these two men, in league with de Batz, had chosen for their denunciation a day when they knew the conspirators were not assembled, in the certainty that the projected inquiry would have no result ? This would be a sure method of warding off suspicion for a long time; but it would be a very bold one !

It is more likely, perhaps, that Maillard, Vergne, and Lafosse, as was asserted by de Batz, had no desire to arrest the conspirator, but merely wished to disturb and frighten

him, and wring some money from him.[1] Be that as it may,
Vergne instantly roused some national guards at the central
guard-house of the section, and, followed by Lafosse, proceeded to the grocer's house. The door opened at the first
summons ; the authorities entered the house, visited every
room, examined even the cellars, and found nothing.[2]

When the patriots found themselves back in the street
after this performance they looked at one another rather
sheepishly. They held a consultation. Everyone knew
that Citizen de Batz owned a little house at Charonne,
where he liked to receive his friends. Charonne was a
long way off ! No matter : the interests of the country
demanded the sacrifice : the night, if dark, was mild.[3]
Levacher, who was commanding the " armed force," cried :
" Right turn ! March at ease ! " and they set off. The
hour was about one o'clock in the morning. The hope of
surprising the conspirators in conclave, or better still, in
bed, gave courage to the most reluctant. They crossed
the sleeping town, reached the Place de la Bastille, and,
through the suburbs, entered the interminable Rue de
Charonne. They passed the barrier, and found themselves
in the open country : the road rose through the vineyards
to the village, which they reached after a march of an
hour and a half.

Vergne then inquired for the house of the mayor,
Citizen Piprel, and relentlessly awoke that worthy man,
who proceeded to do the same for the *procureur-syndic* of
the commune. They both knew the baron's house, and
headed the patrol in the capacity of guides.

[1] See *La journée des Soixante*.

[2] Cortey's house, as we have said, stood at the corner of the Rue des
Filles-Saint-Thomas and the Rue de la Loi, and had a door on both
streets. It is now No. 68, Rue Richelieu, and has been completely
changed. Cortey's widow, Marie Barbe Élizabeth Barré, was still
living there in 1827. At that time it was the Hôtel de Lyon.

[3] *Bulletin de l'Observatoire*, Sept. 30th, 1793.

They marched through the village: then, when the last
house was passed, Vergne and his men took the Bagnolet
road—very quietly, treading gently, speaking only in
lowered voices. Soon Piprel signed to them that they had
reached the place. On the right of the road, in the
shadow of the great elms[1] that overhung it, they perceived
a gateway with a tiled covering. To the right of this
entrance was a little lodge or pavilion with an iron gate
before it; to the left was a long, one-storeyed house—the
house for which they were looking. There was no light
in the windows: the clock of the old church at Charonne
was striking three.[2]

This mysterious house of the Baron de Batz is still in
existence. By a really remarkable chance it has survived
the most surprising transformation that a village could
undergo in the course of a hundred years. A century ago
Charonne was a hamlet hidden among vineyards: it has
become a town with a population of a hundred thousand.
It has been intersected with avenues; its streets have been
straightened and made regular; it has been beautified in
a hundred different ways since it became part of a city
that is more subject to change than any other capital in
the world.

The thing seems so improbable that one might well
think any inquiry on the subject would be futile. It was
without the least hope of success, therefore, that I set
forth to hunt out the probable site of the house, guided
by the rather inadequate topographical information in the

---

[1] Plan of the park of the Château de Bagnolet, in the Cabinet des
Estampes. The gate of the pavilion is still in existence. In place of
the coat of arms that it used to bear are the initials F. P. in wrought
iron. These two letters do not mean François Premier, as is believed
in Charonne, but François Pomerel—the name of the owner of the
Hermitage in 1815.

[2] Report of the Inquiry. National Archives, F⁷, 4732.

report that Citizen Vergne drew up, after his expedition of the 30th September, 1793.

Vague as these directions were they showed me that I might confine my search to the district now included in the Rues de Bagnolet, des Balkans, and Vitruve, and the Boulevard Davoust. I carefully examined every house within these limits that seemed to me sufficiently venerable to be at least a hundred years old, and I thus became certain—morally certain only—that the house of the Baron de Batz had remained intact. It now bears the numbers 148–150 of the Rue de Bagnolet, and is used by the poor-law commissioners to house the managers and various officials of the Hospice Debrouse, lately erected beside the Rue des Balkans. The kindness of these officials facilitated my inquiry, and soon, when I had seen the title-deeds, my belief changed to certainty. I was actually in the Baron's house, which, since 1793, had suffered no changes save in detail.

These little mysteries of Parisian topography, which to many may seem dull, have the power of arousing in some readers an interest that amounts to a passion. And indeed there is no more effectual way of realising the details of an historical scene than by picturing the actors amid the surroundings of their stage. This is my reason for indulging here in a few lines of description.

Beyond the hamlet of Charonne, about the middle of the eighteenth century, the road skirted the park of the Château de Bagnolet, the property of the Duc d'Orléans. At the extreme corner of the park, in the direction of Paris, stood a little pavilion that was built in the time of the Regency for purposes of the chase—and other uses. It contained a *salon d'été* with paintings on its walls, representing "the lives of Abraham and the various saints of the desert,"[1]

---

[1] D'Argenville, *Description des environs de Paris*, 1768.

F

from which curious fantasy the whole of this corner of the park had received the name of the Hermitage. The delightful groves that had been designed by Desforges, the pupil and nephew of Lenôtre, bordered the road all the way to the village of Bagnolet.

It was about the year 1770 that the Duc d' Orléans sold this beautiful property. The park was cut up, and one of the first portions to find an owner was the Hermitage : the hunting-box became a private house. As this pavilion only contained one huge room and six rather small ones the new owner, M. Morel de Joigny, an advocate in the Parlement of Paris, built beside it a very simple but more habitable country-house, with only one storey above the ground-floor. On the one side it overlooked the Bagnolet road, and on the other the demesne of about five acres [1] that had been cut off from the original park of the Duc d'Orléans. And indeed the place being still very solitary, since none of the owners had decided to build on their land, the house at the Hermitage seemed to stand in the midst of woods, for it was only separated by a wall from the forest-trees of the park.

Such was the property that the Baron de Batz had bought in 1787 for 30,000 *livres*, in the presence of the royal notary Maître Minguet, from M. de Saudrécourt, who had succeeded M. Morel de Joigny in 1783.[2] Of course, at that time, he had no thought of conspiracies and could not have foreseen the rôle that the future had in store for him ; but it cannot be denied that fate had served him well.

The place was far enough from Paris to make the vigilance of the patriots, when the Terror was at its height, less easy to exercise than in the town ; at the same time it was included in the limited district within which the

---

[1] Exactly 1 *hectare* 76 *ares* (Survey of 1806).
[2] Archives of the Public Charity Office.

formality of the passport was not required, and it could therefore be visited without the knowledge of the suspicious authorities. And what advantages it had for a conspirator! Four of the barriers of Paris were near it: the Barrière de l'Aunay, the Barrière des Rats, and those of Charonne and Montreuil. It was possible, then, for a man to go twice to and fro between the Hermitage and Paris without showing his face or his certificate-of-safety more than once at the same gate. And moreover a whole labyrinth of lanes made it possible to avoid using the main street of the village: the Ruelle des Vaches, the Rue Aumer, the Chemin du Parc, the Voie Neuve, and others. Finally, if anyone were indiscreet enough to knock at the door, it was easy to go into the garden and plunge into the shrubbery—and *hey presto!* in one bound the fugitive was over the wall, and lost in what had been the park of the Duc d'Orléans, but was, in 1793, a kind of primeval forest. Before the visitor had time even to explain the object of his visit the person he had come to seek had reached Saint-Mandé by a short cut; or, if that seemed too far to go, the huge quarries of Bagnolet offered a temporary retreat that was perfectly safe.[1] The quarries in the outskirts of Paris played an important part during the Terror. It was in the quarries of Montmartre that Rougeville lived for ten days, in absolute peace of mind and body, while the whole police-force of Paris hunted for him. But we must return without further delay to Citizen Vergne, whom we left before the door of the house in which, so many times, the course of the Revolution had received a check.

Vergne made his preparations for the fray. He posted some of his men as sentries in the Ruelle des Vaches, and placed some outposts under the elms of the Bagnolet

---

[1] See the plans of the Survey of 1806–1812.

road; then, followed by Lafosse, Piprel the Mayor, and the rest of his little force, supported by a few national guards from Charonne, he knocked at the main entrance, the door between the Hermitage and the dwelling-house.

There was no answer.

The commissioner waited for a few moments, and knocked again.

The silence was still unbroken.

Ten or twelve minutes passed. At last there was a sound of an opening door somewhere within the walls; of a heavy step upon the gravel; of a second door being opened and shut; of approaching feet and a key turning in the lock.[1] The great door swung ajar.

Vergne pushed past the man who held it, and entered the courtyard briskly, followed by his soldiers. In spite of the darkness one glance was enough to show him the main features of the place. On the right stood the Hermitage Pavilion, a little obliquely, with high, arched French windows; opposite to the entrance-gate were the dark shadowy trees of the garden; on the left, facing the shrubberies, was the long dwelling-house. The door opened suddenly, and a woman appeared on the threshold. It was Citoyenne Grandmaison.

Vergne went up to her, and asked a few questions. She seemed slightly disturbed, or rather, surprised, like one awakened suddenly; and answered that she was the tenant of the house, and lived there alone with her servants. The commissioner accepted her answer for the moment: and, entering the house, crossed the hall and went upstairs. On the first floor was Citoyenne Grandmaison's room, and

---

[1] Though the door is not the old one, the original lock still exists. It is peculiarly solid and heavy. The key, which is also old, is of colossal dimensions.

another near it, in which, when the door was opened, a man was discovered.[1]

"Your certificate," said Vergne shortly.

"Here it is, citizen," said the other, taking from his pocket a certificate-of-safety of the Lepéletier Section.

Vergne hurried away to examine all the rooms. The beds had evidently been slept in, and when he touched the sheets he found them still warm. It was plain that their late occupants had fled.

Vergne went downstairs again and proceeded to the Hermitage Pavilion, ordered the doors to be opened, and hastened through all the rooms. First there was a circular hall with niches [2] round it, then a tiny gallery, and beyond that a large salon with two little rooms off it. The semi-circular salon was painted with charming frescoes.[3] On a table were several plates containing fragments of cake— signs of an interrupted supper-party. The commissioner mounted to the attics, awoke the servants who were sleeping there, and then visited the cellars.

There was no one to be found.

At that moment one of the sentries ran in from the Ruelle des Vaches.

"Citizen," he said, "there is a man in the garden. He has a white riding-coat. We saw him creeping under the trees."

"Search the garden!" ordered Vergne.

He superintended the search himself. They beat the bushes, and hunted all along the walls, and left no shrub unexplored.

---

[1] The entire report of this inquiry and examination, of which an epitome is given here, is in the National Archives, in Citoyenne Grand-maison's *dossier*, F⁷, 4732. It has been published in a similar version, but from another *dossier*, by M. Campardon, *Histoire du Tribunal révolutionnaire de Paris*.

[2] They are still decorated as they were in the days of the Regency.

[3] They have not altogether vanished.

Still there was no one to be found.

Vergne returned to the dwelling-house. As he was crossing the hall a man stood up, facing him at the foot of the stairs.

" Your certificate ? "

" In a moment, citizen."

And without further ado the man showed him a certificate issued to him by the section of the Theâtre-Français, bearing the number 154.

The search was over. Nothing remained to be done but to question the servants separately. The commissioner returned to the salon of the pavilion, to carry on the examinations. He was not a little surprised, on entering the room that had been so carefully searched a few minutes earlier, to find a fourth individual, who seemed to be waiting for him quite patiently. This house that professed to be empty was gradually becoming populous. These men, apparently, had come out of the walls.

" Your certificate ? "

" Certainly," answered the stranger ; and proceeded leisurely to draw from his pocket-book a perfectly correct certificate of the Lepéletier Section, bearing the number 2835.

Vergne turned everyone out of the salon, pushed away the plates, sat down at the table, and having chosen a registrar from among his men gave orders that all the people discovered on the premises should be brought in, one by one.

The official report of this examination is a curious record, and if it be permissible to read between the lines of a document of the kind we may learn many things from it. And first we shall see, without possibility of doubt, that all who frequented the house at Charonne were supplied with a watch-word : it was understood as a matter of course that not one of them had seen de Batz for a long time ; that he seldom came thither ; that they hardly knew him. On this point they were all agreed ; but in matters of detail they had come to no conclusion beforehand ; whence the regrettable contradictions that would have been fatal to the conspirators if Vergne had known his business. But the questions he asked were inconsequent and indefinite ; he seems almost to have been afraid of compromising those whom he was questioning.

To us this document reveals one obvious fact : that de Batz was in the house when Vergne knocked at the door ; that Roussel, Cortey, and Lézardière were there also ; that the reason the cook Rollet delayed so long to admit the commissioner was that the baron and his chief confederates might have time to escape, and that the servants might have time to awaken the conspirators hidden in the attics of the Hermitage, who also tried to slip away, but were unsuccessful. The first witness summoned by Vergne is the gardener, Roblot.[1] He is, he says, in the service of Citoyenne Grandmaison, and it is she who pays him. She lives in the house, alone with the Baron de Batz ; but the latter has not been seen at the place for the last fortnight.

The cook Rollet [2] declares he came to the house " *on the invitation of a friend.* It was he who opened the door to the commissioner, and if he delayed to do so for a short time it was not in order to run to the pavilion to awake the citizens who were there, oh ! no—it was because the keys were *at the locksmith's, and he had to go and ask for them.*" He further remembers putting a cake on the table. It was eaten by Citoyenne Grandmaison, Citoyens

[1] Claude Roblot, gardener by the day, residing in the Rue de Reuilly, Section des Quinze-Vingts, No. 43.

[2] Jacques Claude Rollet, temporary cook, residing in the Rue Pagevin, No. 46.

la Guiche and Marignon, and the little Cortey girl, the daughter of the grocer in the Rue des Filles-Saint-Thomas."

The charwoman[1] has not seen de Batz "for eight or ten days ; she only knows that citizens Marignon and Desardy were at supper, with another man whose name she does not know."

Vergne makes no comment on the name of Desardy,[2] but summons the housemaid.[3] She includes among the frequenters of the house the Citoyenne Féroussac, the Grandmaison's sister ; and Roussel and Marignon, who are very intimate there. "She has not seen la Guiche and the others more than two or three times in the year. De Batz comes to Charonne about every two days."

La Guiche, who is summoned next, gives the lie to the housemaid. He visits the Grandmaison *every Sunday* ; also on Monday ; and sometimes on Saturday. He meets Roussel here fairly often, but de Batz very seldom ; and he does not know where the latter lives. As for this evening, he spent it playing backgammon with Marignon.

" And Sartiges ? " adds Vergne.

" Sartiges ? Yes, la Guiche has seen him once ; he is not sure when. Yes, perhaps it was yesterday at about five o'clock in the afternoon, but he did not spend the evening with him."

Vergne call the next witness : it is Sartiges.[4]

[1] Anne Jouy, wife of Mathieu Bourrier, military waggoner, residing at Charonne, in the house of Citizen Bernard.

[2] It should be remembered that Robert de la Lézardière was hiding his identity at that time under the name of Desardier.

[3] Marie Marguerite Papillon, wife of Cottereau, residing in the house of Citoyenne Grandmaison, Rue de Ménars, 7.

[4] Louis Sartiges, aged 26, man of letters, residing in the Rue de la Liberté, formerly Rue des Francs-Bourgeois, 121, Section du Théâtre-Français.

THE HOUSE AT CHARONNE

"With whom did you spend the evening?" he asks.

"With la Guiche and Marignon; and Citizen Roussel, too, was at dinner."

Marignon,[1] on being questioned after the others, declares that Roussel went away at six o'clock, and took Cortey's little girl with him.

Roussel? For the second time Vergne omits to take any notice of this name. Citoyenne Grandmaison, when questioned in her turn, whispers to the commissioner that Roussel went away early, because he was ill. And so the inquiry continues: always the same irresolution on Vergne's part, and the same evasions and contradictions on the part of the witnesses. Sartiges explains that if he was found in the house though he had slept in the pavilion it was because, hearing a noise, he went in search of Citoyenne Grandmaison; a sudden indisposition made him run for shelter, and he met a soldier in the yard; but he had no intention of escaping through the garden. As for la Guiche, he had slept here, without going to bed. He started off to Paris at about eleven o'clock, but found the night too dark; so, as he had a latch-key, he returned without anyone's knowledge, and threw himself down on a bed in the attics of the pavilion.

All this was suspicious, extremely suspicious, it must be admitted. If there were ever an occasion when the word *suspect* might have been justly used it was in connection with these people, who did not know why they were there, nor how they had got there, nor whom they had supped with. So thought Vergne: and when day dawned he returned to Paris, taking with him the Grandmaison, la Guiche, Sartiges, Marignon, the gardener, the housemaid,

[1] Jean Baptiste Dessabre, known as Marignon or Marignan, formerly an actor at the Comédie Italienne, 78 years old, residing in the Rue Marivaux, 18.

the charwoman, and the cook. The house at Charonne was left empty, and the conspirators met there no more.

The eight *suspects* were led before the Revolutionary Committee of Surveillance of the Lepéletier Section. Their position was serious : their contradictory answers, their embarrassment, their reserves, and, more than all, the fact that they were found together in a house that was, if not the property, at all events the habitual dwelling of a refractory and deeply compromised *émigré*, were reasons enough for lodging them in one of the numerous prisons at the government's disposal. The commissioners, however, treated them with the greatest indulgence. If they did not go so far as to blame Vergne for his ill-timed zeal they showed their disapproval of his actions by setting all the prisoners at liberty on the spot, with the exceptions of la Guiche, who was sent to La Force, and Citoyenne Grandmaison, who was imprisoned at Sainte-Pélagie.[1] And even this, as we shall see, was not for long. The name of the Baron de Batz, decidedly, was one to conjure with ; and of this there was proof on the following day, the 1st October.

On that day Roussel, who was thought to be the secretary of the conspiracy, was arrested in his turn at his rooms in the Rue Helvétius, and taken before the Committee of Surveillance. He admitted without pressure that de Batz had shared his apartments and was then living in Cortey's house ; and that he had now and then met him at Charonne, where a few mutual friends gathered sometimes in the summer to taste the innocent pleasures of the country. He unhesitatingly confessed that he had

---

[1] The names of Marignon, Sartiges, Roblot and Rollet do not appear in the registers of the Prefecture of Police, nor yet those of the women Bourrier and Cottereau.

helped de Batz to obtain a certificate-of-residence, and said that if he had offered him a room it was to save him from the discomforts of lodgings. But when the Committee tried to secure more definite information he said ironically that it was impossible for him to answer questions, as he knew nothing and saw no one, for reasons of prudence, and had even abstained, since the passing of the law against *suspects*, from visiting his own brother ! Finally, when he was questioned as to his means of subsistence and his occupations, Roussel replied that he had no profession, and "confined himself to the title of citizen." [1]

The commissioners were greatly embarrassed. The man before them was an undoubted accomplice and a personal friend of the conspirator. Ought they not to send him to prison ? But this they had no intention of doing. The mere name of the Baron de Batz seems to have acted like a talisman, to have been a kind of sanctuary that made everyone inviolable who sought its protection. There was some question of simply putting Roussel in the central guard-house of the section ; but he observed that his state of health did not permit him to live a sedentary life, and he was at once set at liberty, under the surveillance of two guards who had orders not to lose sight of him.

This was the privileged treatment that was enjoyed by such prisoners as were not very dangerous and had strong protection. It invariably happened that a few days of this close companionship made the two guards into two friends. Their surveillance cost their charge three *livres* per head a day ; but it is quite evident that a modest addition to this sum sufficed to buy freedom, and that vigilance relaxed as

---

[1] National Archives, W, 389. The examination of Roussel is substantially given by M Campardon in his *Histoire du Tribunal révolutionnaire*, Vol. I., p. 508.

the coins multiplied. At that time all Paris was being entertained by the sight of Citoyenne Brissot, who was to be met walking with her son in the streets and public gardens, mingling with the passers-by and speaking to all her acquaintances—and followed, at a distance of fifty paces, by the gendarme assigned to her by the Committee of General Security, who had the tact to exercise his delicate functions from afar.[1]

Roussel, then, was able to attend to his affairs. To put him in charge of two gendarmes was to present two new confederates to the conspiracy. They had no reason, moreover, to complain of the client that fate had bestowed on them. Roussel divided his time between his property at Marolle and the gambling-houses of the Palais Royal. We shall see him again, enjoying a game with his guards in the billiard-room of No 121, to which he was a frequent visitor.

A week later la Guiche, too, began to sigh for freedom. He was of noble birth—a marquis ; all his family had emigrated ; he had emigrated himself ; he was *suspect* and had been arrested in the house of a conspirator. These were reasons enough, one would think, for severe treatment. No matter : de Batz had need of him, and at once an order from the Committee threw open the doors of La Force, and bestowed on him, as on Roussel, the protection of two guardians at three francs a head. In his case we know their names : Citizens Seine and Gonnaz, inspectors of police. La Guiche and his guards disappeared that very evening, and no doubt he taught the two police- men some new tricks, for nothing was heard of them for four months.[2]

---

[1] *Rapport d'un agent secret*, 28th Sept. 1793.—National Archives, F[7], 3688[3].

[2] National Archives, F[7], 4758.

THE HOUSE AT CHARONNE

A week later it was Biret-Tissot who proved his aptitude for baffling the constituted authorities and slipping through the hands of the police. Biret, it may be remembered, was the servant who was employed alternately by Citoyenne Grandmaison and the Baron de Batz. Such was his official position; but in reality he was one of the couriers of the conspiracy. Later on he figured in Élie Lacoste's report as being "in all his master's secrets, and being employed to circulate a very active and continuous correspondence among the conspirators."

Now on the 16th October he happened to be at Saint-Germain-en-Laye. What he was doing there on the very day that the Queen went to the scaffold I do not know. He had arrived on the previous day, and the passers-by had observed him loitering for long hours in the Rue du Pain, as though waiting for someone. When at last a man addressed him the appearance of the two roused the suspicion of a patrol, who seized them, and took them before the general council of the Commune of Saint-Germain.

Biret-Tissot gave his names and described himself as a jeweller. He had been at Saint-Germain for a week, he said, and had also been trading at Versailles, where the autumn fair was going on. Then he became loquacious and played the imbecile. The examination he underwent is so minutely recorded that one can almost hear the very tones of his voice as he lied to the questioning official.[1]

In the first place he knows some people at Saint-Germain : Citoyenne Delaunay, who bought some earrings from him, and the landlord of the *Épée Royale,* and the hairdresser who lives over the way. He lives in Paris, in a street called —called—" I am nearly sure it is Rue Feydeau, No. 7."

[1] From the registers of the Commune of Saint-Germain-en-Laye. National Archives, F7, 4601.

He has stayed there for six months, so he must be right. Before that he lived in the Rue Beaurepaire in the house of a man called Grammont—unless indeed it was in the Rue Grammont with Citizen Beaurepaire. His certificate-of-safety? Here it is, his certificate-of-safety; only it is not signed with his name, because he cannot write. If he has no passport it is because it is unnecessary to obtain one for the department of Seine-et-Oise. He is *doing* the suburbs: he hopes to sell his earrings. Indeed he has already sold some: one pair to a young man, on order, and another to another citizen. How did he make the acquaintance of the citizen who was arrested with him? Why, he met him, and suggested to him to go to a café. If he was loitering about in the Rue du Pain for a long time it was because he had noticed a pretty girl there.

Biret, indeed, had provided for every contingency. When he was searched there were found upon him twenty-seven pairs of earrings, fifteen rings, and a pair of assay-scales.[1] His companion gave his name with some difficulty: he was called Bachelier and described himself as a manufacturer of stockings, Rue des Récollets. Here the examination came to an end, this citizen being—or pretending to be—absolutely and inarticulately drunk. He was sent to the police-station: then a cabriolet was brought to the door, the gendarme Devaux was summoned, Biret was placed in his charge, and the two drove off to Paris, their destination being the Committee of the Lepéletier Section.

The jeweller, during the journey, made himself very agreeable. He probably treated the gendarme to a drink, for the latter was his devoted friend by the time they reached the barrier. When they came to the bridge that was formerly the Pont Royal Biret took his companion's hand.

[1] National Archives, F⁷, 4601.

"Think for a moment, Devaux," he said. "We shall soon be at the Section.. They will keep me there, for I have no one to answer for me: I shall have to pass the night there. I shall not be able, before to-morrow, to send for my brother to come and take me away. Now all this means, you see, that my whole day will be lost."

"Well?"

"Well, let us go and fetch my brother now, and he will come to the Committee with us. Then they will let me go free at once, for, you see, I am a good patriot."

"Does your brother live far away?" asked Devaux hesitatingly.

"Only a few steps from here. Is it all right, eh? Coachman—Rue Montmartre!"

In the Rue Montmartre the cabriolet drew up. Biret sprang to the ground. The gendarme followed him merely as a matter of duty, for he suspected nothing. Biret pushed open the gate of a dark alley, at the end of which was the glazed door of a café. He asked the concierge:

"Are M. and Mme. Clément at home?"

"Yes," answered the concierge from the back of his lodge.

"Good! Wait there, Devaux; I am going to fetch the key."

And Biret darted into the café. The gendarme hesitated for a moment, then in his turn pushed open the glass door and entered the café. There was no one there. The woman at the desk, noticing his agitation, told him that a man she knew by sight, from having seen him at the café several times, had just passed through the room. He had even wished her good-day as he passed; then he went out.

" Where ? " asked Devaux, pale with anguish.

" Out there, of course ! " she pointed to the front of the house, which opened on the Rue Montorgueil.[1]

The unhappy gendarme Devaux returned to his cabriolet and drove to the Revolutionary Committee of the Lepéletier Section, his original destination. Having heard his explanations they put him in the guardhouse, where he spent three days. Had not the General Council of the Commune of Saint-Germain grown uneasy about their gendarme and at last demanded him the poor man, no doubt, would have been included, six months later, among the confederates of the Batz Conspiracy.[2]

De Batz himself appears to have been quite undisturbed by these various incidents. He felt he was unassailable, as indeed he was. How, if he were not certain of his safety, can we explain the fact that this man, who was *suspect* on twenty different grounds and whose accomplices were examined in the hope of tracing him,[3] dared to take part actively in public affairs ? We are driven to believe that he was in league, not only with many of the influential patriots of his own section, but also with certain members of the Committee of General Security, such as Lavicomterie, who was suspected by Chabot, and Louis (of the Bas-Rhin), who was often entertained by Frey. In the Convention he had relations with Alquier,

---

[1] National Archives, F⁷, 4601.

[2] A very strange fact is that the Council of the Commune de Saint-Germain, when demanding the person of their gendarme on the 19th Oct., add : " His negligence was very great ; but, after all, the evil is repaired, since Biret-Tissot has been recaptured." Now the man who had just been captured was not the real Biret, who was only arrested on the 26th Brumaire, that is to say, more than a month after his flight. —(Archives of the Prefecture of Police.)

[3] This was, as a matter of fact, the object of Roussel's arrest (Oct. 1, 1793) : *as a precautionary measure, and in order to have a means of discovering de Batz.*

Simond, Julien (of Toulouse), Bazire, Hérault de Séchelles,[1] Chabot himself, and Delaunay (of Angers), through whom he became allied with Lhuillier, *procureur-syndic* of the department of Paris, and with Hébert. If it is true that he had a hold, through Benoît, on Danton, Lacroix, and their friends,[2] he had indeed little to fear. I know well enough that in making these allegations I am echoing the stories of rather untrustworthy witnesses, such as Chabot, Sénar, and Élie Lacoste; but after all, when one is confronted by an inexplicable fact, one must look everywhere for an explanation. And this explains everything. The Baron de Batz was left undisturbed because he had accomplices in the councils of the government. Because these accomplices did not admit their connivance with the conspirator, can we conclude that they were innocent? Why should we believe those who denied rather than those who accused, when they were all prompted by a single motive—to save their heads?

The various historians of the Revolution have generally had, unfortunately, but one aim: to defend their chosen hero, whoever he might be, and drag all his opponents in the mud. Chabot's accusations, therefore, are not accepted without reserve. Chabot is embarrassing: he accuses too many people. But every historian admits that there are, in Chabot's narrative, "a few truths hidden among many lies," which fact makes it permissible to score a point. Now, we have no theory to support. We are simply trying to explain the known fact that de Batz, with the

---

[1] Lhuillier had been accused by the Committee of Public Safety of having had an interview with Hérault de Séchelles, with the object of allying himself with the Baron de Batz." *Mémoires de Sénar.*

[2] "Danton, Lacroix, and several others have done business with one of my friends from Angers, called Benoît." These were Delaunay's words to Chabot.—*Manuscrit de Chabot:* National Archives, F⁷, 4637.

greatest ease, went to and fro in Paris with impunity. Chabot's narrative gives us this explanation : why should we reject it ? Moreover, to tell the truth, this narrative inspires us with absolute confidence. Chabot does not show himself in a very flattering light. He accuses Danton, it is true—and this is why he is disbelieved—but he exonerates Fabre d'Églantine, whom it was to his interest to accuse. And the simplicity of the story, the prolixity, the informality of the style, everything, even the character of the writing, proves that this general confession was written impulsively, spontaneously, without reticence, and almost without reflection.[1]

Chabot, then, was not lying when he mentioned the men whose names we have just given as being in league with the Baron de Batz. By means of what talisman did the latter secure such powerful allies ? There is but one answer to this question : he bought them ; for it would be ridiculous to suggest that Alquier and Hérault de Séchelles were royalists. And this would be the right moment to speak of the pecuniary resources of the conspirators. Unfortunately this is a difficult point to elucidate. " Batz and his accomplices had about twenty millions between them," said Élie Lacoste. Twenty millions is a considerable sum, and we have no means of verifying the statement. In all the reports that make mention of the conspiracy *Pitt's guineas* figure conspicuously. This was one of the favourite themes of revolutionary eloquence, and received, I fancy, very little attention. It is very possible, however, that England or the *Émigrés* sent money to the royalists in Paris ; and if we

---

[1] We are not now referring to the first statement made by Chabot to the Committee of General Security, on the eve of his arrest, which has been printed several times ; but to the lengthy confidences that he made in writing, in his cell in the Luxembourg, which are now in the Archives, F⁷, 4637.

take the famous English Letter seriously we shall find in it a certain amount of evidence that such a subsidy was actually paid.

Ah, that English Letter—what gallons of ink have been spilt because of it! There are few to-day who know of this affair, and were it not for an allusion in Élie Lacoste's report it would be entirely forgotten. It was simply a correspondence "found at the end of June, 1793, in an English portfolio on the northern frontier." This portfolio was brought to the Committee of Public Safety, who ordered a considerable number of copies of the documents it contained to be translated and printed, and on 4th August decreed that the originals should be deposited in the national archives.

This was giving extreme importance to a fact of no great significance. The portfolio merely contained a letter and a memorandum-book full of notes. With the exception of a few hieroglyphics the letter was not in cipher. It dealt with all kinds of questions : war, money, assignats, provisions, politics, and monopolies. There were passages in this style : " Whatever happens be ready, with all the picked men, for the 10th or 16th August. There are enough lucifer matches, and a hundred of them can safely be given to each of the confederates, since each packet of a hundred measures no more than an inch and three-quarters in circumference, by four and a half long. . . . "—" Money must not be spared. His lordship does not wish you to try and send or keep any account : he even wishes all the papers to be destroyed, since, if they were found, they might be dangerous for all our friends in France. . . . "—" We have 40,000 pounds sterling (equivalent to nearly six million francs, rated at their present value) for the Committees . . . "—" The vault of the Coll. would be suitable for F—G—'s plan."

　　　　　　　G 2

As for the memorandum-book it contained some rather interesting notes.

"*2nd April.*—Letter from Dillon.

"*26th April.*—Paid £600 to effect a change in the Committee's order to remain.

"*27th April.*—Crossed to Dunkirk; arranged with Morel to begin sending couriers, from the 1st May to 30th July 1793, at £30 apiece, in cash.

"*2nd May.*—Received letter from Dumouriez.

"*21st May.*—Burnt all papers and letters up to this date.

"*1st June.*—Gave G. to distribute, £1,050, etc. . . ."[1]

His lordship, the lucifer matches, and the vault, all seem to one at first like fantastic echoes from a romantic burlesque: but it is very unlikely that the Committee of Public Safety would have allowed it to be thought that they had a price, even if that price were six millions, if there had been no proof of the authenticity of the letter. But to conclude, with Élie Lacoste, that all this money was destined for de Batz, is going too far.

We might be tempted to think, however, that he was not unconnected with all this outlay, if we were to take seriously another secret correspondence, quoted by M. Thiers,[2] in which we read the following strange instructions: "See that the price of all provisions is raised. Give orders to your tradesmen to obtain monopolies of all the absolute necessities of life. If you can persuade Cott . . . i to buy up all the tallow and candles at any price, make the public pay as much as five francs a pound for them. His lordship is greatly pleased with the way B . t . z has behaved. We hope that the assassinations will

[1] National Archives, AD[1], 108.
[2] *Histoire de la Révolution.*—Convention, Chap. XII.

be carried out prudently. Disguised priests and women are the most suitable for that performance."

Whatever may be the truth in this matter a great deal of money passed through the baron's hands. A letter that was found in the possession of Devaux[1] gives us an insight into the funds that were at the disposal of de Batz. He had an account with the Vandenyvers,[2] with whom, apparently, he had 216,000 francs. To the stockbroker Arry La Roche he was pledged to repay, at various dates, 1,111,245 *livres* in assignats; but his credit in that quarter amounted to £31,433 in bills of exchange on London, 3,000 florins on Amsterdam, and 1,091 pistoles on Madrid: total, between six and seven millions in assignats.

To Sarrazin his liabilities amounted to 409,500 *livres*, for money borrowed on various occasions. His assets consisted of 8,175 piastres on Livourne, 6,437 on Genoa, £2,630 on London; with 4,500 new *louis d'or* and 400 old, which, considering the scarcity of the metal, represented an enormous sum.

But what is the use of prolonging this list of figures? These will have shown us that de Batz disposed of very considerable sums of money. This is all that it concerns us to know, and it is quite useless to demand a detailed statement of his fortune, which seems to have been essentially variable. One thing is certain: these funds were not his own, but came to him through agents living abroad.

It should also be mentioned that Roussel confessed later on to the fabrication of false assignats, a pastime that was

---

[1] This letter is undated, but is entirely in the writing of Devaux. We may therefore place it in the year 1793, at which time he was secretary to de Batz.—National Archives, VV, 389.

[2] Bankers. They were guillotined with Mme. du Barry.

much in favour in the year 1793. We may even assert, on the word of a document that seems authentic,[1] that this illicit enterprise was carried on in the house at Charonne; in which case the fortune of the Baron de Batz was inexhaustible.

We will now describe how he used this powerful lever for the furtherance of his schemes.

[1] See page 169.

IV

THE INDIA COMPANY.

On the 27th September, a fortnight before his marriage, Chabot left his humble rooms in the Rue Saint-Honoré[1] and repaired to the house of his brothers-in-law. The seals that had been affixed to the property of the Freys, as foreign bankers, had been removed on the previous day. The unfrocked friar was absolutely happy. He adored his Poldine, and did not refrain from boasting, to all and sundry, of her charms, her innocence, and her engaging modesty.

The Freys made him extremely comfortable in the Rue d'Anjou. They gave up the *entresol* of the house to him : it was reached by a wide and dignified staircase. It was only in the ante-room that the arrangements gave some indication of the ardent and austere patriot who lived within : it served the purposes of a signboard. There was a bust of Brutus on a pedestal, and some engravings representing the scene of the Oath in the Tennis Court and the tombs of Marat and Lepéletier ; while from the curtain-hooks hung a fur cap, the favourite emblem of the Jacobins, and a red knitted cap " adorned with four acorns of artificial gold."[2] The rest of the suite was a lovers'

---

[1] He was accused of having burnt a great number of compromising papers when he left these rooms.—National Archives, F⁷, 4637.

[2] Inventory of Chabot's furniture.—National Archives, F⁷, 4637.

bower. The furniture in the large salon was covered with green-and-white damask; the light from the windows was moderated by thick curtains of checked taffetas in the same colours, and in addition to these there were delicately-tinted blinds of striped canvas. On the chimney-piece a sweet little clock of blue-and-white marble served as a pedestal for a cupid in Sèvres china. In the adjoining bedroom hangings of white-and-yellow damask, lined with white taffetas, draped an immense bed of gilded wood, with a canopy supported by four pillars. Two sofas, four arm-chairs, two other chairs, a mahogany toilet-table, a large looking-glass, and a chiffonier with a shelf of blue marble, on which stood a bust of Cicero, completed the appointments of the room.

Certainly a man might live here very comfortably; and no doubt, if Chabot had been free, he would have left the political arena for ever and devoted himself entirely to the peaceful joys of the domestic hearth.

But, when he entered into relations with Delaunay and Julien (of Toulouse), he had thrust his finger into an insatiable machine from which there was no escape. The Baron de Batz, that terrible manipulator of men, was relentlessly bent upon the execution of his plan, and he was not of a temperament to wait patiently while his amorous agent was enjoying his honeymoon.

Delaunay was the first to trouble Chabot's peace by suggesting a new stroke of business to him—an absolutely safe thing, which might produce enormous profits. Delaunay's scheme was to propose in the Convention that the India Company—which, since the days of Calonne's ministry, had been the most lucrative financial operation of the eighteenth century—should be put into liquidation. Forty thousand shares had been issued, and such were the privileges enjoyed by this powerful company that it had been able to pay a respectable dividend to its shareholders. Its prosperity was so firmly established that it had hardly suffered from the Revolution, and the price of the shares had fallen comparatively little.

"You see, Chabot," whispered Delaunay, "nothing could be simpler. My proposal will inspire terror into the hearts of the directors and shareholders of the company.[1] That will make the shares go down : the fall will enable Benoît and de Batz to buy at a low price : then we shall lay before the company at the right moment two different bills, one lenient and the other severe, and say to them : 'Choose. You must pay such-and-such a sum for the decree that is favourable to you.' That sum will be useful to Benoît and de Batz for speculation, and we shall benefit by it. At this moment de Batz is drawing up the two bills."

Here we are confronted by a doubt. We have hitherto depicted the Baron de Batz as a sort of fanatical judge with a single aim : to corrupt, disgrace, dishonour, and defeat the Convention, till that all-powerful enemy should be utterly crushed, even though this work of vengeance were to demand his fortune and his life. But now that we see him at work it is natural that we should ask if it were not simply in his own interests that he proposed to trade with the public funds. When he bought the consciences of these legislators was it not with the object of forwarding his own financial schemes? This disinterested royalist was perhaps, after all, a mere moneymaker, a vulgar speculator.

Well, no. The answer is easy. If he had no object in this speculation but his own individual gain there was

[1] We quote Delaunay's words as reported by Chabot.—National Archives, F7, 4637.

no reason why Chabot should profit by it. Delaunay, to whom his orders were dictated, could have carried the matter through by himself: this is evident from the fact that only Delaunay took part in the discussion in the Convention, and Chabot did not appear. But it was necessary that the ex-Capuchin should be compromised, the whole Jacobin party bespattered, and Danton and others, if possible, dragged into the cataclysm that would result from the revelation of the disgraceful affair. This was the reason for introducing Chabot.

Moreover, the Baron de Batz, who in 1788 owned a considerable number of shares in the India Company,[1] had certainly not sold them after the price had fallen, as it did at the beginning of the Revolution. It was against his personal interests, then, to suggest the liquidation of a company in which he had shares; and yet it was he alone, as we have seen, who proposed the plan to Delaunay. And if, for the sake of argument, we suppose that he had rid himself of his shares, why should he have raised the question? If it were with a view to speculation it was a very imprudent game to play, seeing that he was a man without a citizen's rights, a reputed *émigré*, a prey to a thousand perils, and had now not even a home. A strange position for a speculator! No—we cannot doubt the existence of this well-woven plot. The *incorruptibles* —Saint-Just, Élie Lacoste, Robespierre—so often insisted upon it that we are convinced. This scheme was a device of the Baron de Batz to undermine the integrity of the members of the Convention.

Chabot excused himself, however; not because he was scrupulous, but because he was indolent. Delaunay would gladly have dispensed with him, seeing no reason for

---

[1] Running account of the Baron de Batz with Delessert.—National Archives, T, 699.

admitting another *partner*. But it is plain that de Batz declared he would do nothing unless Chabot were concerned in the affair. Delaunay obediently insisted, but the ex-Capuchin remained supine till they appealed to him through his fears.

One day Delaunay ran into Frey's house in a state of great agitation.

" Chabot," he said to his colleague, " it would be wrong of me to hide anything from you. They are very indignant with you at the Committee of General Security. Panis, Amar, and David, with whom I am very intimate, are actually speaking of bringing an indictment against you."

" An indictment ? But why ? "

" On account of your marriage. They say you have married an Austrian, which cannot be denied ; but they add that your wife's fortune is purely fictitious, and that you have settled 200,000 francs on her—the fruit of your speculations."

" What nonsense ! My brothers-in-law are rich, they are patriots, they detest tyrants, and are so much attached to France that they sacrificed their position in Vienna, where their name and fortune were assured, in order to live in Paris."

" That," continued Delaunay with assumed hesitation, " is just—just——It is said they never had either name or money. They are called Tropuska and are Moravian Jews. The only fortune they are known to have consists of a number of debts in Austria, where they were hanged in effigy after certain shady adventures concerning which the Committee is being bombarded with denunciations." [1]

---

[1] We simply give a résumé here, as far as possible in the exact words, of the denunciations of the Freys received by the Committee of General Security.—National Archives, W, 342, *dossier* 648.

"But Leopoldine?" asked Chabot in consternation.

"That is a long story. The elder of the two Freys is married: his wife stayed in Vienna with their two daughters. He has also a son of sixteen, whom he passes off as his nephew and whom he has brought to France. He has put him into the revolutionary army, for he endeavours to have spies everywhere. As for the boy's two sisters, one of them is vegetating in Austria, and the other is kept in luxury by a German baron."

"But Léopoldine?" asked Chabot again, anxiously.

"That is a more serious matter. They declare she— she—came from the seraglio of the Emperor of Austria, to whom her brothers sold her when she was hardly more than a child. Personally I do not believe a word of it," added Delaunay hastily; "but these rumours are spreading rapidly from mouth to mouth."

"They are infamous slanders. What can I do about it?"

"We will support you. De Batz has great power with the Committee; but of course you must be careful not to displease him just now. If his speculation on the India Company were to fail, you would lose your most powerful supporter. Besides, if it turns out that your wife has no dowry, you must think of the future. Look here, we will put you into this affair—you can have 100,000 francs. Benoît will undertake to pay you that sum, and if you like it can be done directly in your wife's name, so as to assure her future and prevent any suspicion from attaching to you." [1]

It was with the help of this argument and many others of the same nature that Delaunay finally overcame Chabot's hesitation. The latter, indeed, was overwhelmed by the revelations that had been made to him, and was but the

[1] Chabot's Manuscript.—National Archives, F⁷, 4647.

shadow of the proud and fiery *sans-culotte* of the past.
Like Hannibal he had been transformed by Capua ; and
in his case Capua was the comfortable *entresol* in the
Hôtel Frey, the pretty room with the silken hangings in
which his beloved Poldine went to and fro. But what a
blow had been dealt to the poor lover ! The shipwreck of
his integrity was a small matter to him when he was
mourning the loss of his illusions, and trying to save from
ruin the last fragments of the passion that he had naïvely
taken for an idyll.

It is possible that he succeeded. He tried to persuade
himself that the Freys were slandered by men whom the
pure civic virtue of these patriots had made jealous, and
he actually became convinced that this was the truth. It
only dawned upon him gradually that a mysterious force
was controlling the whole course of events, upsetting all
his calculations, and dragging him towards inevitable
catastrophe.

It was during the sitting of the 8th October that
Delaunay made his speech against the India Company.
Ah, that was a fine harangue ! How artistically its composer, the Baron de Batz, had accumulated diatribes
against the corruption and robbery of the Monarchy !
He must have taken special delight, I fancy, in attacking
the iniquity of the old régime through the mouth of this
contemptible man, this venal Delaunay, this traitor who
was cynically making trade out of his office.

The orator worked hard for his wages. He trembled
with indignation as he spoke of the monstrous jobbery
and shameful reign of Louis XIV, of the pillage and
scandalous speculations carried on by Calonne.

It will be well for us to recall, as briefly as possible, the
theme of his argument. The laws of August 27 and
November 28, 1792, had made all bonds subject to a

registration-fee for every change of ownership. The India Company had met this by substituting for its shares a receipt similar to those used in connection with the National Debt. In this new form the bond was no longer made payable to bearer, the name of the holder was entered in a register, and the transfer was effected by means of a few words in the books of the Company. Thus the law was evaded, and the Company had avoided payment of £2,249,786 in registration-fees, since over 128,000 transfers had taken place in the course of the year 1793.

Delaunay thundered against the capitalists and melted over the sorrows of the people : his speech was "a fulminating blow" to the Company.[1] Then, when he thought his colleagues' attention was relaxing, he cut his eloquence short and in a few hasty words brought forward a Bill for the liquidation of the India Company, with a clause to the effect that the liquidation should be carried out by the existing directors. This gave the Company a pretext for remaining as it was.

The trick was done : the violence of the speech could not fail to make the shares fall "to nothing"; while the ambiguous terms of the Bill left an opening for the Company to proceed as before, while awaiting an opportune moment to secure the best value for its effects.

There was so much talk in this Convention, so many meaningless speeches, that the members, being accustomed to the verbiage of their fellow-legislators, were more resigned than attentive to Delaunay's ceaseless stream of words. No one seemed to notice the inconsistency of the orator's indulgent conclusion with the extremely severe tone of his arguments. Yet as Delaunay, convinced of his success, was leaving the rostrum, a member of the

[1] See the *Moniteur* of the 19th of the 1st month, year II.

Philippe François Nazaire Fabre d'Eglantine.

assembly rose and began to speak. This was Fabre d'Églantine. Although he was better qualified to deal with questions of art than with financial affairs, his quick, alert mind had been struck by his colleague's inconsequence.

"After the vigorous attack made by the last speaker on the India Company," he said, "I am surprised that he did not move its complete annihilation. No measures can be too strong to take against people who have cost the Nation fifty millions. I propose that the government should lay hands on all goods belonging to the India Company, and should sell them through its agents. I propose, further, that seals should be affixed to the papers of all the directors, with a view to discovering fresh proofs of their rascality."

These words left Delaunay dumfoundered and gasping. If Fabre's proposals were accepted the India Company was doomed. Happily, Cambon expressed an opinion that Fabre's motion was a little radical. Robespierre replied, insisting that Fabre's suggestion should be followed. Other amendments were proposed, and the question grew complicated : and at last the weary Convention put the whole matter into the hands of a Commission of five members, who were to make a final draft of the Bill. These five were Delaunay, Chabot, Ramel, Cambon, and Fabre d'Églantine. The two first were already sold to the Company : a single vote in addition to theirs, therefore, would secure a majority in the Commission.

When the chapfallen Delaunay returned to de Batz, and told him how the intrigue had been on the point of utter failure owing to Fabre's motion, the baron, we may be sure, set his mind at ease at once.

"Fabre?" he said. "Well, what does it matter? I will buy him too."

A GASCON ROYALIST

This same Fabre was a Bohemian, and his past life seems to have been a poor preparation for the functions of a legislator. In 1763 [1] he forsook his home and his father, "a humble draper," and set out, with absolutely no resources, to try his fortune in Paris. Fortune proved kind at last, but only after being assiduously wooed for many years and imposing cruel tests upon the wooer. Figaro's agitated life was that of a peaceful *bourgeois*, compared with the varied existence of the future Conventionist. And the comparison strikes one as apt : there was a touch of Figaro in this man.

His first care was to make a living, and as he knew no trade he joined the Montansier troupe, who were then giving comic operas at Versailles. Since the extremely small parts that were all he was able to play were miserably paid he threw in his lot with one of the actresses, named Dubocage, but called *La Borgnesse*, or the *woman with one eye*. Such hours as were free from domestic and professional occupations he spent in painting flower-subjects, composing music, and scribbling erotic verses. It is generally believed that one of his poems was rewarded, at the Floral Games of Toulouse, with a golden Eglantine, and that this gave him the happy idea of adding to his name the graceful ornament by which, chiefly, he is known to fame. This is a mistake. Fabre was never crowned at the Floral Games. No doubt he had aspired to win the golden Eglantine, and, having failed, deemed the futile attempt gave him a sufficient right to the poetical title with which he ennobled his obscure name. Thenceforward he thought himself a man of importance. He undertook the management of the theatre at Beauvais,

[1] Fabre was born on July 29th, 1750. His certificate of baptism was published by M. Faber. See *Carrière dramatique de Fabre d'Églantine*.

forsook his comic troupe soon afterwards, and proceeded to Paris with no resources in his pocket save the manuscript of a poem called *L'Étude de la Nature*, which he dedicated to Buffon. The illustrious naturalist paid for this act of homage with a gift of ten louis.

We next find Fabre singing bass in the theatre of Namur, in 1776. There he ran off with a young *bourgeoise* belonging to the place, Mlle. Deresmont [1]; and as abduction was a capital crime in the Low Countries, he was arrested, imprisoned, put in irons, and condemned to be hanged.[2] But he escaped the gallows, and went off to act a less dangerous comedy on the boards of the Luxembourg theatre.

He soon returned to France, and spent a few days at Thionville without finding employment; then, still with empty pockets and a light heart, walked to Sedan, where he announced himself as a painter of portraits in miniature, at a louis apiece. The first order was not long in coming—but it was also the last, for the enthusiastic patron of art who had yielded to the temptation did not think his portrait a good likeness, and had the bad taste to reject it. Fabre, disgusted

---

[1] Catherine Deresmont was aged fifteen-and-a-half. She was familiarly called *Catiche*. Fabre had contrived to win the good graces of the Deresmont family. There is still in existence a letter he wrote to Catiche's mother, giving a fairly favourable view of himself: "I do not wish to flatter myself," he says; "but, quite apart from my talent for acting—a line in which I could go as far as any man—I think there are few who combine, like myself, birth (!) and education with so many and various talents, all fine, all useful, all relevant to one another, all independent of one another . . . etc."

[2] Fabre was condemned to be hanged on the 20th March, 1777. His fellow-actors sued for pardon for him from Prince Charles of Lorraine, Governor of the Low Countries. His judges described him as an adventurer "addicted to the most subtle libertinism, with perverted and dissolute morals, and no resources but a mediocre talent for the stage." He was pardoned on the 31st March.

with painting, raised a troupe of actors, and was on the point of crossing the frontier when it occurred to his landlady to claim what he owed her. The actor took a haughty tone, and was arrested. He slept in the police-station, escaped again, arrived safely in Belgium, sang in opera at Liège, married as he passed through Strasburg,[1] and returned to Maëstricht, where a son was born to him.[2] Thence he went off to act at Besançon, inadvertently leaving his wife and child behind him; and going on to Lyons found a post at the theatre there through the good offices of a fellow-actor who, though his name was Collet, insisted on being called d'Herbois. Collet and Fabre were hissed in company. The former, later on, made the men of Lyons expiate their irreverence; the latter was soon consoled, and happening to meet, in one of the squares of the town, his brother Fabre-Fons,[3] who had set up as a quack and sold ointments to simpletons, he borrowed a little money from him. This was soon absorbed by a theatrical enterprise; and this time—disillusioned, discouraged, despairing—he took the coach to Paris, where he arrived penniless and weary of the world. "He was on the point of being parted from it by twenty fathoms of water," when he met his Almaviva in the person of the poet-philosopher Ximenès.[4]

We now find Fabre frequenting the houses of the

---

[1] On the 9th Nov., 1778, to Marie Nicolle Godin. The marriage took place in the church of St. Pierre.

[2] Oct. 3rd, 1779. The child was baptised in the church of St. Jean Baptiste by the name of Louis Théodore Jules Vincent (*Inter-médiaire* of August 25, 1886). The son of Fabre d'Églantine became a naval engineer and died at Versailles in 1840. He had a daughter and two sons, of whom the last died in Paris unmarried, in the Rue du Dragon, 1888. He was a copying-clerk in the Ministry of Marine.

[3] Fabre d'Églantine's mother was called Jeanne Marie Fons.

[4] Born in Paris in 1726 of a family from Aragon: died 1817.

literary, playing the dandy, and flouting his creditors.
He wrote some plays, and was hissed; he lost his temper
and made the audience listen to him. Then suddenly he
produced two quasi-masterpieces; a long comedy of
character named *Le Philinte de Molière ou la Suite du
Mysanthrope*, and a song: *Il pleut, il pleut, bergère*.
Fame smiled upon him, but fortune was still cold: Fabre
possessed nothing but debts. He was about to be
thrown into La Force when a safe-conduct from the King,
dated 1789,[1] secured him his liberty. Then the Revolution broke out, and Fabre flung himself into it with
eagerness, deeming it a fertile field for intrigue. He
threw in his lot with Danton and made him his friend—so
much so that after the 10th August we find him living
in the Chancellerie as secretary to the Ministry of Justice.
He was not there long—only six weeks—but long enough
for him to have ten thousand pairs of shoes made with
cardboard soles, of which his influence enabled him to
dispose to the army-contractors, at a profit to himself of
35,000 francs.[2] This proof of civic virtue won him a
seat in the Convention. Behold him a legislator! He
lived sumptuously in an *émigré's* house, forgot to share
his good fortune with the wife and son he had left,
"to wait till called for," in the inn at Maëstricht, provided
himself with a companion from among the actresses of
the Théâtre de la République, and finally died on the
scaffold, leaving behind him a good deal of property, an
actress, and two brothers, of whom one was a general and
the other a drummer!

Such, briefly, were the adventures of the personage
whom we are about to introduce into our story. His
antecedents, it must be confessed, were not of a nature to

---

[1] National Archives, F7, 4434.
[2] *Histoire parlementaire de la Révolution*, vol. xxxii, p. 232.

discourage the Baron de Batz in his work of corruption. The ground, it seemed, was thoroughly prepared. It might be presumed, without too much rashness, that 100,000 francs would overcome an integrity that had already suffered shipwreck so often.[1]

What seems incredible is that a man like this—though his talent, and cleverness, and gift for intrigue cannot be denied —should have contrived to make his way into the Convention and to play the part of a statesman there. His past was no mystery. Those, at least, who took him seriously must have made inquiries into it. Danton, who knew him well, having employed him as secretary, said of him: "That man's head is a collection of comical notions"—and yet admitted him to the councils of the government! Camille Desmoulins, who had been Fabre's colleague at the Ministry of Justice, and was destined to die with him, certainly had him in his mind when he wrote: "Close beside the guillotine where the heads of kings are falling is the guillotine of Punchinello, and they share the world's attention." And yet this man, who was judged so severely by his friends, lifted up his voice from the rostrum with-

---

[1] I confess I do not agree with Dr. Robinet on the subject of Fabre's *correspondance amoureuse*, published in 1796. The correspondence itself is merely a bookseller's speculation : that is obvious : but it seems to me that the introduction, recording the chief incidents in Fabre's eventful life, has been too severely judged by my eminent brother in letters. It is, as he says, so far from uncomplimentary that it has misled some writers into believing it published by the heirs of the Conventionist. This is, however, untrue : and the man who wrote it, Roussel d'Epinal, was thoroughly conversant with the men and things of the Revolution : his book on the Palace of the Tuileries proves this : and, moreover, what inclines me to regard it less severely than Dr. Robinet is that some of its facts can now be verified. For instance, the story of Catiche Deresmont's abduction was considered mythical : and now all the documents of the trial have been found by M. Gachard in the Archives of Belgium. (See, on the subject of Fabre's dramatic career, Victor Fournel's fine study in the *Revue des Questions Historiques*).

out being sent back to the boards from which he came, and Cambon was willing to discuss with him the gravest questions of finance, and he was one of the most important members of the Convention !

De Batz judged him more sanely ; he gave his orders.

" Take 100,000 francs to that play-actor," he commanded. " He will trouble us no more."

Neither had Delaunay many illusions as regarded his colleague. In his opinion Fabre's motion that the India Company should be dissolved proved that he had an interest in its annihilation.

" He must be speculating against it." said Delaunay. " We must insure him from loss." [1]

This was an important point to discover. The Commission of Five seemed in no hurry to meet, and this delay gave Chabot the impression that they were waiting for offers. " If they were not all wanting to make something out of the business," thought the ex-Capuchin, " they would have drafted the Bill on the spot." [2]

In default of the Commission it was the Baron de Batz who drew up the Bill, for Delaunay brought a copy to Chabot " written by the hand of Benoît," and begged him to submit it to Fabre.

" If he approves of it there are 100,000 francs in assignats waiting for him."

Chabot took the Bill, put it in his pocket, and prepared to dissemble. Approaching Fabre quite casually in the Hall of Liberty he asked him what day he would like the Commission to meet.

" Any day that suits you and Delaunay," answered Fabre, and passed on.

Chabot was disconcerted. He had hoped that Fabre

[1] Chabot's Manuscript, F⁷, 4637.
[2] National Archives, F⁷, 4637.

would make the first advances ; that he would at all events allude to the speculation that was in question. But no. Fabre spoke altogether like a man who could afford the luxury of being honest. It was very bewildering, and one can imagine the consternation of Julien and Delaunay when Chabot came to report the failure of his attempt. The obstinacy of their colleague was the downfall of all their hopes.

To one who follows, step by step, the progress of this affair, the mere statement of the facts makes one point clear: the part played by the India Company was simply that of a pretext, a pretext that was necessary to de Batz to explain, in the eyes of the men he paid, his interest in buying them ; while his real aim was to sow corruption on favourable ground, in the hope that the strong winds of the Revolution might blow the seed over the whole Convention.

Chabot, who was now become a docile tool, undertook to buy Fabre, and make him sign a bill drawn up by de Batz and copied by Delaunay. The ex-friar was provided with 100,000 francs, and strong in this irresistible argument he approached Fabre in the Hall of Liberty.

" See," he said, holding out the draft, " we have been working without you. Here is a Bill. If only you approve of it we will bring it forward."

Fabre took the paper and examined it. Seeing at a glance that its terms were opposed to his amendment and favourable to the Company he took a pencil from his pocket, and, scribbling on his knee, proceeded to revise the text in accordance with his motion.

Chabot was on the point of remonstrating. In the portfolio under his arm was the roll of assignats, but, though he had actually opened his mouth to offer them, he held his peace. What silenced him ? The fear of colliding with Fabre's integrity? It is unlikely. The hope of overcoming his colleague's obstinacy without buying him? It is doubtful. We think rather—and Chabot's own confessions confirm our belief—that the ex-Capuchin, who was certainly not over-scrupulous, designed to play a trick upon his own confederates. They had given him 100,000 francs; he would keep this sum for himself. Let the decree ruin the India Company or no: it matters little to him, when he has the money in his pocket. And this manœuvre, too, saves him from compromising himself; for after all one sees strange things, and Fabre may be an honest man.

Whatever his motive, when he left his colleague he took away the 100,000 francs with the corrected draft of the Bill. Julien and Delaunay, who were awaiting him impatiently, were filled with consternation by this fresh obstacle.

" He refused the 100,000 francs, then ? "

" Not at all, he took them," declared Chabot.

" What are we to do next ? "

" *Dame*, we must be cautious! He insists on there being no sign by which his consent could be discovered. The fact of his taking the money shows that he agrees—if only tacitly—to go with us. We can act accordingly."

"Good. Let us talk it over, for we must get the matter finished." [1]

Julien and Delaunay, assisted by Benoît, who was an

[1] In all this troublous business there seems to be but one authentic fact, namely that Chabot received, in addition to his own 100,000 francs, another sum of 100,000 francs for Fabre, which he kept himself while assuring his confederates that Fabre had received it. This may be gathered from Chabot's confessions and Fabre's defence. We have related the facts in the order that seems to us most lucid, and have deliberately sacrificed many details that would have added picturesqueness to our story, but would have over-weighted it and perhaps made it less clear.

expert in these little financial tricks, went through Fabre's alterations word by word. They saw that, by the addition of a few words here and there, his version could be made to serve their interests admirably, and they determined to use it.

Delaunay had it copied in the government offices in the form—save for a few modifications in detail—of which Fabre had approved; and on the following morning Chabot ran off to the Hôtel d'Aumont, in the Rue de la Ville l'Évêque, where the retired actor had lately been living. He sent his name in; and though Fabre was in bed he gave orders, without waiting to dress himself, that his colleague should be brought to his room. He ran his eye over the paper that was handed to him, and signed it hurriedly.

Chabot returned home, where he found Delaunay, Benoît, and Julien at breakfast, and with them Glandy, the cousin who had been so much enamoured of the young Léopoldine.[1] This party of friends then proceeded to alter the Bill. One of the guests—Glandy, no doubt, for the writing in the interpolations was not recognised afterwards as that of any of the Conventionists—added, after the clause ordaining that "the Company should be put into liquidation," the words: "in accordance with its statutes and regulations," which restored to the Company the right of carrying it out itself. At the end of the paragraph relating to the triple "fee to be paid on transfers," they inserted "fraudulently made"; and these words dispensed those who professed to purchase in good faith from paying the fees.

This done, Delaunay erased the first two words of the title *Projet de Décret*, and thus transformed the Bill into a Decree. Above Fabre's signature he wrote *signed by*,

---

[1] Chabot's Manuscript.—National Archives, F⁷, 4637.

and added the names of Cambon, Julien, Chabot, and Ramel. He then signed his own name in his capacity of Reporter to the Convention, and sent off the document thus produced to the offices of the government, where it was slipped among the papers ready for printing.

The end was attained : the next move was to secure the pay. The shameful traffic that took place in connection with these payments cannot be better described than in the words of Chabot's cynical, or unconscious, confession.

"On the following day," he writes, "Delaunay and Benoît brought me twenty-four or thirty-four thousand *livres*. I did not count them because they told me they would bring me the rest of the 100,000 *livres*. The next day they gave me enough to bring the sum up to 60,000 *livres*, and, the day after that, 40,000 *livres*, which I sealed up. I wrote on it : *To the Committee of General Security of the Convention, at the National Palace. I can count sufficiently on the affection of my wife to be sure that in case of my death she will promptly send this packet to those to whom it is addressed, since its contents are of the first importance to my honour and to the Republic.*

"This envelope was burnt by Jagot against my wish. It would have proved that the packet was done up at the time, and that I firmly intended to frustrate the plot.[1]

"For my share Delaunay offered to divide with me the property of de Batz at Charonne or in the department of l'Allier. I refused on various pretexts. On the following day Benoît and he came to bring me some blank bonds of the India Company, with an offer to give me the value of

---

[1] It must not be forgotten, in reading Chabot's confidences, that they were written three months after the forged decree, and that then Chabot, in prison, denied having received money for himself. The money he sealed up is put forward as being intended for Fabre d'Églantine, whereas it was really given him for himself. Benoît and Delaunay thought Fabre had been paid the day before.

50,000 *écus* for my share. I refused, and insisted that all who were to have a share should be present. They pressed me, and offered to make them payable to my wife. I answered that I would not consent. They offered to make them payable to my brothers-in-law. I again refused, on the pretext that the property of foreigners was not safe. They offered to make them payable to any friend I might choose, or to give them to me blank and let me fill in an imaginary name myself.

" ' I will do nothing of the sort,' I told them, ' for if the Committee, as you said, are going to affix seals to my possessions, they would find this store of bonds, and would want to know who owned them. I will not compromise myself. Let us share it all like good comrades, and then I will do what seems best to me with my share. And besides, there ought to be more of us to share it. There is too much for each. Bazire ought to be there : he is in need of it ' (and I was in need of witnesses, to enable me to carry out my scheme of having them all seized).

" They made difficulties, both with regard to sharing the money with everyone present, and also to the addition of Bazire. They promised to return, and so they did, but only to offer me a bill of exchange on any foreign bank I chose, on the ground that it was absolutely necessary for me to send my own money and my wife's abroad, as proceedings were going to be taken against me on account of my marriage. I told them there was now no safety for me outside the Republic, and that I would stay and defy those who attacked and slandered my marriage. Finally, after many and daily disputes of this kind, they allowed Bazire to have a share . . ."

One thing may be gathered from these confessions : Chabot could have no doubt as to who was paying him. It was evidently de Batz, since he had begun by offering to reward him with the property at Charonne ; that house having become useless, on account of the close watch that was kept upon it. But that the directors of the India Company played any part in this affair is quite out of the question. Michelet, the man of powerful deductions, guessed the truth ; but his wide mind would not lend itself to the microscopic work indispensable for the correlation of a thousand separate little facts that might have given substance to his conclusions. " What makes this strange affair still more mysterious," he says,[1] " is that, the more one reflects upon the subject, the more one sees that the Company could not hope to derive any benefit from the crime. Did no one read this published, printed Decree ? Would it not have been denounced at the end of two days by the Commission that was appointed to direct and superintend the liquidation ? I shall be told that the guilty men, Fabre and Delaunay, would certainly have emigrated as soon as they had received their money. Quite true. But were the bankers of those days so silly as to throw money into an enterprise of such an ephemeral, such an obviously uncertain nature ? There is not a man of any weight who would do so to-day. I am much more inclined to believe that the principal investor, the Baron de Batz, threw away his 100,000 francs as the first move in an affair in which, through Chabot perhaps, he hoped to entangle certain others. The affair of the company was a mere pretext."

One point remains to be elucidated. Why did Chabot associate Bazire with his evil deeds ? Why did he wish him to have a share in the spoils ? " In order to secure a witness "—would he say ?—" whose honour was above suspicion." If this were true he could not have made a

---

[1] *Histoire de la Révolution*, Book XV, Chap. IV.

worse choice. Bazire, who had sat with Chabot at the table of the Baron de Batz, and had already been strongly impressed by the confidences of Delaunay and Benoît at Charonne, was on the contrary a witness to be accepted with extreme caution. Chabot chose him because he did not wish to be alone in his treachery; and because he thought, quite correctly, that the greater the number implicated the less would the Convention dare to strike. Bazire enjoyed a certain degree of popularity in that assembly: he was a man who commanded attention: and Chabot was delighted to disgrace himself in good company.

Moreover Bazire, as was well known by all his colleagues, was one of the poorest men in the Convention. Among the papers seized in his rooms [1] were various scraps covered with figures—the accounts of his daily expenditure, which leave no doubt in one's mind as to this legislator's state of penury. He could not even contrive to pay his servant Agathe, to whom he entrusted the house-keeping:—

"*Received from M. Bazire the sum of 100 livres for the months of November and December of the year 1792, on account of the note he gave me, promising to pay my wages. Paris, 11th Jan. 1793. Being unable to sign my name I have made a cross. +.*"

No doubt this illiterate cook persuaded the concierge or some other kind neighbour to set down her master's accounts for her, for here is another document that throws a pathetic light on the destitution of poor Bazire:—

Memorandum of my expenditure through Agathe.

Given to the washerwoman . . . . 1 *livre.*
Mending . . . . 1*l.* 8 *sols.*

[1] National Archives, T, 699.

Carriage of letter . . . . 4s.
Two carcases . . . . 1l. 4s.
Coiffure and luncheon . . . . . . 1l. 10s.
Chicken . . . . 4l.
Load of wood . . . . 27l.
For a cab . . . . 3l. 10s.
For shoes for Citizen Bazire . . . . 9l.
Ink . . . . 18s.

If he lunched on two carcases Bazire made up for it in coffee. He had a running account with Salle, the manager of the Café de la Liberté :—

November 6.

5 cups of coffee . . . . 1l. 10s.
1 oz. tobacco . . . . 3s.
2 cups of coffee . . . . 12s.

November 7.

2 cups of coffee . . . . 12s.
½ oz. tobacco . . . . 1s. 6d.
3 cups of coffee . . . . 18s.

Chabot, we can well believe, thought there would be no difficulty in corrupting a man whose poverty was evidently greater than his scruples ; 100,000 francs would be well spent thus. This was Chabot's view, in his friendship for his colleague, and Bazire's integrity did not give him the lie.

Thenceforward Chabot thought himself safe. But de Batz had a cruel disappointment in store for him. On the 19th Brumaire Benoît came to Frey's house in a state of great anxiety.

"You are making a great mistake," he said to Chabot, "in refusing to secure your own fortune and your wife's by one bold stroke: the counter-revolution is a certainty."

Chabot thought he was joking. Benoît, quite calmly and amiably, revealed the whole plot to him. All the Conventionists were doomed to the scaffold : the first to go would be the seventy-three imprisoned Girondists, and then all the Moderates : next, it would be the turn of Danton, Lacroix, Legendre, and Rovère : after them Thuriot, Bazire, and Chabot himself would die : then there would be a hecatomb of the Commissioners to the army, against whom denunciations were being fabricated in the Ministry of War. Even Billaud-Varennes would be attacked, having been involved in certain sales of corn : and, if Robespierre himself could not be convicted of corruption, it was easy to prove the corruption of one of his intimate friends. In this way the national representation would be decimated, and, when the departments found that their deputies were guillotined one after another, not a man would be willing to leave the provinces and replace the victims. The Convention would then be reduced to a handful of men whom no one knew nor respected—a body that could be used as a tool or dissolved at will.[1]

Chabot's surprise was immense. He saw that he had fallen into a trap, and was merely an instrument in the hands of the conspirators.

" Pitt," added Benoît, " has agents in the Commune, in the revolutionary army, in the Ministry of War—everywhere."

Chabot was not listening to him. He believed himself capable, by the exercise of finesse, of deceiving them all. His mind was already busily constructing a scheme ; the mixture of half-confessions and reserves and hypocritical denunciations by means of which he hoped to save himself,

[1] These are the actual words of Benoît's revelation, as reported by Chabot.—National Archives, F⁷, 4637.

and would have done so had his partner been a man of less ability than the Baron de Batz.

"I felt more than ever," he wrote in his vindicatory Memorial, "the necessity of making Benoît talk in the presence of witnesses. I persisted in my refusal to emigrate, but I consented to see de Batz, *which hitherto I had always refused to do.*[1] My object was not only to discover the whole secret, but also to obtain possession of an important memorandum on the embezzlement of the public funds under the Constituent Assembly, which might have put further secrets into my hands, and which was offered to me by de Batz in return for an interview. Well, he came; but as he was in hiding and I always had visitors with me he went away by the back-stairs before I could get anything out of him."[2]

It may be that my imagination deceives me, but personally I think no writer of romance ever conceived a more dramatic situation than this. Chabot, the powerful Conventionist, who, with a word, can send his enemies to the scaffold, who has conquered the Monarchy, condemned the King, and defeated the Girondists, receives in his rooms a homeless outlaw, who is forced to hide himself and use the back-stairs—yet it is the outlaw who assumes the masterful tone, because he has bought the right to treat his host like a valet. Ah, if the others had only written like Chabot! If all the actors in this vast intrigue had given us so detailed a confession of their corruption as he, what a picture we might draw, and how strange it would seem to see this fugitive suddenly appearing before each of his hirelings—giving his orders, dictating his conditions, paying their wages, and revelling in their disgrace!

No doubt, when de Batz paid this visit to Chabot, he

---

[1] And the luncheons at Charonne to which Chabot himself confesses?
[2] Chabot's Manuscript.—National Archives, F7, 4637.

wished to see for himself that everything was going on as he desired.   He made sure that the complicated machinery of his intrigue was all in order and ready to work.   Like the stage-carpenter in a huge theatre, bringing all his skill to bear upon the arrangement of the ropes in a complicated scene, de Batz came to give a final glance at his stage, and disappeared again into the wings.   Presently, at the tinkle of a bell, the transformation-scene would unfold.

On the day following this interview, the 20th Brumaire,[1] Philippeaux rose in the Convention and—at whose instigation ?—pronounced these terrible words :

"The time has come for unmasking, that virtue may be seen uncovered.   It is time for the people to know whether all who profess to befriend them are really working for their happiness.   But let us begin by being severe upon ourselves.   I propose that every member of the Convention . . . shall be called upon to produce, in the course of a decade, a statement of his income before the beginning of the Revolution ; and if it have increased since that time, to show by what means it has done so.   With every law a penalty is associated.   I propose that such members of the Convention as fail to satisfy the requirements of your Decree shall be declared traitors to their country and prosecuted as such."

Great sensation on the benches !   A voice was raised : that of the upright Romme.   He supported the proposal and moved that the discussion should be postponed until the morrow, since a great many of the members were absent.   Philippeaux agreed to this : but Bazire rose to plead his own cause.

"If I oppose the motion of Philippeaux," he said, " it

[1] November 10th, 1793.

is not on my own account. I am the poorest man in the Convention . . . . I wish to point out that the projected Decree will be powerless to reach rogues : crime invents all kinds of tricks : to hide his money the rogue uses an assumed name, whereas the honest man, supported by his conscience, proudly displays the fruit of his labours and economies. Do not be too quick to swallow the baited hook that is dangled before you by knaves, whose only object is to tear us asunder, one from the other. It is not patriotism that prompts these denunciations and calumnies : they are born of counter-revolutionary intentions. I know well enough what fate awaits me for having given my opinion so frankly ; but the man who dares to speak thus from the rostrum dares to die. . . . The loss of my head will be the price of my courage ; but I have learnt to defy death ! " [1]

" President," cried Montaut, " call the speaker to order. The Convention attacks none but conspirators."

The President, who was Laloi, tried to still the storm ; but the assembly insisted upon an immediate discussion, and now it was Chabot who rose to speak. For he too considered himself in danger, and thought it well to take precautions.

" I propose that deputies shall enjoy the same privileges as private individuals, that is to say, that they shall not be condemned until they have been heard. Unless you adopt this measure what honest man will be willing to care for the interests of the Republic, if he knows he may be struck down in the very act of serving her ? Death has no terrors for me ; if my head can be of any use or help to the Republic, let it go. What seems to me important is that there should not invariably be but a single opinion on every Decree. If there should be no

[1] See Bazire's speech in the *Moniteur* of Nov. 12th.

Right I will form one by myself, even though it should cost me my head, so that there may be an opposition, and that people may not be able to say that we pass Decrees on trust, without discussion."

Then Chabot spoke in veiled terms of the conspiracy that had been revealed to him on the previous day. All Benoît's confidences were retailed in his discourse.

"How do you know, citizens, that the counter-revolutionaries do not design to send you to the scaffold? One of your colleagues has heard it said: 'To-day it is so-and-so's turn, to-morrow Danton's; the day after to-morrow it will be the turn of Billaud-Varennes; we shall end with Robespierre.' To republicans these are alarming words. How do you know that someone will not come, on the strength of a forged letter, and demand a Decree against the truest patriots?"

In these words we can detect Chabot's desperation. An unexpected light is thrown upon these unemotional lines in the *Moniteur* when one knows what lies beneath them! The ex-Capuchin looked down from the rostrum upon all his colleagues, and saw that the predicted storm was on the point of bursting. He did not know the strength, nor the numbers, of his enemies. He thought the Convention could read his shame upon his forehead. The revelations of the previous day made him see conspirators everywhere. Whenever a fresh orator rose to speak Chabot asked himself the agonising question: "Is that one of them? In whose pay is he? How much does he know? Is he going to denounce me?" It was to save his own life that he fought, and clung to the rostrum, and implored the assembly not to let any of its members be condemned without first being heard.

"And the Girondists, Chabot? Were the Girondists heard?"

It was Bourdon (of L'Oise) who gave utterance to this apostrophe. Bazire answered.

"Those people," he cried, "had already been condemned by public opinion! To-day it is the true friends of liberty who are being attacked on vague grounds. . . . I support Chabot's motion; I demand its adoption."

"I am quite willing," replied Bourdon, "that a deputy should be heard before being condemned; but if he tries to escape when a warrant is out against him he ought to be outlawed!"

"You cannot punish a man for trying to escape," answered Bazire, "for he is only obeying his instinct of liberty. Marat, when he was put under arrest, hid himself. Will you blame the conduct of that great man?"

Julien (of Toulouse)—he, too, had sold himself—intervened at this moment.

"A private individual who runs away," he observed, "is not outlawed. Why should you punish a representative of the people more severely?"

This ended the discussion. Chabot, Bazire, and Julien were triumphant. The substance of Chabot's motion was made law by the Convention, and all the other motions were despatched to the Committee of Legislation to be put into writing. The fight had been warm, but to the traitors it seemed that they had been victorious.

On the following evening they were attacked in a fresh quarter, at the Jacobin Club. The intractable Dufourny, who seems to have thought it his vocation to demolish Chabot and his band, and could not have played his part better if de Batz had been prompting him, undertook to teach the Conventionists a lesson. He expressed his indignation that Bazire, in his excessive sensitiveness, should have permitted himself to say: "When will this butchery of deputies be ended?" As for Chabot he had dared to assert "that it was only terror that made all the deputies of the Right go over to the Mountain, and that he would form a Right by himself to save the Republic. Dufourny finally proposed that a solemn deputation should be sent to the Convention to ask if Frenchmen of revolutionary principles could still count on the firmness of their representatives.

Montaut, Hébert, and Renaudin fulminated in their turn against Chabot and his friends. "These gentlemen are very sensitive! They are afraid lest the heads of patriots should fall beneath the blade of the law! The Jacobins will let the Convention know that *it has no right* to act in opposition to the people's will. Let us go to them in a body; let us vote that the conduct of Chabot and Bazire shall be inquired into!"

This resolution was carried with hearty acclamation.[1] France was no longer governed by the Convention. That *Assembly of Giants* fell back in terror before the Jacobin Club, and nothing could be more pitiable than the scene in the Hall of the Tuileries on the following day, when,

---

[1] "My sister was in the women's gallery on this occasion, and afterwards overheard, her identity being unknown, the plot to send us to the scaffold within the week. She said to me as we went out: 'I know your honesty, but I think your courage is failing. You are pensive: are you guilty? Speak; I will put a dagger into you. Perhaps you will be arrested this evening; and though I could see you ascend the scaffold without shedding a tear if you were dying in the cause of liberty, I do not wish you to die as a conspirator. At least bequeath to us the memory of a just and honest man.'"

Déclaration de Chabot.—He adds that after this he took some precautionary measures. He wished at first to burn the 100,000 francs in assignats that he had accepted for Fabre, but the idea of such a thing made Léopoldine cry.

in obedience to an order from Dufourny, who was not a deputy, the terrorised Convention weakly repealed the Decree that had been discussed and carried on the 20th Brumaire.

The sittings of the 22nd and 23rd are full of instruction : they show how fatuous a parliamentary majority may become when under the influence of fear : and they recall the *lits de justice* of the old Monarchy, when the king, by the mouth of his chancellor, dictated *his good pleasure*. But now the master was the sordid populace that always rises, in the ferment of a revolution, to the surface of society.

First, by way of prologue, a numerous deputation from the Commune of Franciade [1] appeared at the bar, bearing the treasure of the basilica. They were received with thunders of applause.[2] The spokesman of the deputation held in his hands the skull of St. Denis, which had been taken from its reliquary.

"By a miracle," he cried, "this saint's head that we bring you was transported from Montmartre to St. Denis. Another miracle, greater and more authentic, the miracle of the regeneration of thought, brings back this head to you in Paris. The only difference between the two journeys is this : the saint, says the legend, kissed his head respectfully at every halting-place ; whereas we felt no inclination to kiss this decaying relic. . . . At last this skull and the holy trumpery that goes with it will cease to be the ridiculous object of the people's veneration. . . . To you, legislators, we bring all the gilded rottenness that was at Franciade. . . . There are six cartloads of it."

The Convention, in its enthusiasm, ordered this address to be inserted in its official Bulletin. But this incident

---

[1] Saint-Denis.
[2] *Moniteur* of 14th Nov., 1793.

was merely a *lever de rideau*; the chief piece was yet
to begin. Bar, meeting the wishes of the Jacobins half-
way, moved the repeal of the law passed on the 20th in
accordance with Chabot's motion. Billaud-Varennes
supported Bar, and the Assembly reversed its own
judgment *unanimously*. Another interlude followed:
"The section of the Gravilliers entered the Hall; at its
head marched a body of men dressed in sacerdotal and
pontifical garments; the band played the airs of the
Carmagnole and *Malbrough s'en va-t-en guerre*. They
carried banners and crosses, and as the canopy entered they
played *Ah! le bel oiseau*. All the citizens of the section
removed their robes at the same instant, and from beneath
the disguises of fanaticism emerged the defenders of the
country, clothed in the national uniform. Every man
flung into the air the garments he had just removed;
so that stoles, mitres, chasubles, and dalmatics were flying
in all directions, to the sound of musical instruments and
repeated shouts of *Liberty for ever! Vive la république!*
The spokesman of the deputation held up a little child
at the bar: 'His ears,' he cried, 'have never yet heard
lying words: he has learnt nothing but the Declaration of
the Rights of Man, which he knows by heart.' The child
gracefully read aloud a discourse in praise of the Convention
and of reason. There was repeated applause. Amid
transports of the most ardent enthusiasm the president
was begged to bestow the kiss of fraternity upon the child.
He was then carried to the president's chair, while the
hall resounded with acclamations and the band played
patriotic airs." [1]

Such were the masquerades to which the Convention was
reduced to submitting! It had lost all sense of dignity
and had become a mere machine, with no end save to

[1] *Moniteur* of 15th Nov., 1793.

applaud the most grotesque performances and obey the orders of every kind of fanatic.

On the following day the frolic began again. One of the secretaries read aloud a letter addressed to the Assembly by the commune of Orgeville.

" We too wish to deserve well of our country . . . and purge it of the noxious brutes that pollute it. We had one in our commune of a very dangerous kind : one that tormented the poor in every kind of way, and not only enraged the living but even ill-treated the corpses of the dead. If there are any devils in hell this creature must have escaped from that place, to the sorrow of every one of us. This animal is called a *curé*, or otherwise M. Flichy. We do not want this M. Flichy, nor yet his holy-water . . . etc." [1]

These fatuities are not irrelevant to our subject : it is important to show how low the Convention had fallen. On the 22nd September, 1792, its deadliest enemy would not have dared to predict such degradation for it.

Dufourny, finally, appeared at the bar, followed by a deputation from the Jacobin Club. His speech was long. With the calmest effrontery he lectured the Conventionists severely, blamed them for their weakness, and laid down a complete plan of action for them. The assembly applauded him, and ordered the speech to be inserted in the *Bulletin*. But Bazire and Chabot understood that the Jacobins were expecting them to apologise. A pitiable sight, therefore, was seen : two legislators humbly retracting from the rostrum, by order of a band of irresponsible fanatics, the motion they had brought forward in the same place.

Bazire expressed his regret at having taken part in the discussion of the 20th. He recalled his claims on the gratitude of patriots, and thanked his comrades the

[1] *Moniteur* of 15th Nov., 1793.

Jacobins, "with whom he wished always to live," for bringing him back to the right way. He ended by calling upon "the Convention to vote that the Society of Jacobins had deserved well of the country."

"The Society has never ceased deserving well of the country," thundered a voice that was instantly drowned in applause.

Bazire slunk away from the rostrum, where he was replaced by Chabot. He too gave thanks to his brethren for their active supervision. "If I should chance to err," he said, "I should thank them again for denouncing me and sending me to the scaffold. If I am sometimes caught nodding I can be awakened with whips." Then he boasted of having largely contributed to the death of the Girondists, and swore to be a Jacobin till death.

But the Jacobins were tenacious in their rancour. Or, rather, the stage-manager had resolved to hasten the action of the drama. If we refuse to believe that it was de Batz alone who directed the blows dealt to Chabot the fury of the ex-Capuchin's enemies becomes inexplicable. The report of the sitting of the 26th Brumaire, in the Jacobin Club, mentions among the opponents of the husband of Léopoldine Frey *a voice, a citizen, another citizen, a member.* Who were all these anonymous people? For ourselves, we have no doubt that they were agents of the Baron de Batz. It was they who muttered words of disapproval when Chabot tried to exculpate himself, and kept eager watch for any indiscreet expression he might let fall in his anxiety, and distracted him with one crushing interruption after another. The ex-friar himself knew the truth.

"These cries showed me," he writes, "that the conspiracy was being carried out." [1]

[1] Chabot's Manuscript.—National Archives, F⁷, 4637

THE INDIA COMPANY

We will abridge into a few lines the report of this sitting, which should be read in its entirety : [1]

Chabot, after boasting the purity of his intentions, tried to explain his motion of the 20th.

" In spite of my enemies, whom I defy," he cried ; " in spite of the revolutionary women "—the galleries were filled with viragos yelling *To the guillotine* ! [2]—" no one can deny that I saved the Commonwealth."

A VOICE.—" The Commonwealth can save itself." Chabot retracted this unfortunate expression. He suggested resigning his post as a deputy and enlisting with the volunteers ; but nothing disarmed *his brethren.* Dufourny reproached him for marrying a foreigner. " A woman is a garment ; if Chabot required a garment of that kind he should have remembered that foreign stuffs are proscribed by the nation. . . . Before a man marries any woman he should first find out whether those to whom she belongs are not justifiably *suspect,* and allied with our enemies."

Dufourny's inflammatory speech was greeted with three cheers : the tumult became such that Anacharsis Clootz, who was presiding, was reduced to putting on his hat. Peace was gradually restored, and Chabot was subjected to a fresh attack.

A VOICE. " Before their sister's marriage the Freys [3] cut no great dash ; but since that event everything has changed, and now the housemaid is better dressed than her mistress used to be. When the seals were affixed there was no linen belonging to the household that is worth 700,000 *livres,* and the cupboards were empty ! "

---

[1] *Moniteur* of 17th Nov., 1793.
[2] Chabot's Manuscript.—National Archives, F7, 4637.
[3] They were present at this sitting of the 26th Brumaire.

121

ANOTHER CITIZEN.—" In the house where Chabot lives there is a nephew of the Austrian Minister."

Chabot, weeping and bewildered, lost his head. He protested that all these tales were false; offered to give himself up as a prisoner; called upon all good citizens to help him unmask his calumniators.

A MEMBER.—" I demand that Chabot be called to order for appealing for help when no one is persecuting him."

The ex-Capuchin admitted his fault, and tried to continue speaking; but his voice was drowned in the uproar. He left the rostrum and struggled to the door of the hall, pursued by shouts and insults. Surely in this hour of crisis, the thick veil that had covered his eyes must have been torn away; surely he understood that a powerful enemy had him by the throat, and that the moment of his fall had been foreordained by someone great and invisible. But by whom?

He passed a night of agony. He felt that he was lost; he foresaw that he would be arrested: that to-morrow, perhaps, the tumbril would come to take him to the scaffold. But no—there was still one hope left!

When dawn broke [1] he went with all speed to

---

[1] We are following Chabot's recollections; but it seems more probable that this occurred after the Jacobins' sitting of the 23rd, when Hébert demanded Chabot's exclusion. Robespierre did not remember the exact date of the interview: he left a blank space in the rough draft of his report: but we have calculated the course of events as follows. On the 23rd Brumaire Hébert demanded Chabot's expulsion. On the 24th or 25th the latter, seized with panic, went to see Robespierre: on the 26th Chabot made his declaration to the Committee, and the Jacobins held the sitting of which we have given an abridged account: on the 27th Chabot was arrested: and on the 28th Amar announced his arrest to the Convention. It matters little whether Chabot knew that he was lost after the sitting of the 23rd or that of the 26th: they were equally ominous. The important thing to show is that Chabot only spoke under the influence of fear, and not with the object of *saving his Country* as he professed.

Robespierre. As he crossed the threshold of the only man of the Revolution whom it has been possible to name the Incorruptible—a name that is very hard on the rest, we may observe incidentally—as he faced the ice-cold eyes of the omnipotent ruler, as he glanced round at the modest room and its scanty furniture, at the white-wood table and the bed and the few chairs that contrasted so strikingly with the damask draperies of the Hôtel Frey, Chabot's last illusion fled. Robespierre looked at him coldly while he explained the object of his visit. There was nothing to be hoped for from a man of this kind.

However, the sometime friar put a bold face on the matter. He had brought with him the 100,000 francs that had been entrusted to him for Fabre. He drew them from his pocket.

" I have awakened you, Robespierre," he said,[1] " but it was to save our country that I did it. I have in my hand the clue to the most dangerous conspiracy that has ever been devised against Liberty."

"Well you must reveal it."

"Yes; but to do so I must continue visiting the conspirators ; for I have been admitted to their confederation. They led me on gradually, and at last offered me terms ; they tempted me with a share of the fruit of their robberies. The day is fixed for their meeting, and I, too, am to be there. They think I do not guess the rest of their scheme ; but they are aiming at a complete counter-revolution. If it be thought desirable I can have all the conspirators seized red-handed."

---

[1] This dialogue was recorded, in the words we give, by Robespierre himself, in his *Projet de Rapport* on the Chabot affair, a report that was never read to the Convention.

See *Histoire parlementaire de la Révolution*, Vol. XXXII.

"It would be doing the greatest possible service to your country: you should not hesitate in the matter. But what are your proofs?"

Chabot held out the roll of assignats that was in his hand.

"Here is a packet," he said, "that was given me in order that I might try and persuade a member of the Mountain to withdraw his opposition to the financial schemes of some of his colleagues. I did not wish to refuse the commission lest I should thereby make it impossible for me to discover and reveal the whole of the plot. But my intention is to go, this moment, and place this packet in the hands of the Committee of General Security, and denounce the traitors. And, further, I can give the Committee an opportunity of seizing them all together in a place where I shall be myself."

"Lose no time, then, in going to the Committee of General Security: they will doubtless accept your offer eagerly."

"Yes, but I wish to guard against my presence among the conspirators being taken as a sign that I am one of them. I must ask for a guarantee. I am ready to die for my country, but I do not wish to die like a criminal. My mother and sister are here: I do not wish them to die of grief. My sister said to me the other day: 'If you have betrayed the cause of the people I shall be the first to plunge a dagger into you.'"

"The Committee of General Security, you may rest assured, will with your help take the necessary steps for discovering the conspiracy. Your intentions, and the information that you will have given them, will be your guarantee. You might as well at the same time report the matter to the Committee of Public Safety: they will seize any available means of saving France."

THE INDIA COMPANY

This amounted to a dismissal. Chabot, greatly cast down, left the Maison Duplay. He had hoped that Robespierre would fling himself into his arms at the news of the conspiracy, and that they two would go off together to *save their country*—an occupation to which Chabot was quite accustomed. The reception given to his revelation showed him that the Incorruptible liked business to be conducted according to rule, and that the Committees alone were empowered to receive denunciations.

He therefore hastened to the Committee of General Security. Here, doubtless, he would be received with acclamation. Not at all. It was in vain that he boasted of his own finesse, and extolled his devotion, and showed the 100,000 francs : his colleagues remained quite calm. He begged for a safe-conduct *to follow up the business*— or, more likely, to take him to the frontier—but it was refused him. He insisted that he ought to be given an acknowledgment of his deposition : they answered that it was unnecessary.

Then Chabot carried his devotion to the uttermost limits of self-sacrifice.

" To-morrow," he said, " at eight o'clock in the evening, Benoît, Delaunay, Julien, Bazire, and de Batz will be in my rooms. Have us all arrested together, the innocent with the guilty. This will clear your minds of any possible doubt as to their complicity, or my honour."

" To-morrow, at your house, at eight o'clock in the evening ? We quite understand : we will surprise you all together."

And Chabot, filled with pride at his stratagem, returned to the house in the Rue d'Anjou with his head in the air.

It would be very interesting to know which member, [1] or

[1] Chabot seems to accuse Lavicomterie.—National Archives, F[7], 4637.

spy, of the Committee of General Security ran off as soon as Chabot was gone, to warn the Baron de Batz of the treacherous blow that his confederate was making ready to deal him.

The Baron de Batz no doubt laughed heartily.

" To-morrow, in Chabot's rooms, at eight o'clock in the evening ? " he asked.

" Yes, you are to be surprised with him."

" Very well, it is quite simple. See that he is arrested at eight o'clock in the morning."

And on the morrow, *at eight o'clock in the morning*, by order of the Committee of General Security, Chabot was arrested—all by himself—to his unspeakable astonishment.[1]

---

[1] " Camille Desmoulins declares, in his *Notes sur le rapport de Saint-Just*, that Chabot asked the Committee to have him and Bazire arrested at eight in the evening, promising to hand over the Baron de Batz and Benoît (of Angers), who would be with him at that hour ; but the Committee, instead of arresting the denounced and the denouncer at eight o'clock in the evening, arrested the denouncer at eight o'clock in the morning, which allowed de Batz, Benoît, and Julien (of Toulouse) to escape."—Louis Blanc, *Histoire de la Révolution*, Book XI, Chap. VIII.

V

THE EPILOGUE TO CHABOT'S LOVE STORY.

On the same day Delaunay and Julien (of Toulouse) were arrested, and taken, like Chabot, to the Luxembourg. Here, too, was lodged Bazire, who, in the eyes of the Committee of General Security, had associated himself with Chabot's actions.

Thus, in the course of three months, this strange thing happened twice : twice the counter-revolutionary schemes of the Baron de Batz were revealed to the Committee, and twice it was the denouncers who were imprisoned. One would naturally expect that steps would be taken, if only for the sake of appearances, against the conspirator himself ; that there would at least be some show of looking for him. Not at all.

And yet, at the very hour when Chabot was denouncing the plot to his colleagues, an incident was taking place that might have hastened the end of the story.

The reader, perhaps, has not forgotten Biret-Tissot, the confidential servant of the Baron de Batz, who acted as an intermediary between the confederates, and slipped so cleverly through the fingers of the gendarme under whose charge he was travelling from Saint-Germains to Paris. He had not been heard of since his escape ; but on the 25th Brumaire the Revolutionary Committee of the Lepéletier Section received an anonymous letter, in disguised handwriting.

It ran thus :

A GASCON ROYALIST

" Citizen Commissioner, Member of the Revolutionary Committee of the Lepéletier Section, my duty obliges me, as a good republican of your own section, to give you news of a certain individual who is more than *suspect* whom you have long sought whose nickname is tissot, but whose real name is birette or birelle; his father and mother live in the rue beauregard bonne nouvelle he was valet to the ci-devant baron de bast, rue de menars, and afterwards to citoyenne grandmaison his *bonne amie*, who is in prison at Sainte Pélagie. You will find tissot, in the faubourg Saint Martin in the house of a man called Constant, mounted gendarme, inside a carriage-entrance facing the rue des marais next the lemonade-shop; he has lived there since his master's *bonne amie* was arrested on information given by me; I saw him in the street a week ago in his ordinary clothes and again since that with the gendarme, in striped waistcoat and breeches and I followed them; that was how I made sure of the fact by the conversation I found out that they walked about together every evening; I know on good authority that a certain grocer said that de bast, his master, had taken refuge with a deputy of the Convention; to surprise Tissot have the door watched as early as possible in the day and do not go in till after midnight or before daylight as though you were going to tell the gendarme to go on duty. For fear of any mistake the woman in the lemonade-shop told me that the way to the gendarme's is by a little staircase on the left beyond the gate—a door at the foot of the stairs on the second storey. The republican who writes to you is of your own section, he will give you other information after this expedition and he does not wish to be known he was on guard the day that a false tissot was arrested try to be quick over the business for fear of any change." [1]

[1] National Archives, F⁷, 4601.

THE EPILOGUE

The Lepéletier section did not hurry : but none the less it acted, and, at six o'clock in the morning of the 27th, the Commissioners Aliaume and Cornet repaired to the place described. The anonymous letter was quite correct : Biret-Tissot, who certainly had the gift of undermining the proverbial integrity of gendarmes, was found with Constand. He was taken before the Committee of the Section, and examined.

He did not deny that for five years he had been in the service of M. de Batz ; but on the latter leaving Paris eighteen months earlier he had entered the employ of Citoyenne Grandmaison as domestic servant. Unfortunately she was in prison, and he was now without a place : so he lived sometimes with one person and sometimes with another. He had three domiciles, and moved from one to the other often, because he was afraid of being arrested, " though he did not think he deserved it." [1]

He was questioned on the subject of the house at Charonne, on the various dwellings of de Batz, and on the *liaison* between the baron and the actress : his answers were rather vague, and gave no new evidence on the subject of the inquiry.

This incident—we must draw attention to the fact, for it is significant—took place on the 27th Brumaire, while Chabot was revealing the vast schemes of the Baron de Batz to the Committee of General Security. The Committee therefore received, simultaneously with Chabot's deposition, the news of Biret's arrest and the report of his examination. They had in their power one of the chief agents of de Batz, and certainly one of the cleverest. They even knew that de Batz *was hidden in the house of a deputy of the Convention* : that the author of the anony-

[1] National Archives, F⁷, 4601.

129   K

mous letter was well informed had already been proved.
By dint of a little diligence Amar, when he reported to
the Convention on the following day that the four deputies
had been arrested, might have been able to announce at
the same time that their corruptor was under lock and
key, or at all events that he was being traced. One
expects to hear of orders quickly given, of the instant
despatch hither and thither of the entire police-force. But
no: the affair came to nothing. Almost incredible as it
seems, neither Biret nor Constand was even detained. They
were left at large![1]

Who can it possibly have been that tied the Committee's
hands in this fashion? Ah—that is the baffling, endless,
impenetrable mystery that confronts us at every turn
throughout this story, the mystery to which, no doubt,
de Batz alone had the clue!

From the day when the actions of the Baron de Batz
were officially denounced to the Convention, and the
government could therefore no longer decently pretend to
be unaware of his existence, we can detect two perfectly
distinct factions in the Committees. De Batz, as we can well
believe, had not bought all the influential members of
the government. Those whom he did not pay saw in
him merely a clever and dangerous conspirator who must
be secured at any cost; but their zeal was rebuffed every
day by the spirit of clemency that was rife, though
unexpressed, among such of their colleagues as were sold
to the conspiracy. We have no document nor record of
any kind to prove the influence that de Batz exercised
over the Committees; but the facts speak for themselves;
the indolence shown in repressing the conspiracy, the
unskilfulness of the measures taken, the sluggishness of the

In the *répertoire Labat* Biret's arrest is dated 17th Frimaire, and
that of Constand 13th Floréal.—(Archives of the Prefecture of Police.)

search, are a sure indication that the course of justice was impeded by a powerful hand.

For instance, on the 1st Frimaire (21st November), Voulland came to the Convention with the piteous tale that Julien (of Toulouse), one of the four deputies against whom a warrant had been issued, had escaped. He was known to possess a passport, by means of which, it was to be feared, he would be able to reach the frontier.

The Assembly annulled Julien's passport, and issued orders to "all the constituted authorities, both civil and military, and all citizens of the Republic,"[1] to seize the fugitive and bring him back to Paris. This was an ineffective measure : Julien was well hidden. He was living peacefully in the Rue Saint-Lazare, with one of his colleagues of the Convention, Lacroix, who sheltered him for nineteen days ; at the end of which time he dressed himself in a blouse and gaiters, and, with a whip in his hand, escaped with a transport-officer in the service of the Republic.

It was said that the transport-department was altogether in the power of the conspirators : it was asserted that de Batz had so many agents in it that he could, had he wished to do so, have stopped the revictualling of Paris or put an end to the famine that reigned there. This, no doubt, was an exaggeration, but the evidence that gave rise to the belief was of a fairly convincing nature.

The ex-Abbé d'Espagnac, who was one of the heads of this department, had been among the frequenters of the house at Charonne, and the men in his employ were chosen on a truly curious principle. A list of the employés attached to the depôt of Marcoussis was read

---

[1] The *Moniteur* of 4th Frimare (24th November, 1793).

2 K

aloud one day in the Jacobin Club, and all the "brothers" shuddered with indignation. It ran thus:

Murphi, huntsman of the *ci-devant* King; Bouchéri, Macherer, Blanchard, coachmen of the *ci-devant* King; Hugué, domestic servant of the *ci-devant* King; Rouarre, bodyguard of the *ci-devant* King; Martin, steward of the *ci-devant* King; Allain, postillion of the *ci-devant* Comte d'Artois; Le Commandeur, postillion of the *ci-devant* Duc de Coigny; Bournaut, servant of the *ci-devant* princesses the aunts of the *ci-devant* King (his wife was still in their service); Bouquet, who emigrated with the *ci-devant* Comte d'Artois; Garnier, coachman to the *ci-devant* Marshal de Broglie; Piédecoq, servant of the *ci-devant* King; Mazuet, refractory priest; Cazalisse, huntsman of the *ci-devant* Princesse de Lamballe; d'Arvilliers, *ci-devant* noble, a violent aristocrat . . .[1]

As we may divine, the civic virtue of these individuals was not altogether likely to be immaculate, and it is easy to believe that a word from de Batz was enough to ensure the escape of Julien, with the help of all these *ci-devant* royal servants, who were delighted to trick the Convention.

That assembly was obliged to resign itself: Julien was never recaptured.[2] But some compensation for the mishap was secured by the arrest, on the 3rd Frimaire, of the patriot Junius Frey and his brother, who were taken to Sainte-Pélagie.[3]

A few days later a strange incident roused the attention of those members of the Committee of General Security who were trying to gather up the threads of the vast conspiracy revealed by Chabot. Six young men presented themselves before Citizen Payot, the major of the second

---

[1] *Moniteur* of 8th October, 1793.
[2] He did not reappear till long after Thermidor.
[3] Archives of the Prefecture of Police.

squadron of the revolutionary army of Versailles, and expressed their intention of joining his force. Payot asked for their *Certificats de Civism.* The young men had none, and retired.

The appearance of one of them being particularly suspicious he was followed. He went to the park, crossed the Plaine de Trappes, entered the Bois de Saint-Hubert, and on arriving at the village of Rochefort knocked at the door of the château. He was arrested. He gave his name: Prince Jules Armand Guethnoë de Rohan-Rochefort. He was twenty-four years of age; all his relations had emigrated except his mother, who was in the prison of the Récollets at Versailles.

A Prince de Rohan asking to be enrolled as a volunteer in the revolutionary army! This sounded bad. It was learnt on inquiry that, two days earlier, the said prince had been arrested by a patrol of patriots between Charonne and Belleville: he had been taken under a considerable escort to the guardhouse of the barracks of La Courtille: but on the following day, when he was required to appear before the Committee of the section, he was nowhere to be found. He had escaped during the night, had reached Versailles safely in a hired coach, had spent the rest of the night " at the sign of the Honest Innkeeper," and had quietly returned on foot to Rochefort, whence he came back to enlist in Citizen Payot's troop.[1]

He was questioned as to his motives in going to Belleville. He answered that he had been to sell a cow to Citizen Champgrand,[2] at whose house he had once or twice met Proly.

[1] See, for this very obscure incident, *Dossier,* W, 389, in the National Archives.

[2] Champgrand had a property at Saint-Mandé. He was arrested at the same time as Rohan-Rochefort.

Now this Proly was none other than that "son of the Austrian Minister" who lived at the Hôtel Frey, and who, as we know, after being employed as a political spy by the Committee of Public Safety, had some time ago become terribly *suspect*.

The Prince de Rohan was committed to the prison of La Bourbe till the matter could be investigated. But the incident had recalled Charonne to the mind of the Committee. It was there that the clue to the mystery was to be found, no doubt; and a fresh and very careful search in that place was resolved upon.

Citizen Delorme, superintendent of police in the Lepéletier Section, went therefore to fetch Citoyenne Grandmaison from the prison of Sainte-Pélagie, where she had been in confinement since the 30th September, and took her, first, to the rooms in the Rue de Ménars where she and de Batz had lived. They consisted of a bedroom, a large boudoir, a dining-room, another small room, and a kitchen. Delorme inspected all the cupboards, broke open all the furniture, explored all the places that sounded hollow, and discovered nothing. He was about to draw up his report and affix the seals when one of his assistants perceived, in the boudoir, that a cupboard had been walled up and papered over.

Citoyenne Grandmaison remained calm. She had condemned the cupboard herself, she said, " to protect herself against the bad smell in that corner, which was near the drains." Nevertheless, the workmen were summoned and the partition was taken down. There was nothing there.[1]

At Charonne the same operation was carried out, with Citoyenne Grandmaison again present. Walls, floors, and cupboards were explored, with no more success than before. The pavilion of the Hermitage was inspected

[1] National Archives, F⁷, 4732.

from cellar to attic; and the Grandmaison even amused herself by pointing out to the superintendent a small room that was the "kind of place where something might be hidden." The simple-minded official had all the flagstones removed and the ground dug up, with no result.[1]

The superintendent affixed the seals, put Citizen Nicolas Fouré in charge of them, replaced the Grandmaison in Sainte-Pélagie, and returned to the Committee of General Security to report the result of his mission. The Committee, in the bitterness of their disappointment, were moved to wrath, and resolved at last upon a measure that had been too long postponed. On the 12th Frimaire (2nd December) they issued an order that "the persons named Batz and Benoît should be seized and brought before the Committee of General Security by Citizen François, member of the Revolutionary Committee of the Section of the Tuileries, as well as all persons whom he considered suspicious in Romainville and its environs."[2]

I know nothing of this Citizen François. If he took his mission seriously he must have suffered many disappointments, and without wishing to judge too hastily of his talents as a detective I think it probable that he was not capable of outwitting the terrible adversary whom the Committee had allotted to him. However, this order had a strange result. Hardly was it signed before silence fell on the subject of the Baron de Batz: for a whole month his name was not heard.

Chabot, in the Luxembourg, was living a very peaceful life. The proof of civic virtue that he had given in

[1] This room no doubt was in the space now occupied by the staircase of the first floor. This, according to the old plans of the Hermitage, was the only part of the house that was flagged.

[2] National Archives, F7, 4588. The order is signed: Voulland, Louis (of the Bas-Rhin), Guffroy, and Jagot.

denouncing his corrupters must surely, he thought, have added a halo to his popularity. Being for a few days in close confinement, and forbidden the use of ink, pens, or paper, he had contrived, with the help of a piece of coal and a scrap of paper he found in his pocket, to scribble a petition to the Convention that he might be allowed to continue his revelations in writing.[1] This privilege was granted, and the ex-Capuchin overwhelmed the Committees with *copy*. He narrated his whole history in every detail ; he denounced without intermission ; he denounced everyone ; he *saved his country* without a moment's pause.

In material matters he had little to complain of. At this time the prison regulations still allowed prisoners to provide themselves with food at their own expense ; and Chabot, who was in no want of money, was able to satisfy the taste for good cheer that he had acquired at the table of the Freys. He obtained his supplies from Coste, who kept a restaurant in the Rue de Tournon ; and, judging from his bills-of-fare, there was nothing democratic about his appetite.

On the 17th November he had some soup with bread in it, four cutlets, a larded chicken, a pear and some grapes : the meal cost him 8 *livres* 6 *sous*. On the 18th he had bread and soup, boiled beef, and six larks : on the 19th, to the bread and soup and boiled beef that he never omitted, he added a partridge. Nearly every day he ate a pullet worth six or eight *livres*, and sometimes a fricassee of two pullets. On the 7th December he indulged in a red-legged partridge, and on the 8th he ate a chicken cooked with truffles, and a pullet. That day his meal cost 14 *livres*.[2]

He also had his portrait painted in miniature by

---

[1] *François Chabot à ses Concitoyens.* National Archives, F⁷, 4637.

[2] Memorandum of food supplied to Citizen Chabot, deputy to the Convention.

THE EPILOGUE

Citizen Bénard, and bought, probably for his sister, his mother, and Poldine, three rings and a sweetmeat-box in yellow tortoise-shell.[1]

He made verses, too, with *bouts rimés* that were suggested to him ; and did not fail to make use of this opportunity to display his patriotism, and celebrate the serenity of his clear conscience, to the tune of *Comment goûter quelque repos ?*

> Un amant de la *liberté*
> Brave les fers de l'*esclavage ;*
> S'il s'élève quelque *nuage*
> Pour troubler sa *sérénité,*
> Il en appelle à la *justice*
> Qui ne peut pas tarder *longtemps*
> À le rendre à ses chers *parents*
> Dont le chagrin fait son *supplice* (*bis*).
>
> Il se console en ses *malheurs ;*
> La vertu respecte ses *chaînes*
> Ses amis partagent ses *peines,*
> Elles se changent en *douceur.*
> La prison n'est un triste *asile*
> Qu'au crime qui ronge le *cœur :*
> On goûte partout le *bonheur*
> Quand la conscience est *tranquille* (*bis*).
>
> Les jours de sa *captivité*
> Ne sont que des moments *d'orage*
> Qui purge aux yeux de l'homme *sage*
> L'horizon de la *liberté.*
> D'un plus beau jour il voit l'*aurore.*
> Il dit toujours à ses *amis :*
> Les traîtres seuls seront *punis,*
> L'éclat du crime est un *phosphore* (*bis*).[2]

However, from time to time, incidents occurred to trouble this happy calm. A few days after his imprisonment, for instance, he heard of the arrest of his brothers-in-law : the letter he wrote on this occasion to the

[1] Memorandum by Citizen Bénard. These articles cost 545 *livres.*

[2] *Bouts rimés, proposés à François Chabot au Luxembourg et remplis par lui le 24.*—National Archives, F⁷, 4637.

Committee of General Security is full of the enthusiasm he felt for the patriotism of the two German Jews; but his ardour seems a little artificial, and his words even convey a vague hint of suspicion.

" I thank Providence," he says, " for having made you at last resolve to arrest my brothers-in-law. I believe them to be pure as the sun, and true Jacobins, and if they were not so they would be the greatest hypocrites in the universe."[1]

Providence, indeed, plays a prominent part in all his effusions. The renegade appears to believe in God almost as much as in Robespierre, and he uses the two names indifferently in a hymn of adoration.

" Robespierre! In the name of the humanity you cherish hasten the moment when my sufferings shall end. What! I am punished as a conspirator, and all my relations and friends are arrested! Why does death flee from me when I call? I have brought to the grave a mother of eighty years and a father of eighty-five. And why? Because I married a foreigner of sixteen!

" What—was I faithful to my country when I lived with mistresses who sought to injure me, and did I become a conspirator the instant I married a virtuous woman?

" Great God! thou art punishing the errors of my youth now that I have begun to be virtuous!! I adore the hand that chastises me. . . I address myself to you, Robespierre, with the confidence that your virtue has always inspired in me. I confess to you that I am no longer Chabot. My courage has fled since it became impossible for me to die for the cause of liberty. . . "[2]

[1] *Le Citoyen Chabot aux membres du Comité de Sûreté générale*, 11 *Frimaire an II.*—National Archives, F[7], 4637.

[2] Letter dated 27 Frimaire, year II.—National Archives, F[7], 4637.

THE EPILOGUE

And in one of his manuscripts he has the temerity to write these words: " Eternal thanks be given to thee, O infinite Providence of my God, for that thou hast always sustained me in the path of virtue!"

All this was the merest farce: Chabot was playing the buffoon to save his head. Of the conceit that lay in those words: " *I am no longer Chabot!* " and of the unreality of his appeal to a Providence in whom he did not believe, he afterwards gave proof. Great indeed was the cowardice that he could not altogether disguise in his apostrophe to *death that fled from him*—an apostrophe that was composed between a truffled pullet and a dish of rare game! And abject indeed was his flattery of Robespierre, the only man, as he well knew, who had the power to defend him. Not that Robespierre thought, for a single moment, of doing so.

It was with the aim of winning the indulgence of the Incorruptible that he spent his days in committing to paper those precious memories that served, later on, as themes for many a discourse from the platform of the Convention. For everything that Chabot wrote was taken day by day to the Committee of General Security; where it was read, and re-read, and then communicated to the Committee of Public Safety. His continual denunciations gave rise to suspicions, vague at first, but afterwards more definite. There was not a name that was absent from this general confession of the unfrocked friar: Hébert, Fabre, Lacroix, David, Danton—all were there; and those who began by rejecting the idea that such illustrious patriots could possibly do wrong, came at last, little by little, to wonder if the tale after all were true. Thus the scheme of the Baron de Batz was slowly working its way towards fulfilment. The mud that Chabot scattered in his struggles besmirched the whole Convention.

He had now no illusions left : he saw clearly what had befallen him : he was aware both of the identity and of the power of his enemy.

" I have denounced a system of corruption intended to disgrace the members of the National Convention, an attempt whose sole object was to dissolve the Convention itself, and I have been in solitary confinement for two months, while, perhaps, the heads of the Conspiracy are still secretly carrying out their infernal plot !

" *When I denounced the ci-devant Baron de Batz I ought to have expected this subversion of the principles of justice.* His only object in remaining in France was to act as the most energetic agent of the *émigrés* and the foreign powers. The care he took to have all his moveable property nominally owned by other people [1] proves that he was afraid of being recognised, sooner or later, as an accomplice of the *émigrés*."

The cell next to Chabot's had been apportioned to Delaunay. There was little intercourse between the two comrades : but once or twice Delaunay had sent to Chabot, by the hand of one of the turnkeys, some punch or liqueur which the ex-Capuchin declined to drink—"for fear of my life," said he. This shows us very clearly that his avoidance of death was after all more sedulous than death's avoidance of him.

One day, while the *conclaviste* [2] Besse was making Chabot's bed, Vernet the turnkey entered the room with a letter for the ex-friar. It was a note in a woman's handwriting, demanding from the prisoner the sum of 100

---

[1] Chabot was well-informed : the reader will remember the fictitious sale by de Batz of the house at Charonne, in July 1792.

[2] This was the name ironically given at the Luxembourg to the servants who waited on the prisoners, in allusion to the attendants assigned to the cardinals while they are in seclusion during a conclave.

écus, for which the unknown correspondent declared he was liable.

Chabot, who was unaware of owing any money, suspected a trap, and made a movement to throw the paper into the fire. But, as he approached the fireplace, and glanced at the note again with a view to divining the object of it, he saw that the heat of the fire was bringing out, between the lines, some reddish-brown characters that had been traced in invisible ink. He quickly read this strange communication, and re-read it four times to impress it on his memory. It ran as follows:

"Be calm. The A's are gone or in hiding. Hé . . . holds firm and will defend you. Deal carefully with B. Accuse the A's and, above all, C. Dufo . . . is still his sworn enemy. He will help us. His marriage annoys the fr. . . . His brothers and relations will be arrested. All is going well. Be brave and cheerful. The rep . . . is his sworn foe. The rascal has deceived us, but he will be sorry for it. The A's will accuse him, and the p. is against him. You are not spoken of. I told you not to trust the C. The f. will be the dupe in the matter, however."

When he was certain of being able to remember the words of this note Chabot called Vernet.

"Who gave you this letter?" he asked.

"A citizen who is waiting downstairs for the answer."

"But I owe nothing," continued Chabot. "They are asking me for money, and I do not know the signature."

"He assured me that you knew him well."

"To whom did he tell you to give this note?"

"Why, to Citizen Delaunay of Angers, the deputy."

"Well, I am not he!"[1]

---

[1] We give the precise words of Chabot's narrative. See National Archives, F⁷, 4637.

Vernet took the note and carried it off to its owner, leaving Chabot to his reflections.

After turning over the enigmatical sentences in his mind a hundred times he contrived to make sense of them, and to substitute names for the initials. He interpreted it thus: one of the confederates was informing Delaunay that the A's, or *amis*, Julien and Benoît, were in safety. The blame might be put on the absent, but B—de Batz—must be carefully dealt with. Hébert held firm, and Dufourny was inclined to blame the rascal Chabot, who had denounced the conspiracy. They had been wrong to trust the C.—the Capuchin. But it would be the f.—the friar—who would be the dupe. The reporter was his sworn foe and the people were against him.

In recording this strange incident we have followed Chabot's notes. He expected to derive great advantage from it: for to be called a rascal by the conspirators was a piece of good fortune for which he had not hoped. This simple note, with its key, vindicated him completely; and he hastened to enter the facts in his Confessions.

In our opinion there is not a word of truth in the whole story: it is altogether the fruit of a desperate man's imagination. In the first place, the incidental circumstances will not stand examination: if a man intends to burn a useless paper he throws it into the fire; he does not slowly carry it to the fireplace. Moreover, is it likely that Chabot, once having in his possession a document so compromising to his enemies and so advantageous to himself, would have meekly yielded it up on the ground that it was not addressed to him? So delicate a scruple is by no means consistent with what we know of this individual. But though the ancedote is an invention from beginning to end it is worth preserving. It shows us at least one fact : that Chabot knew even more of the habits and movements of the conspirators than he admitted. He knew that de Batz transmitted his orders to his agents by means of invisible ink : he was not ignorant of the fact that Mrs. Atkins used this method of correspondence when the Queen's rescue from the Temple prison was in question. De Batz thought it an ingenious plan, and used it on occasion. It is even probable that Chabot—when he was free and was selling himself—had often received notes written in this way. He remembered the fact, and tried to wring a proof of his innocence from this fresh revelation. He only succeeded in providing his judges with a new weapon : and we shall see how Amar and Élie Lacoste, in their reports, referred to the *invisible ink* to which Chabot had so imprudently called their attention.

It will easily be believed that the news of a wide-spread conspiracy, having for its object the destruction of the National Convention and the restoration of the Monarchy, had made a great sensation in Paris. The Committees, who prided themselves on governing "in full daylight," had not kept the revelation to themselves. Nothing else was discussed in the Assembly ; the Jacobin Club lost its head over the matter ; the whole population of Paris— demoralised by five years of ceaseless revolution—was feverishly awaiting some stirring event. And there was no limit to the theories that might plausibly be held : it was known that immense numbers of aristocrats were pre- paring a final assault upon the Republic ; but no one knew their names, which made it permissible to suspect everyone. The police spies with whom Paris was swarming were having fine sport ! They could denounce whom they would, being well assured that the most unlikely tale would be accepted as a fresh indication of the power of the conspirators. If de Batz had paid them to disseminate distrust they could not have succeeded better.

"Some citizens, speaking of Chabot," wrote one of these spies, "said that he would soon win back the confidence that he had never really lost, and that, if this were not the case, *they could never trust anyone.*" [1]

Here is another note : "There is a rumour that the Chabot affair is a myth invented by Hébert and Chaumette to concentrate upon one man's head all the weight of the people's indignation." [2]

A third spy is on the track of one of the conspirators : "He is often to be seen in the Revolutionary Tribunal," he writes," [3] "wearing a peruke, but in the Jacobin style ; age, about thirty four, height 5ft. 5in., face oval, eyes brown, eyebrows chestnut, beard red, and in his expression that particular quality that the *ci-devants* have never yet entirely lost."

The same suspicious character was often remarked in the large café at the Porte Saint-Antoine. He wore a great-coat with blue lapels, and shoes with cork soles : sometimes he spoke English, and reviled the course of events. [4]

Rousseville, the famous police spy—to whom the Committee of General Security had granted, for the furtherance of his work, two horses from the stables of the *ci-devant* King [5]—was persuaded that the isolated house at the end of the Champs-Élysées, the house known as the Petit Luxembourg, was the meeting-place of the conspirators. He saw it entered by a great many *gentlemen.*

[1] Report dated Décadi, 1st decade of Nivôse, year II.—National Archives, F[7], 3688[3].
[2] Report of 20th Nivôse. National Archives, F[7], 3688[3].
[3] 9th Nivôse, year II.—National Archives, F[7], 3688[3],
[4] Report of 14th Nivôse.—National Archives, F[7], 3688[3].
[5] Register of the Committee of General Security.—National Archives, AF[11], 221.

THE EPILOGUE

"It is, moreover," he wrote, "uninhabited, and has a garden as suitable for political plots as it is for lovers' secrets."[1]   The café situated at the end of the Rue Saint-Benoît also seemed to him terribly suspicious.   When he entered it "someone gave a low whistle and there was absolute silence."[2]

One of these *observers of public opinion* saw conspirators wherever he went.

"Having been with a deputation to the Convention I went to dine with some of my colleagues in the *ci-devant* Jardin Breteuil, in a large room with a fine inlaid floor. I saw at once that I was going to spend my day's pay on my dinner; but there was nothing to be done—I resigned myself to the experience.   My friends asked for the bill-of-fare, and I found, after having had some soup and rice, some beef, a bottle of wine, and two potatoes, that I had spent 8 *livres* 10 *sols*.   They charged me this, they said, because I was not rich.   'Confound it,' I said; 'what do the rich pay here?'   It is really ridiculous— the passage of the old riding-school of the Tuileries[3] is too dear for *sans-culottes!*   I ought to say that I saw, coming into this big room, *ci-devant* marquises and counts and knights of the dagger[4] of the old Monarchy, and deputies, etc.   But I confess I could not recall the names of these *ci-devant* nobles, for when they are disguised as *sans-culottes* the devil himself would not know them. But I shall find out, for a man I know has promised to take me behind the scenes at the Opera when they are

[1] National Archives, F⁷, 3688³.
[2] National Archives, F⁷, 3688³.
[3] The Jardin Breteuil adjoined the passage between the Riding School and the Feuillants.
[4] *Chevaliers du Poignard* was the name given by the people to the royalists who went secretly, with concealed weapons, to defend the royal family in the Tuileries, in February 1791.—(*Translator's Note*).

there. They make signals to each other there, and the actresses call them by their names. There—that is all that I can do, d—n it! To-day I am going to the assembly-general."[1]

All these rumours and theories gradually became public property, and were repeated and exaggerated. At this time the general feeling of apprehension was at its climax, and not a man in Paris would have been surprised, during these first three months of 1794, to learn one fine morning that the entire Convention had been massacred, that Louis XVII was on the throne, and that Danton was at the head of his ministry. The *Moniteur* thought it was its duty to calm this harassing excitement by quoting a semi-official paragraph from the *Salut Public*. "It is impossible," it said, "to form a correct idea of the meddling lies and libels on their country that the aristocrats are repeating on all sides. . . . There is a kind of malevolent person whom we wish the public to regard as the most dangerous of all—the kind of man who is always trying to read between the lines. . . . Do not believe any news that is not published by the Convention."[2]

This was throwing oil on the fire, for the Convention gave no news at all. It was in vain that one member or another, about every ten days, rose to beg the Committee to put an end to the feverish expectation of the people by revealing the whole plot, and publishing the long-promised report on Chabot's denunciations : the Committee answered that they were working night and day at that important document, and that unless they were given the time that was needful they could not conscientiously fulfil the arduous task they had undertaken.[3]

[1] National Archives, F7, 3688³.
[2] *Moniteur* of 15th Frimaire (5th December, 1793).
[3] See, especially, the *Moniteur* of the 1st Nivôse (21st December, 1793).

THE EPILOGUE

This was regarded as an excuse. If the government hesitated to give the names of the conspirators it must surely be that the names were very illustrious. The general feeling of suspicion grew stronger; it extended to the whole Convention; its unpopularity increased, and, to make the demoralisation worse, every man who feared to find himself included in the anonymous accusation hastened to denounce a colleague in proof of his own civic virtue.

There are no words that can describe the tempest of denunciation that raged at that time throughout France. Every day brought its own scandal, either in the Jacobin Club or the Convention, and the story of these sickening scenes, as told in the *Moniteur*, makes one realise how triumphantly the Baron de Batz, in his place of concealment, must have rejoiced over the storm he had raised. The drama he had composed was being acted under his eyes: his enemies were tearing one another to pieces, hurling the most unexpected accusations at one another's heads and vilifying one another in the most revolting revelations. In the Jacobin Club Nicolas denounced Camille Desmoulins; Hébert denounced Bourdon (of L'Oise) and Fabre d'Églantine; Collot d'Herbois denounced Philippeaux; Camille Desmoulins denounced Hébert; Goupilleau denounced Rossignol; Lachevardière denounced Goupilleau; Legendre denounced Hébert; Hébert denounced Lacroix. The Jacobins denounced the Cordeliers; the Cordeliers referred to the Jacobins as *sans-culottes* with incomes of 8,000 francs. The horrified *brothers* resolved to " purge themselves," and the process of purging made suspicion and insult the order of the day. Nor was the Convention more self-controlled. Bourdon (of L'Oise) called upon the Minister of War, Bouchotte, to give his reasons, within twenty-four hours, for bringing to

Paris and its neighbourhood a large number of Austrian prisoners and deserters.[1] This question reduced the assembly to a state of panic. A cry was raised that the Committee of Public Safety had distributed arms to these foreigners. Taillefer declared that these Germans were clothed "—how do you think, citizens? In the national uniform! The pretext is that they must unavoidably be clothed, since they are naked!" Another member reported that the Austrian prisoners quartered in the barracks of La Courtille had shouted *Vive le roi!* Yet another, speaking of the great number of foreign soldiers then in Paris, declared that the Committee had announced their intention of sending them away, but had done nothing further. Finally Merlin demanded an explanation of the object that was expected to be attained by thus massing *Coburg's army round the capital.*[2]

The Convention was distraught. It had a vision of itself besieged, taken by assault, and massacred by the foreign troops whom " a vast combination " had gathered round the gates of Paris; and it had additional reason for anxiety in the fact that the guidance of the machinery of government was apparently being taken from it. No members were subjected to strict supervision. In this town where German soldiers were walking about in perfect safety, wearing French uniforms and armed with weapons provided by the Committees, the deputies were treated as *suspects.* Pons (of Verdun) was arrested by the police-inspector Marino in the act of entering his own house, at eleven o'clock at night. He showed his deputy's-card, but Marino paid no attention to it, and Pons spent part of

---

[1] There were, as a matter of fact, 2,000 Austrian prisoners at Meaux, 2,300 at Chartres, 2,000 at Saint-Germain, &c. See the *Moniteur* of the 30th Ventôse.

[2] Sitting of 29th Ventôse.

the night in the guardhouse. He lodged a complaint. Marino, on being questioned by the Committee of General Security, alleged by way of defence that he had never seen a deputy's card! And when he was asked why he had not at once reported the incident to the Committee of General Security :

"*I did not know,*" he said, "*that there was a Committee of General Security of the National Convention.*"

"But was it not your duty to take the alleged representative of the people before the president of the Convention, to be identified ?"

"I have no more to say." [1]

It was thus that the government was served during these early days of 1794. There was reason enough, it must be admitted, for any number of fears ; and all the more that it was known beyond all possibility of doubt, since Chabot had revealed it, that an immense conspiracy had the government in its power.

It would be easy to multiply instances of the disorder that reigned in the Convention : the reports of the sittings plainly show that the assembly knew the ground beneath them to be undermined, and expected every day to see the outbreak of the gigantic conspiracy that was always referred to in veiled terms, and seemed invulnerable to every attack on the part of the Committees. This was a fine opportunity, truly, for suspicion, and calumny, and personal hatred! And suddenly comes the news that Fabre d'Églantine has been arrested. What!—is he too in the plot ? Oh yes! Delaunay's depositions have led to the discovery of a document—the draft of the forged Decree—that proves his guilt. And now Hérault de Séchelles and Simon are accused of complicity with the

---

[1] See in *Moniteur*, the sittings of 29th Ventôse and 24th Germinal, year II.

enemies of the Republic. They helped an *émigré*[1] to evade the officials of the Lepéletier Section—it is always the Lepéletier Section—and where do you think the fugitive was found? Why, hidden in Hérault's rooms!

Thus the suspicion of treason, like an irresistible flood, seemed to be on the point of submerging the assembly that had once been so proud of its strength, but was now utterly disabled by the blows of its invisible foe. Every man who rose to speak was suspected before he opened his lips. He was heard with attention. If his proposal were moderate he was regarded with suspicion, as a man who had evidently been corrupted: if it were not so, he was suspected still more, as one of those false patriots whose object was to drive [the Republic into excesses and thus hasten its end. It was in their desperation at this time that the legislators in the Hall of the Tuileries, in Michelet's phrase, "shot each other with their eyes."[2]

One man, however, seems to have seen clearly through all this war of extermination that threatened the Assembly. This was Robespierre. He alone of them all, perhaps, was gifted with the statesmanlike mind that seeks to understand the cause behind the event; and he divined

---

[1] His name was Catus.

[2] The archives of the Committee show how great was the terror of the government. Here is the record of a contemplated measure: "Once for all, the Committee of Public Safety should try to discover the truth with regard to the principles and schemes of the Republic's enemies both great and small. To attain this end there is a simple means, but a very bold one: namely to intercept: 1st, all correspondence leaving Paris; 2nd, all correspondence arriving in Paris; the whole to be carried out on one day, and for one day only. I admit it is a subversion of all principle; but in times of revolution, as every-one allows, the affairs of this world are regulated by one great goddess: Necessity. Two men, *one to keep an eye upon the other*, should stop the mails on all the roads for three hours. . &c." (National Archives, AF[11], 60.)

THE EPILOGUE

the hidden hand that was controlling the fatal struggle in which the Revolution was now engaged.

"Only a blind man could fail to see that the aristocrats have been laying a trap for the patriots, by stirring them up one against the other. Our quarrels are the strength of our enemies: they are delighted to see us fight: they will stand round and watch us, waiting for the moment to cut our throats." This is the theme of all his speeches: he often returns to the idea: he cherishes it: it serves him for a programme. Thenceforward the plot of the Baron de Batz had a name of its own: it was called the Foreign Conspiracy. "It is the foreigners," says Robespierre again, "who are dragging the patriots into fatal recklessness and are pushing them into inconsistent excesses. This is the source of all these precipitate accusations, these quarrels with their tone of menace. The object is to make Europe believe that the representatives of the nation are not respected, that not a single patriot is safe, that patriots and counter-revolutionaries are all exposed to the same dangers." [1]

It was at this time that the Incorruptible wrote the following note, which was found among his papers after his death: "The days that have lately dawned are big with the destinies of the universe: the two spirits that dispute the rule of it are face to face. . . . At the head of the criminal faction that believes the hour is at hand when it shall bathe in the blood of the faithful representatives of the people *is the Baron de Batz.*"

Thus, by a series of really remarkable deductions, Robespierre, like a true statesman, arrived at the discovery of the baron's plan, the plan whose aims, briefly expressed, were to discredit the Convention and crush it under the foot of popular displeasure. And, when once this idea

[1] Robespierre in the Jacobin Club, 6th Nivôse, year II.

151

had taken shape in Robespierre's mind, he associated with it everything that seemed to him inimical to the good name of the Revolution. The anti-religious masquerades by which the assembly-hall was disgraced, and of which we have given an example, were, according to Robespierre, prompted by the conspirators. The bloodthirsty excesses of Hébert's faction were encouraged by the confederates. The policy of mercy towards which Danton and Desmoulins presently inclined was insisted upon by the aristocrats. This conspiracy of de Batz was in a fair way to become the scapegoat of the whole governmental system.

These observations may appear trifling, but they explain certain facts that would otherwise be inexplicable. It was thanks to this theory that the Revolutionary Tribunal was thenceforward enabled to word its sentences of death in this invariable manner : " *So-and-so . . .* being convicted of complicity in the conspiracy that has been formed against the Unity and Indivisibility of the Republic, the liberty and safety of the French nation. . . ." This formula, from this time onward, served for all condemned prisoners alike, for Danton as for Mme. Elizabeth, for Hébert as for Malesherbes, for André Chénier as for the venerable Duchesse de Noailles, for working-men and dukes, for members of the Parlement and generals, for girls, and priests, and *septembriseurs*—for all those whom Fouquier-Tinville sent indiscriminately, *to play hot-cockles*, as he put it, in the Place de la Révolution.

And now that the baron's schemes are being carried out, now that the Jacobins and the Cordeliers and the Convention are at sixes and sevens, and on the point, as he foresaw, of cutting each other's throats, all that remains to us to do is to follow the course of events : to record the efforts made by certain members of the Committee of General Security to secure the person of the leader of the conspiracy, and the still greater efforts made by others to save his head. Finally, we must relate how the Convention, in its exasperation at failing to seize that impalpable spectre—always at hand, yet always invisible—indemnified itself for its defeat with a hecatomb of innocent people.

It was Saint-Just who made himself the interpreter, from the rostrum of the assembly, of Robespierre's views: he revealed the whole fabric of the conspiracy. Had de Batz himself divulged his vast schemes, his methods of action, his hopes, his attempts, he could have said nothing that Saint-Just left unsaid. In his long speech [1] he alluded to everything, he brought the most insignificant facts into relation with one another, he considered the plot as being on the point of success. "The kings of Europe are watching the clock," he cried; "the death of our liberty and the destruction of Paris have been promised to them!" But he was, so to speak, theoretical throughout: he confined himself to anonymous allusions: he mentioned no names. The Convention had hoped for something more satisfactory: the important things to know were the names of the confederates, and the details of Chabot's revelations, which everyone seemed bent on concealing.

So much was it the case that these were the points on which the Convention desired enlightenment that when, three days later, Amar mounted the rostrum as the representative of the united Committees of Public Safety and General Security, to read his report on the recent cases of corruption, he was greeted, before he opened his lips, with thunders of applause. Now, at last, the whole secret would be revealed!

Great indeed was the disappointment! Amar, it must be said, had only undertaken the report under pressure

---

[1] *Moniteur* of 24th Ventôse, year II.

and compulsion. He had been evading the Committee's orders for the past month, and threats were required to make him speak.[1] It is true that he made a virtue of necessity, so to speak, in as far as he sacrificed Bazire, Chabot, Delaunay, Julien, and Fabre, who were already doomed ; but he said not a word of the conspiracy. I am wrong : by a very singular chance, if chance it were, the names of the Baron de Batz and the banker Benoît, who should have figured in his report as persons of the first importance, became the *Baron de Beauce and Benoîte—* as though pains had been taken to make them unrecognisable.

It should further be noted that Saint-Just's speech, also, had been printed so carelessly that the text had become incomprehensible in some places, and grotesque in others.[2] Mischance, apparently, pursued those who attacked the Baron de Batz. Robespierre, however, regarded the matter otherwise, and expressed his surprise vigorously that Amar "should have forgotten the most important object of his report." Billaud-Varennes supported this motion, and demanded that Chabot should be accused, not merely of double dealing, but especially of being implicated in an immense intrigue of which Amar had not said a

[1] Letter from the Committee to Amar : "We sent our colleague Voulland to you to express our impatience in the matter of the Report for which you have kept us waiting for four months. He told us, in your name, that you would attend the Committee in the evening. You again broke your word. You must, absolutely, end these delays. You will force us to take measures that will be very disagreeable to us, as your friends." (11th Ventôse) National Archives, Register of the Committee.

[2] 1st Germinal (21st March, 1794). "There is a report by Saint-Just being circulated, on the foreign factions, which swarms with misprints. Is it due to malevolence or ignorance that a report that should intimidate all our enemies has been made ridiculous in this way ?" Report of a secret agent, See *Tableaux de Paris pendant la Révolution*, by Schmidt,

word. Poor Amar made no reply. He withdrew his report, to revise it before it was printed.

We have no documentary authority for believing Amar to be a confederate of the Baron de Batz, but had he been so he must have acted as he did. For not only did he refer to the conspirator as to a person of secondary importance, but he did excellent service to the cause of the conspiracy by reducing Chabot's affair to a mere trial for corrupt practices. Far from having a soothing effect, this report gave fresh life to the prevailing mistrust, and turned every man's hand against his neighbour. Since no one knew in which direction to strike, it seemed the safest course to decimate the advanced party. Robespierre was right when he said : " The two extremes meet : the fanatic covered with scapularies and the fanatic who preaches atheism have much in common ; and sometimes red caps are nearer to red heels than one would think possible."[1] So Hébert, Ronsin, Momoro, Vincent, Proly, Clootz, and other kindred spirits were driven off to the Tribunal. Their indictment was no difficult matter to Fouquier-Tinville ; he had but to repeat the phrases that had appeared in every speech since Chabot made his revelations : the projected annihilation of the representative assembly, the foreign powers directing the whole conspiracy with the help of perfidious agents—we know the theme. We know, too, the formula by which the accused were sent to their death ; " convicted of having attempted to dissolve the Convention and to destroy the republican government. . . ." The same methods that had been employed for the *ultras* were made to serve for the *cis-*revolutionaries (the word is Fabre d'Églantine's) ; and it was on the same grounds, soon afterwards, that Danton and Desmoulins were sent to the scaffold.

[1] Speech in the Convention. *Moniteur*, 7th Nivôse, year II.

But before we go on to the next scene in the story that we have undertaken to tell we must return to our two principal characters, de Batz and Chabot.

What was the baron doing, we may ask, while the terrible machine that he had set in motion was grinding among its revolving wheels the most notable heads of the revolutionary party? No doubt he was terrified into silence, and was hiding in some hole, or in some confederate's house, horrified at the work he had done? Not at all. De Batz was chiefly concerned with two matters. First, he was trying to obtain the release of Citoyenne Grandmaison, in which attempt he succeeded without much difficulty.[1] Secondly, he was much engrossed in buying a country-house to replace the house at Charonne, which had really become uninhabitable owing to the indiscretions of the police. His dream this time was to possess a large property, where he might enjoy, from time to time, the peaceful pleasures of the fields. He fixed at last upon the demesne of Chadieu, in Puy-de-Dôme, and on the 7th Nivôse a Swiss watchmaker called Jean Louis Nathey acquired possession of it, in the presence of Maître Cabal, notary, for the sum of 530,000 *livres*. Nathey was careful to state in the contract that in buying the property of Chadieu he did not intend nor aspire to exercise his rights as proprietor, since the place belonged to—(here there is a blank line)—to whom he was merely lending his name " to give him pleasure." [2]

Now, we are in a position to fill in that blank line. It was at Chadieu that de Batz, who was its true owner, died in 1822. If there were any doubt in the matter it would be finally dispelled by another document in the same

---

[1] Citoyenne Grandmaison was released on the 14th Nivôse, year II. (Archives of the Prefecture of Police *répertoire Labat*).

[2] National Archives, F[7], 4774[56]. Found among Nathey's papers.

dossier, which proves that Nathey acted as the conspirator's man of business and representative. This document is " the inventory of plate from the house of the person called Batz, presumed to have emigrated," for which plate a receipt is given to the said Nathey. The plate, we may add, consisted of an electro-plated dinner-service of a considerable number of pieces, including, among others, three dozen plates, eighteen large dishes, eight oval soup-plates, twenty-eight small oval dishes, etc. All these crested pieces of plate were sent to the Mint.[1]

As for Chabot, he did not accept his position nearly so philosophically. When he read Amar's report he was filled with consternation. What? was it possible that the reader of this report could have vilified the denouncers and said not a single word of those whom they denounced? The ex-Capuchin saw that the tactics he had thought so clever had completely failed. He recognised that he was a doomed man.

On the 27th Ventôse, at about three o'clock in the afternoon, Citizens Peyre, Maine, and Forest, who were confined in the Luxembourg in the Chambre de l'Indivisibilité, heard the bell that was connected with the various rooms on that landing "ringing repeatedly and very energetically."[2] Being curious to know the cause of this unwonted summons they went into the corridor. A carpenter who was repairing the floor near the door of Chabot's cell, which was the next cell to their own, told them "he had heard a voice calling *help!* and he thought someone was doing away with himself." On listening at the door they heard groans, and "a curious noise." One of them ran to fetch Benoît the head-jailer, who had already been summoned by the turnkey Besse,

---

[1] National Archives, F7, 4774⁵⁶. Found among Nathey's papers.
[2] National Archives, W, 342.

and was hastening up the grand staircase. They all entered Chabot's cell together, and found him stretched upon his bed, convulsed with sickness and writhing with internal pains.

This was what had happened. As his watch struck three o'clock [1] the ex-Capuchin, who had no doubt fixed upon this for his last hour, called the turnkey Besse, and showing him a paper that lay on the table, said:

"Take this. It is a letter addressed to the National Convention. Now go and fetch the head-jailer, Benoît: I have an important communication to make to him."

Besse put the letter in his pocket and left the room. Hardly had he reached the foot of the stairs before he heard the bell ringing repeatedly. He immediately went upstairs again with Benoît, whom he had just met. He opened the door of the cell. Chabot had poisoned himself.

Without a moment's delay a hasty summons was sent to the doctors who were imprisoned in the house. Marenski and Loupé ran to the spot. Chabot silently drew their attention to an empty bottle that was on the table. The label was thus inscribed: *Application to be used outwardly and on no account to be taken.*

Between two paroxysms they questioned him, and in a hardly audible voice he made the following statement:

"I have made my last testament. . . I thought my death was necessary to the happiness of my country . . I resolved to drink some of a lotion that was given me for an external ailment that I suffer from. . .[2] As I drank it

---

[1] This was not the exact time. Chabot stated that his watch *did not go well.*

[2] It is true that Chabot had been ill from the 6th to the 30th Ventôse. There is in his *dossier* a bill from Citizens Charras and Duchatelle, chemists, who supplied him with emollient herbs, Sydenham's white decoction, diascordium, &c.

THE EPILOGUE

I cried ' *Vive la République!* ' for I felt I was offering a sacrifice to my country."

Chabot was a mountebank to the end. A man who swallows the contents of a bottle of poison, crying ' *Vive la République!* ' with the intention of offering himself up as a sacrifice to his country, and then promptly rings his bell violently for help, is plainly endowed with less courage than love of melodrama. However, the doctors saw that there had been corrosive sublimate in the contents of the phial, and that the state of the suicide was alarming.

He was able, nevertheless, to utter a few words. Asking Besse for the letter he had confided to him he gave it to Benoît.

" Here," he said, " take my will, and tell my persecutors that I forgive them, since I believe they sentenced me to death to save my country." [1]

Benoît, in the presence of the dying man, put the will into an envelope, which he sealed ; and Chabot wrote his signature near the seal.

That envelope is still in existence. There it lies, in the *dossier ;* and this little scrap of crumpled paper seizes the imagination strangely. Close to the red circle of sealing-wax is Chabot's signature, obviously written with a trembling hand and with a great effort. He even adorned his name with an elaborate flourish, as though he took pleasure in this last manifestation of the vitality that he felt was ebbing from him.

---

[1] Chabot's will is in the Museum of the National Archives. The following is an extract from it : " Chabot disowns the son of Julie Berger ; but none the less wishes him to be supported till he is fourteen years of age." Julie Berger was the housekeeper whom Dufourny blamed him for deserting. These words, too, should be noted : " There have been errors in my life. I hope the Divinity will forget them, and receive me into His bosom, which I adore in spite of all the modern atheistic fanatics."

159

In the evening there was a terrible crisis. At about five o'clock they gave him some sweet-oil and milk to drink ; but the pains returned with increased violence at eight o'clock, and continued till eleven. They gave him a strong dose of laudanum to alleviate them.[1] For three days he was at death's door ; but on the 30th Ventôse the medical officers Bayard and Naury signed the order for his removal, and poor Chabot was carried off, on the 2nd Germinal, to the Hospice de l'Évêché, which had been turned into a hospital for all the prisons in Paris.

The end was near. Ten days later Danton, Camille Desmoulins, Philippeaux, and Lacroix were arrested: the *batch* was being made ready in which Chabot was to play his last part.

We have done our best to show how the Committees, being unable to lay their hands on the leaders of the de Batz Conspiracy, seized everyone who could, rightly or wrongly, be suspected of intrigue, corruption, or lukewarmness. The Foreign Conspiracy—to use the historical name of the vast plot whose chief incidents we are trying to put together— had already sent Hébert and his faction to the scaffold ; it was now the turn of the Dantonists. Their ever-famous trial has so often been described that we shall not repeat its details here. We must, however, point out the links, hitherto insufficiently recognised, which connect this trial with the conspiracy of the Baron de Batz.

The accused numbered sixteen : Danton, Camille Desmoulins, Chabot, Bazire, Delaunay (of Angers), Fabre d'Églantine. Hérault de Séchelles, Lacroix, and Philippeaux were all deputies in the Convention. To these were added Lhuillier, *procureur-général* of the department of Paris, the ex-Abbé Sahuguet d'Espagnac, Junius and Emmanuel Frey, Diederichsen, advocate of the royal courts of

---

[1] National Archives, W, 342.

Denmark, General Westermann, and Gusman, a Spanish noble.

That seven of the accused had relations with de Batz was clearly proved by Chabot's revelations, and therefore we shall not further discuss those cases. The seven in question were Chabot and his two brothers-in-law, Delaunay, Bazire, d'Espagnac, and Lhuillier.

Fabre d'Églantine, in my opinion, was innocent of the crime of which he was accused: the alteration of the Decree. But the retired actor was doomed to expiate his dubious past, and his too sudden accession of wealth. A police report, dated the 15th Nivôse, gives us in a few lines the charges that were indirectly brought against him.

" Since Fabre d'Églantine was arrested many people have been saying things to his disadvantage. Yesterday I was in a café where he was being discussed. Two years ago, said one man, he was not at all rich, but for some time past he has been behaving as if he were. He took a fine house belonging to the *ci-devant* Duc d'Aumont, in the Rue de la Ville-l'Évêque, at the corner of the Rue d'Astorg, which is not at all suitable to a *sans-culotte*. This house, in which he lived alone with a young lady, is adorned with pillars, and has two main buildings, a pretty garden, stables and coach-houses. The decoration of the rooms is perfect : there are fine mirrors and tapestries and furniture of a refined and tasteful kind, and statues and china. Everything in the house indicates wealth. They say he gave large and splendid entertainments. But, said the other man, of what use were stables and coach-houses to d'Églantine? Surely he had no horses nor carriages?—I do not know whether he had any carriages, but I can assure you he had three horses. I have been into that house, and I saw them.—Speaking

M

of horses, said a third man, you remind me of an answer I heard given to d'Églantine, which did not amuse him at all. I was dining in company with him and David, the representative of the people. The conversation turned on the horses that were being requisitioned for the army. D'Églantine complained, on this occasion, that seventeen horses had been taken from his brother Fabrefont.—And how, asked David, did your brother come to have seventeen horses? D'Églantine was greatly embarrassed, and answered in a way that satisfied no one."

A man of whom such things could be written, and who could, moreover, be accused of careless conduct, if of nothing worse, in connection with a case of embezzlement, was already condemned. Fabre, however, defended himself well; but was finally sentenced on the deposition of his colleague Cambon.

Hérault de Séchelles, as we have already said, was accused of sheltering an *émigré* of suspicious character : this fact was enough to include him among the conspirators. Philippeaux was expiating his pity for the Vendéans, while Westermann was expiating his severities towards the same people : these two being an illustration of the dilemma of Robespierre, who included in the Foreign Conspiracy both those who were too indulgent and those who were patriots of too violent an order.

Gusman and Diederichsen were foreigners who, with others at that time, were leading rather mysterious lives in Paris, and could not fail to figure in the repression of a conspiracy called *foreign*. Diederichsen who was half Austrian, half Danish, had been denounced as an agent of Junius Frey. This being the case he deserved a place by Chabot's side.

Lacroix was accused of marrying a *ci-devant* countess, of living in luxury, of having recently adopted moderate

views, and of proposing that the Convention should be
re-elected. There remain Danton and Camille Desmoulins.
On what grounds did they figure in the Batch? Can they
reasonably be suspected of conspiring with the Foreign
Powers? Can we really believe that Danton turned
royalist, and after conspiring with d'Orléans was making
ready to proclaim Louis XVII—of all of which he was
accused? Can we admit that Robespierre sacrificed him
to his personal hatred? For my part I believe none of
these things. Danton was sent to his death on the same
two charges that doomed the rest: embezzlement and
moderate views. Yet he was no thief— ah no! But he
led a life of comfort that was at variance with his necessarily precarious position. In connection with the
Belgian campaign millions passed through his hands: did
none of that money stick to them? Would he even have
been aware of it? Was he a man to worry himself with a
ledger and columns of figures? "I am accused of having
sold myself . . . Men of my stamp have no price!" Such
were Danton's accounts! His fire, his intense vitality,
his prodigal expenditure of energy sufficiently explain
how money melted in his hands. But to steal, to trade
in cold blood like Chabot and Delaunay, were altogether
inconsistent with his character. Of his lukewarmness—
Danton's lukewarmness!—what can we say? Did he go
so far as to wish for the restoration of the Monarchy?
Was he really a conspirator? Did he dine three times a
week with de Batz, as Élie Lacoste declared afterwards?
No : but like many of the revolutionaries he thought the
Revolution was over as soon as it had placed him in a
pleasant position. He had a young wife whom he loved, he
had comfortable rooms, a large estate in the country, a horse
and carriage in his stable, wine in his cellar. What more
need a man desire? Was it not time to take a little rest?

What was the use of revolutionising the whole world? Camille reasoned in the same way, no doubt quite unconsciously. The Terror, he thought, had done all that could be expected of it. He had a charming wife, an income of 20,000 francs, and a nice property at Bourg-la-Reine ; and the gay child of genius who had come to Paris without a shirt began to talk of mercy, and in perfectly good faith thought it a mistake to go too far.

All, except Lhuillier, were condemned to death. The two tumbrils that took them to the scaffold on the 16th Germinal, towards evening, had some difficulty in cleaving the immense crowd that thronged the quays and streets. Camille was uttering cries of despair, and struggled so violently, in spite of the cords that bound his hands, that he was nearly naked when he reached the foot of the scaffold. Danton never lost his air of calm disdain, and tried to soothe his friend. Hérault de Séchelles seemed sad and preoccupied. Lacroix was apparently crushed. Chabot, who had been cured by the doctors and seemed, throughout the trial, to be feeling no bad results of his attempted suicide, hung his head as though he were ashamed. They all died unresistingly, if not resignedly ; and when night fell their bodies were carried to the Parc de Monceaux, where they were flung pell-mell into the common trench.

Thus tragically were fulfilled the expectations of the Baron de Batz. By his audacity and daring, by his Gascon astuteness and craft, he had succeeded, from his obscure position, in aiming the thunderbolt at the highest peaks of the Convention : through Chabot and his confederates he had now struck Danton. But the death of the ardent tribune did not put an end to suspicion : indeed it did but add fuel to the fire. The corrupt were destroyed, but when would the corrupters be attacked ? On the evening

THE EPILOGUE

of the same day, the 16th Germinal, Robespierre begged, in the Jacobin Club, that the conspiracy might be included in the order of the day. "If any good citizen," he said, "can throw any light on the terrible circumstances that have resulted from this conspiracy, let him mount the rostrum!" They were all conscious that their victims had been merely scapegoats, while the real heads of the plot were unpunished. The trial of the Dantonists had been no more than a platonic satisfaction, an illusive spectacle intended to give the impression that the Convention was wide awake to its enemies' schemes; and many facts clearly proved that the chief conspirators were still at large and had by no means renounced their designs.

De Batz was the man to be seized at all costs. The Committee of General Security had no doubts on this point: as long as that evasive foe were at large there would be no safety for the Republic. Barely a fortnight had elapsed since Danton's death when Fouquier-Tinville received the following letter:

"3rd Floréal, year II of the One and Indivisible Republic.

"The Committee enjoins upon you to redouble your efforts to discover the infamous Batz. Remember, in your interrogatories, that his agents are everywhere, even in the prisons; that this Catilina has always been the soul of every plot against liberty and national representation; that, after preaching tyranny in the Constituent Assembly, he held, in Paris and at Charonne, meetings of the Austrian Committee that was directed by the wife of the tyrant; that he was one of the four who tried to save Capet on the 21st January, and were heard on the boulevard shouting: '*À nous*, all who wish to save the King!'; that, with the help of the rascals Michonis and Cortey, he was on the point of carrying away the Capet family from the Temple, to which the said Cortey admitted him as one of the guards in his Company, and had it not been for Simon, he would have posted his infamous accomplices, as yet mostly unknown, at the doors of the Tower staircase ; and that this rascal is all the more dangerous that he has as yet succeeded in hiding from us his methods of procedure.

"In conducting an examination neglect nothing that may lead to a discovery ; spare no promises, whether of money or anything else ; ask us to release any prisoner who will promise to find him for us, dead or alive, and also anyone through whom we might catch him without their knowledge, by dogging their footsteps ; tell everyone that he is outlawed, and has a price upon his head ; that a description of him is published everywhere and he cannot escape ; that everything must be discovered and there will be no mercy for those who could have given him up and did not do so. We mean by this that we wish to secure that rascal at any price, and that the Committee counts above all upon yourself. Read the enclosed note ; it will enlighten you.

"*The members of the Committees of Surveillance and of General Security of the National Convention* :

"Vouland, Jagot, Louis (of the Bas-Rhin), Élie Lacoste, Amar, Vadier, La Vicomterie."[1]

"Tell them there is a price upon his head." It is said that the Committees had promised 300,000 francs to the man who should deliver up to them the Baron de Batz alive ;[2] but this is merely an unproved assertion. A very conscientious search has failed to reveal any evidence of

---

[1] National Archives, W, 380.
[2] *L'Ombre du Baron de Batz*, by Eckard, Paris, 1838.

this measure, either among the papers of the police department, or in the registers of the Committee.

Whatever the truth may be in this matter, it is certain that Fouquier must have been greatly dismayed by the receipt of this letter. " Discover the infamous Batz ——." But where should he be sought? Was there the least hope that such of his alleged accomplices as were already under lock and key would be persuaded to denounce him? It was hardly probable : these people were not renegades like Chabot, and showed considerable obstinacy in preferring their honour to their heads. But though there was little chance of an interrogatory wringing their secret from them, something might possibly result from bringing them all into the same prison. It would transpire whether they knew each other, for instance ; and spies skilfully mingled with the prisoners would surprise them conversing, or corresponding, or making some sign that might set the police on the track of the Baron de Batz.

The correspondence between dates and facts is significant. On the 13th Floréal the Committee decreed " that the head-jailer of the Anglaises-Lourcine Prison should proceed at once to the Tuileries to answer certain questions that were to be put to him." [1]

The members of the government, we may observe, were not above conferring personally with a jailer : they and he together drew up a list of all the prisoners, at that time confined in the various prisons of Paris, who, before their arrest, could have been directly or indirectly acquainted with the Baron de Batz. For these prisoners a trap was to be laid : they were to be confined in the same prison, in order that they might be more closely watched.

On that very day the following prisoners were committed

[1] National Archives, Register of the Committee of General Security. AF, II, 275.

to Sainte-Pélagie : Citoyenne Grandmaison, who, after two months of liberty, had been taken back to the Anglaises ; Biret-Tissot, who had been in La Bourbe since the 17th Frimaire ; Constand the gendarme ; Rohan-Rochefort, who, it may be remembered, has figured in our story ; several nobles, such as Baussancourt and Sombreuil, and with them Mme. d'Esprémenil, who might all be reasonably suspected of regretting the old *régime ;* Cortey and Devaux, two undoubted agents in the conspiracy ; Jardin, who was accused of helping Julien (of Toulouse) to escape ; Pottier (of Lille), secretary to the Lepéletier Section, who was more than suspected of favouring the conspirators ; and the banker Jauge, whose name had been found in the accounts of the Baron de Batz. Having united all these people under the same lock and key the authorities waited for them to compromise themselves.[1] It would have been satisfactory to add to this heterogeneous collection a certain Abbé d'Alençon, a mysterious personage who lived in the Rue Helvétius, near the house that had formerly sheltered de Batz ; but when the police went to arrest him he had disappeared.[2]

Of all the accused, Roussel alone committed an indiscretion.[3] When he was taken to the Registrar's office of the Tribunal to be examined he met there several *suspects* who, like himself, had been summoned before the authorities that were conducting the inquiry. Roussel appeared uneasy. As he sat on a bench awaiting his turn he confided in his neighbours, hoping, no doubt, to find among them someone who could help him.

" I would gladly give twenty-five, or even forty, thousand

---

[1] Archives of the Prefecture of Police.

[2] Register of the Committee of General Security. National Archives, AF*, II, 254 (16th Floréal).

[3] This incident occurred before the 13th Floréal. The denunciation that followed took place on the 25th Ventôse.

francs to be out of this. If I could only get a letter into the jailer's hand it would be a good thing for me. They are going to accuse me of fabricating false assignats. . . . In that case I am a dead man, but I defy them to discover our manufacturing plant—it is well hidden. In spite of all the care that the National Guard took to surround a certain house, and in spite of all their searches, they found nothing! If I can only manage to keep alive for two months more! By that time the Republic will have gone to the deuce, and the enemy will be in Paris!"

These confidences were overheard by one of the prisoners: a certain Dubiez, known as Dignancourt, whose real name was Houdart. Who this Houdart was, and what misdeed brought him to the bench of the Registrar's office, are matters of little importance. It was, no doubt, with a view to securing the favour of the authorities, which might be useful to him by-and-by, that he reported Roussel's conversation to the Committee of General Security,[1] who saw in it a fresh proof of the existence of the conspiracy. The house that the National Guard had surrounded, and that had been so carefully searched without any discovery being made of the implements for fabricating false assignats, must surely be the house at Charonne.[2] Here at last, then, was the clue that would guide them into the labyrinth! It was imperative that it should not be lost: the matter was entrusted to Héron and Sénar, than whom none were more skilful in unravelling an intrigue. These two, escorted by Ducange, repaired to Roussel's lodgings to carry out a thorough search.

[1] National Archives, W, 389.

[2] Possibly the plant is there still. As we have already said, the house at the Hermitage has not been altered except in minor respects, and there may have been a hiding-place there. A certain well that has been filled up, in the cellar, seems to me particularly *suspect*.

The situation was dramatic. Here, on the third floor of a house in the Rue Helvétius, were the most famous police-agents of the Revolution, in a room that had recently been inhabited by de Batz. Roussel, indeed, admitted that he had taken the baron into his rooms " to save him from paying too high a rent."

" So Batz is a poor man ? "

" He seems very comfortable."

" What has become of his furniture ? "

" He brought none with him. I gave up my room and my bed to him."

Héron and Sénar, seeing that they would discover nothing by this method, opened all the cupboards, searched all the drawers, collected all the papers, and examined them minutely. Then the examination began again.

" Here is a letter signed *Saint-Mauris*, but not dated. Who is this Saint-Mauris ? "

" A person who lives in the Rue Choiseul, near a carpenter's shop."

" In this other letter, which is unsigned, we read : ' M— left some parcels in the carriage, and will go and take it at five o'clock. As for the people of the house, I do not think this will have a bad effect. A rumour of my approaching departure has already been spread. . . . What are we risking now ? Everything is confessed, everything is decided, and will result, I hope, in our common satisfaction.' Do you know the meaning of these words, and to whom this letter is addressed ? "

" To Citoyenne Grivois. It merely concerns a love-affair."

" The woman Grivois ? Is she not the owner of the house in the Rue de Ménars, where de Batz and Citoyenne Grandmaison lived ? "

THE EPILOGUE

" Yes."

" Do you know the girl called Nicole ? "

" I have seen her at Citoyenne Grandmaison's, where she was in service, and also with Duchesne, who used to be my tailor, but is so no longer." [1]

They learnt no more that day. Roussel was taken to Sainte-Pélagie. Héron and Sénar, who were not in the habit of bestirring themselves for nothing, and felt it incumbent on them not to return empty-handed, went off to arrest, while they had the opportunity, Citoyenne Grivois, the servant-girl Nicole, and the *ci-devant* Saint-Mauris. Their names had been mentioned : that was enough. They were all sent off to join the rest at Sainte-Pélagie. [2]

As for the Baron de Batz—that elusive Proteus, who seemed to take a sort of coquettish delight in giving fresh proofs of his nimbleness and activity at the very moment when it seemed he must inevitably be defeated—he took it upon himself to send the latest news of his doings to the Committees.

In accordance with custom, Chabot's rooms had been sealed up on the day after his execution. [3] In the inventory of the ex-friar's possessions we find, among other details of considerable piquancy, a mention of *forty pairs of trousers!*—which seems a large supply for a *sans-culotte* who was in the habit of attending the meetings of the Convention with bare legs. But this is by the way. The magistrate and the commissioner fastened the customary strip of paper, sealed with red wax, on all the

[1] This interesting interrogatory, which we do not quote *in extenso*, is in the National Archives, W, 389.

[2] Archives of the Prefecture of Police.

[3] The seals were affixed for the first time on the 17th Germinal, and again after the inventory was taken, 23rd Floréal.—National Archives, F, 4637.

171

doors of the rooms; notably the door of a little room in which all the papers were collected together.

Five days later two citizens appeared at the house in the Rue d'Anjou. They stated their names and offices: Nice and Laporte, "commissioners of the department and of the municipality." They mounted the stairs to the *entre-sol*, broke the seals, took the papers and plate, and retired quite calmly.

On hearing of this outrage the Committee of General Security were stupefied. They despatched the deputies Delcher and Baudot to institute an inquiry in the Rue d'Anjou, and issued a warrant against Nice and Laporte. But their stupefaction was turned into terror when, as the result of the inquiry, it transpired that the offenders had been accompanied on the occasion by *a third individual whose name and residence were unknown.*[1] De Batz again!

He alone had the audacity and the presence of mind needful for so bold a stroke as this. The Committee had no delusions on the subject: the unknown was certainly the Baron de Batz.[2] They were forced, however, to content themselves with the mere knowledge of the fact: they did not even attempt to push the inquiry any further. They resigned themselves to awaiting the moment when it should please this man to finish his undertaking, and give the word to all his thousands of accomplices to carry out their final work of destruction, and massacre the whole Convention. For this, it was said, was his ambition.

[1] National Archives, F⁷, 4637. Report of the representatives, Delcher and Baudot.

[2] Élie Lacoste's report is quite clear on that subject.

VI

THE AMALGAM

The Conspiracy has broken out !

Such was the cry to which Paris awoke a week later, on the 4th Prairial. Collot d'Herbois had just been murdered.

As a matter of fact he was not dead ; he was not even wounded ; but such is the nervous sensibility of the Parisian populace in moments of crisis that this detail was of little consequence. A man had fired two pistol-shots at Collot d'Herbois—therefore the Convention was being massacred. The immense sensation caused by this event was still at its height, when, at nightfall of the same day, a still more astounding rumour spread through the town.

" Robespierre has just been assassinated ! "

Every house was instantly emptied ; the throng streamed towards the Rue Saint-Honoré ; the most fantastic tales passed from mouth to mouth.

" Is he dead ? "—" He died on the spot."—" Is the murderer caught ? "—" Yes."—" No."—" It is a woman ! " —" A countess ! "—" The army of the Émigrés is at Compiègne ! "—" At Saint-Denis ! "—" Little Capet has come out of the Temple ! "—" The Revolution is over ! "

There were many who expressed grief, from motives of prudence ; there was a still greater number who sighed

173

with relief. There were very few who dared to say boldly : *So much the better* !

Meanwhile Robespierre was in no worse case than Collot d'Herbois. This story of the massacre of the Convention had a very slight foundation : namely, two unconnected facts that have no place in history, but that none the less we must consider in detail, because the Committees, by associating them with the conspiracy that was having so demoralising an effect, placed them to the credit of the Baron de Batz.

These are the facts. On the 3rd Prairial, at about 9 o'clock in the morning, a fairly tall man, with a wide forehead, a large nose, grey eyes, and a long face,[1] approached the courtyard of Duplay the cabinet-maker, in whose house Robespierre lived, and addressed a fruit-seller who had set up her wares beside the entrance-gate :

" At what hour does Citizen Robespierre go to the Committee ? " he asked.

" Inquire at the end of the courtyard," answered the good woman : " that is where he lives."

The visitor passed through the gate and advanced a little way into the courtyard, which was littered with planks. Here he found a woman, and a volunteer with his arm in a sling. He repeated his question.

" Robespierre is busy at this moment," said the soldier, " and can see no one. I do not know when he will go out."

The man then went away without making any remark. He was seen going into Raulot's restaurant, at the end of the Terrasse des Feuillants, where he breakfasted. Then he crossed the garden, entered the hall of the Convention, settled himself comfortably on a bench, and slept for an hour or two. After this he posted himself beneath the

---

[1] Admiral's certificate-of-safety.—National Archives, F⁷, 4762.

COLLOT D'HERBOIS.

peristyle of the Tuileries, but soon left it, and lingered for
a time near the door of the Committee of Public Safety.
Several deputies passed him, entering or leaving the
building : he asked them their names. He then proceeded
to the Café Mauri and the Café Gervoise, where he played
a game of draughts with a young man. At about nine
o'clock in the evening he sat down at a table in the
Restaurant Dufils, in the Place du Théâtre Favart, and
ordered his supper.

As he ate he talked to the waiter.[1] He said his name
was Admiral, and his mistress was a baroness.

"Serve me well," he said, "and I shall come back here
with her. Are there private rooms in this establishment ?
My mistress is rich. Her husband lives in the South, but
he is soon coming to Paris to get hold of 1,700,000 *livres*
that the Nation owes to him. If he is not paid there will
be a row ! "

Beneath the formality of the depositions that have
handed these details down to us we can detect the fever
that was consuming Admiral, the nervous excitement that
he tried in vain to hide.

"Ah—but you don't know ! " he went on, still speaking
to the waiter. "The lady is at the same time the mistress
of a deputy—yes, a deputy who lives in the same house as
myself. I play the part of the clown in the affair. I
have not slept for a fortnight. I have taken opium, but
nothing is of any use. Bring me another bottle."

As Admiral had already drunk, in the course of this
conversation, a bottle of wine, two glasses of malaga, and
a glass of brandy, the waiter thought it his duty to refer
the matter to his master, who gave orders that no more
drink should be supplied to this already too loquacious
customer.

[1] A man called Cabale.

Admiral went away grumbling. He returned to his lodgings on the fifth floor of No 4, Rue Favart. It was then eleven o'clock at night.

Instead of entering his room he remained on guard upon the landing, listening to every sound in the house. He waited thus for two hours. He had drawn a pair of pistols from his pockets, and held one, loaded, in each hand.

At about one o'clock there was a sound of knocking on the front-door. Like a madman Admiral leaped down the stairs in a dozen strides ; then, prompted by some equally mad impulse, he rushed up the five flights as quickly as he had gone down. Citizen Collot d'Herbois' servant,[1] having heard the knock and feeling sure it was her master coming home, was descending the stairs [2] with a candle in her hand, to open the door. As Admiral dashed past he jostled her ; but he said nothing, and returned to mount guard on the topmost landing.

Collot quietly mounted the stairs, preceded by his servant with the light. They had reached the third storey, and the servant was fitting the key into the lock, when Admiral suddenly rose up in the darkness before the deputy, shouting :

" Stop ! Your last hour has come ! "

At the same moment he fired the pistol full in Collot's face. The weapon missed fire. Collot had dropped his walking-stick in his alarm, and stooped to pick it up ; and at that moment Admiral discharged his second pistol point-blank. Collot's movement had saved his life : the bullet passed into the wall.

While the distracted servant took refuge in the room

---

[1] Her name was Suzanne Prévot.

[2] Collot's rooms in this house were on the third floor above the *entresol*.

within, and, opening the window, cried *Murder!* loudly, Collot d'Herbois rushed down the three flights of stairs, dashed into the street, and roused the whole neighbourhood with his despairing appeals for help. A member of the general council of the Commune, one Bertrand Arnaud, who lodged in the same house, heard this commotion, and springing from his bed invested himself, over his nightshirt, with the emblem of his office, the tricoloured ribbon. Thus habited, he ventured with bare legs into the entry. He found there, he said, " a hat, the point of a sword, and a handful of hair ! "

But already the entrance was full of soldiers. Collot d'Herbois had run to give the alarm at the guardhouse hard by ; and moreover a patrol that had paused for a few minutes under the porch of the Théâtre Favart [1] had heard the servant's cries and rushed to the spot. In the midst of them was struggling Collot d'Herbois, who had armed himself with a sword and wished to pursue his murderer, " expressing with great violence his desire to rid the Republic, with his own hands, of an odious monster." They all entreated him not to risk his precious life any further, declaring that they would do their duty, and the scoundrel should not escape.

What they feared was that the scoundrel was still upon the stairs, and had reloaded his weapons. They held a consultation. Bertrand Arnaud, still in his nightshirt and tricoloured scarf, made a speech ; Collot suggested that they should go up to his rooms, where they could arm themselves with his pistols and muskets, pikes being insufficient for an expedition of this kind. To reach this point, however, it was necessary to venture upon the terrible staircase. They made up their minds to the measure at last. Citizen Jean Baptiste Pelletier marched

[1] The Théâtre Italien, afterwards the Opéra Comique.

at their head; Collot followed him; and the rest brought up the rear.

The staircase, after all, was unoccupied. Admiral had shut himself up in his room, and was not stirring. They grew gradually bolder, and climbed to the fifth storey: the assassin's door was closed. They knocked: a terrible voice answered from within:

"Come on, *canailles!* The first man that enters I shall shoot!"

This created a chill. Should they break open the door? It opened suddenly, and Admiral, with flaming eyes, appeared upon the threshold. He fired a pistol at random, and one of the men, called Geoffroy,[1] uttered a cry and fell. The rest flung themselves upon the assassin, bound him, and carried him off to the guardhouse amid shouts of triumph. He was searched; in his pocket were four bullets, wrapped in a *billet de garde*. To the first questions that were put to him he answered: "That he was heartily sorry he had missed his mark: it would have been a fine day's work, and he would have been admired by the whole of France."

"And what a misfortune," he added, "to spend 90 francs on pistols for the purpose—and then for them to miss fire!"

Then, turning to Nailly, the man in charge of his house, who was present in his capacity of captain of the second company of the section, he said with a laugh:

"Well, Captain, I shall have to walk off to the little window![2] My only regret is that I missed those two blackguards!"

At dawn he was taken to the guardhouse at the convent

[1] A locksmith, of No. 5 Rue des Petits Champs.
[2] The guillotine.

of the Filles-Saint-Thomas, whence in the course of the morning he was removed to the Conciergerie.[1]

We have referred to the excitement that this attempt caused in Paris: the strange incident that occurred at Robespierre's dwelling on the same day, the 4th Prairial, created a far greater sensation.

At the corner of the Rue de la Lanterne and the Rue des Marmousets, a few yards distant from the Law Courts, there lived in 1794 a stationer called Antoine Renault. He had a daughter aged twenty, named Cécile, and three sons, of whom one, Jacques, was in his father's business, while the other two had been called upon to serve in the army nearly two years before. The Renaults were simple folk, neither ambitious nor violent, but honest, steady, and economical, as is the typical character of the small shopkeepers of Paris. They enjoyed a certain degree of comfort, Père Renault being the principal tenant of the house in which he lived.

Cécile Renault, though her education had been so much neglected that she was unable to read, appears to us not altogether guiltless of pretension. She had a weakness for dress and personal adornment, in any case: she indulged in discussing millinery, and in buying on credit, without her father's knowledge, little trifles for which she paid in small sums saved from her pocket-money. In a word, she was something of a coquette, and this is all we know of the character of this poor girl. Her mother had long been dead.

---

[1] We have described as accurately as we could the scene of Admiral's attempted crime, with the aid of the depositions of Citizens Dutils, keeper of the restaurant, Cabale, waiter, Bertrand Arnaud, Jean Baptiste Pelletier, and Citoyenne Suzanne Prévot, the interrogatory of Admiral, and various reports of the Lepéletier Section.

See National Archives, W, 389, and F[7], 4757, 4762, etc.

A GASCON ROYALIST

Towards the end of Floréal Cécile had taken to a dress-maker in the Rue des Deux Ponts, Citoyenne Dématin by name, a few yards of white muslin with which to make a gown.

" I am in a great hurry for it," she said, " for in a week from now I am going to my cousin's wedding, and I want my gown to be ready."

" You are going to a wedding, Mademoiselle ? " asked the dressmaker.

" That has nothing to do with you. But be quick over it ; there is no knowing what may happen. In a week I may be guillotined ; I want none of my affairs to be behindhand." [1]

On the 4th Prairial, as we have seen, Admiral's attempt at murder was the talk of Paris. It is certain that the story had been heard in the City, as elsewhere ; but it does not seem to have made much impression on the various members of the Renault family. At two o'clock in the afternoon the stationer returned home, having just come off guard, and no doubt it was he who told his son and daughter the news that was the chief topic of conversation in the town. He ate his dinner, and, the weather being oppressive, fell asleep in his arm-chair on leaving the table. At about five o'clock Cécile persuaded him "to take a turn by way of diversion," and Père Renault, thinking the idea a good one, went out to pay 25 *livres* that he owed to Citoyenne Maré, seamstress, at the end of the Rue Saint-Antoine.

Cécile settled herself, with some work, behind the windows of the shop. Seeing in the street one of the lodgers in the house, a girl called Papin, she tapped on the glass to attract her attention.

" Look here," she said, " I owe sixteen sous to Citoyenne

[1] We give the exact words of Citoyenne Dématin's deposition.

180

THE AMALGAM

Jules.[1] Will you undertake to give her the money for me?"

The girl Papin took the money, and turned to go away.

"You are in a great hurry. Let us have a little talk," said Cécile.

They talked of various indifferent matters. When it was nearly six o'clock Cécile left her friend and her brother chattering together in the shop, and went upstairs to her room, saying she would return.

Cécile, it must be observed, was brought up very strictly by her father, and never went out alone : this accounts for the fact that Jacques Renault, when it was half-past six and he had not heard his sister come down again, became somewhat uneasy and called her from the foot of the stairs. Receiving no answer he went up to the first floor. Cécile was not in her room.

We are going to follow her ; but first we must call attention to a circumstance in this extraordinary adventure which seems to be a complete mystery. It was six o'clock in the evening when Cécile left the Rue de la Lanterne — on this point all the witnesses were agreed—and it was not till nine o'clock[2] that she reappeared in the Rue Saint-Honoré. How did she spend these three hours? I am surprised that no historian should ever have asked this question ; but I am still more surprised that the minute inquiry instituted by order of the Committee of General Security should have done nothing to throw light upon it.

[1] Cécile had just bought from her a little mirror worth 36 sous, for which she had paid 20 sous on account.—(Deposition of Citoyenne Jules).

[2] Barrère's report to the Convention. *Moniteur* of 10th Prairial. See also *Histoire du Tribunal révolutionnaire*, by Compardon, Vol. I, p. 352.

At nine o'clock, then, Cécile appeared at the door of Duplay the cabinet-maker and asked to speak to Citizen Robespierre. Éléonore Duplay, the cabinet-maker's daughter, answered that he had gone out. Cécile replied, with some temper :

" It is very strange that he is not at home. It is the business of a public official to see everyone who comes."

Didier and Boulanger, two of Robespierre's friends, were crossing the yard at this moment, and heard this answer. It seemed to them to be lacking in reverence, and they threatened to take Cécile before the Committee of General Security. At the same time Didier took her by the arm to push her into the street.

" In the old régime," cried Cécile, " when people went to see the King they were admitted at once."

" So you regret the days when there was a king ? "

" Ah—I would give the last drop of my blood to have one. In my opinion you are no better than tyrants." [1]

Didier and Boulanger seized her, and led her before the Committee of General Security. When they arrived at the Tuileries Cécile begged them to let her go into the Café Payen to pick up a parcel she had left there. They consented ; and she appeared before the Committee with her modest luggage in her hand. She was questioned without further delay.

She astonished the Committee by her coolness and the mocking clearness of her answers. She gave as her reason for visiting Robespierre that she wished " to see if she liked him," and was, moreover, curious to see what kind of person a tyrant was. She upheld the opinion she had already expressed in opposition to the principle of Liberty, and added that she would rather have one king

[1] Deposition of Didier and Boulanger, *Moniteur* of 10th Prairial.

than fifty thousand tyrants. The parcel she had in her arms was opened: it contained a dress, a jacket, and some linen.

"I brought these clothes with me," she said, "because I shall be glad to have a change with me in the place where I am going."

"Where do you think, then, that you will be taken?"

"To prison first, and then to the guillotine."

It happened that a woman [1] bringing a petition was in the antechamber of the Committee-room: she was brought in, and ordered to search the prisoner. Nothing was found on Cécile but the mirror she had bought that day, and two little pocket-knives: one, with an ivory handle, had been given her by her brother; the other, which had a handle of tortoise-shell, was a souvenir of her sister, who had been dead for some years. [2] It was nearly midnight when Cécile Renault was lodged in the Conciergerie. As she turned the corner of the Law Courts she could see in the distance, for an instant, the house in the Rue de la Lanterne wherein anxiety and despair were reigning at that moment.

Jacques Renault, when he found that an hour had passed and at seven o'clock his sister had not returned, was seized with such a panic of anxiety that he fainted away. The girl Papin, who was still with him, was alarmed by this excessive sensibility, and ran off to fetch her mother to the Renaults' house. This woman undertook to inform the stationer of Cécile's absence. At eight o'clock he returned home to supper.

His despair was violent. He searched the whole house, and in his daughter's room found a little cape flung upon the bed; but he was sobbing so wildly "that he could not

[1] Citoyenne Lamotte.
[2] Deposition of Père Renault.

discover whether she had taken anything with her." With his son's help, however, he was able to put up the shutters of the shop; and he then returned to his room and locked the door.

Citoyenne Papin explored the neighbourhood. She made inquiries at the house of the confectioner whose daughter was Cécile's dressmaker; she visited Citoyenne Gentilhomme, another seamstress whom the girl sometimes employed. Nowhere had Renault's little daughter been seen. It was now nearly midnight. Mme. Papin postponed the rest of her inquiries to the following day, and returned to the stationer's house, of which she occupied the second floor.

An hour later, soon after she had gone to bed, she heard a knock at her door.

" Who is there? "

" It is I, Madame Papin," answered the voice of Jacques Renault.

" Has Cécile come home? "

" No, Madame Papin. I have brought you our cat. We have just been arrested."

" Arrested! But why? "

" I do not know. Will you take care of our cat while we are away? You will see that he has everything he wants." [1]

The next morning the stationer's shop remained closed. The whole neighbourhood was excited. The gossips, on their way to fetch their bread from Besançon the baker, related to one another how the little Renault girl, having been warned that her father and brother were about to be arrested, had run away to save herself from the same

---

[1] Deposition of Mme. Papin. It was Héron who undertook the arrest of Renault and his son.

fate. It was not till ten o'clock that Madame Prévot announced that Cécile had tried to assassinate Robespierre. This was an opportunity for idle tongues. Père Renault was greatly blamed for allowing his daughter to visit some of the neighbours, such as, for instance, Citoyenne Gentilhomme. Riotter the goldsmith had never thought very well of those people ; he had been talking about it only the other day with his neighbour Pelé. Citoyenne Villiaume the laundress remembered that Renault had shown great satisfaction at the time that Lepéletier de Saint-Fargeau was murdered, and had said, rubbing his hands : " There's one of them gone—there will soon be more ! "

It is appalling to see the eagerness with which all these worthy women, and porters, and shopkeepers threw stones at the neighbours whom they had held in respect only the day before ; and this with the sole object of *appearing to know something*. " Ah ! I knew well enough that this would happen ! " was a phrase that was heard a thousand times on that 5th of Prairial, from the Rue de la Lanterne to the Rue des Marmousets. The police heard all the tales, and made of them a *dossier* that Fouquier-Tinville afterwards found useful.[1]

No characteristic detail, I think, has been omitted from this story of two incidents which at the first glance seemed of slight interest. Remembering the rudimentary state of justice in 1794 one would expect to see Admiral and Cécile Renault tried, condemmed, and executed in the course of a single day. It was thus that Fouquier-Tinville interpreted his mission. When reporting Admiral's interrogatory in the Convention he expressed

[1] All these depositions are preserved in the National Archives, W, 389.

his intention " of passing judgment on that scoundrel this very day at two o'clock.[1]

This, however, was not the intention of the assembly. The idea of connecting these incidents with the Batz Conspiracy, of making an *amalgam* (the word was Amar's, it is said) which should associate Admiral and Cécile with the confederates who were already in prison, seems to have sprung up almost instantaneously in the minds of the Committee. Fouquier's zeal was checked with a word, and an inquiry set on foot ; for it was not enough that Barrère, Couthon, Robespierre, and the rest should blame the Foreign Conspiracy for the two attempted crimes ; it was further necessary to find some semblance of a link between de Batz, Admiral, and Cécile.

It is the opinion of every historian, without exception, that this link never existed save in the imagination of the Committee at bay. As for Cécile Renault there can be no possible doubt that she yielded to an impulse of her own, and we shall presently set down all that can be said in excuse, in our opinion, of her incomprehensible action.

In the case of Admiral, on the other hand, we have been led, by a minute study of all the depositions, to regard him as an unconscious accomplice of the conspirators, who took advantage with rare skill of the violence of his passions.

There was nothing in his past to explain the action of which he had been guilty. He had always been in service ; his last employment was as porter of the lottery-office ; he was not known to have any resources beyond his modest salary of 600 *livres ;* his papers were perfectly correct— certificate-of-*civisme,* certificate-of-safety, receipts for rent and patriotic subscriptions ; he was provided with all the

[1] Letter of the Public Prosecutor to the Convention, 4th Prairial,

documents that proved, in 1794, the immaculate political morality of a citizen.

One fact was surprising: this man, who had but 50 francs a month at his disposal, suddenly began to lead a somewhat expensive life. Citizen Trillié, whose restaurant he patronised, remarked that, about the 1st Germinal, Admiral began to order meals every day that cost forty or forty-five sous, exclusive of wine.[1] He would then go and amuse himself at the Palais Royal, where he lost considerable sums of money. In the billiard-room at No. 121 he had made the acquaintance of an undoubted accomplice of the Baron de Batz, Roussel, who spent his evenings there with his attendant gendarme. Roussel and Admiral, indeed, had become very intimate, and the one was never seen without the other.[2]

It also transpired in the course of the inquiry that Admiral's mistress was a woman named Lamartinière, who lived in the Rue de Chabanais. This was the alleged baroness, whose favours he boasted of sharing with a deputy to the Convention.[3] This *liaison* evidently flattered the vanity of the office-porter. It was proved, however, that this woman was not, as Admiral declared, the mistress of Collot d'Herbois, who was not even acquainted with her. To whom, then, did the lover owe this unfortunate piece of information? What was the motive of those who sought to infuriate him with the Conventionist? These two questions are not irrelevant; for to us, who know how Admiral spent the evening of the 3rd Prairial before his criminal attempt, how he drank much

[1] Inquiry by Citizens Jobert and Junck, 5th Prairial.—National Archives, W, 389.

[2] Denunciation by Citizen Joseph Huitville, 5th Prairial.—National Archives, F7, 4762.

[3] Deposition of Citizen Cabale, waiter, quoted above.

more than was good for him, and how he confessed that for a fortnight he had vainly been taking opium to make him sleep, it is obvious that he was a man half mad with jealousy.

The police were struck by one coincidence : namely, that Admiral's expenditure had increased since he made the acquaintance of Mme. Lamartinière. The woman was therefore served with a warrant, and while her interrogatory was in progress her house was searched.

She revealed some rather strange facts. It was at a sale of furniture that she had met Admiral for the first time. After a few weeks of constant intercourse [1] he had suggested selling his furniture to her, and she had accepted the offer. Admiral therefore conveyed to her house everything he had, except a mattress, a bolster, a jug, and a looking-glass, which he wished to keep in his possession *till the 4th Prairial*. On the day of this removal of his property she was much alarmed to see him " draw a pistol from his pocket, and come towards her, saying : ' Do you wish to die ? ' : she answered *No*, and he went on : ' What is the use of living now ? ' She said ' Are you mad ? I am in no such hurry to die.' Then he put away his pistol, saying : ' Ah, you are afraid ! ' and went away." [2]

The story throws a good deal of light on this obscure incident. It had been whispered to Admiral that Collot d'Herbois was his rival, which was not the case. He promptly resolved to avenge himself : he sold his furniture in order to buy pistols : [3] then, as soon as the purchase was made, he longed to end the matter, and suggested to the woman he loved that they should die together. She,

---

[1] *Only three weeks*, she said. *Two months*, declared Admiral.

[2] Examination of Mme. Lamartinière.—National Archives, F⁷, 4762.

[3] Admiral would never confess where, nor when, he had bought his weapons.

being altogether mystified, declined the offer, and he reverted to his original idea of killing his rival.

While the woman Lamartinière was being questioned in the registrar's office of the Tribunal a search that was not altogether unfruitful was carried on in her rooms. A sealed letter was discovered, with a superscription that roused the interest of the Commissioners. It was addressed:

To CITIZEN D'ALENÇON.
Rue Helvétius, No. 179, Paris.

This Citizen d'Alençon, it may be remembered, was an ex-Abbé, an enigmatical personage whose arrest had been ordered by the Committee of General Security at the same time as that of the accomplices of the Baron de Batz. The police had been unable to take him, because he had been warned in time, and had escaped.

The letter was opened. It bore the signature of Citoyenne Lamartinière, who admitted having taken it herself to d'Alençon's address. As he had not returned to his rooms she thought she ought not to entrust it to the porter, and had kept it herself through carelessness. The letter was as follows:

PARIS, 22nd Floréal, year II.

CITIZEN,

I received your letter a little late, and I should have expected you to adopt quite different measures. . . I waited for you till midnight, having with me what you so greatly desired. I thought you would have given me the preference, and would not have gone to supper with Citoyenne Rine, but how completely you forgot me and all the fine promises you made me. I may tell you, that I was, thanks to you, in a state of the greatest anxiety.

A GASCON ROYALIST

As I do not really know you at all well, and know nothing
of your movements and actions, it is impossible for me to be
answerable for you, and I even think it is dangerous to
answer for a person who conceals his address.   However,
for the last four days I have done nothing but run risks,
both to find out what has become of you and to ensure
your safety, and I warn you that, in spite of my hopes of
success in the matter of your last request, I shall take no
further steps till you have paid me the 600 francs that
you owe me in the eyes of the law. As I do not like
double-faced people it is natural to me to insist on frankness and honesty. I should have liked to find similar sentiments in you ; but I have met with nothing but barbarity,
ingratitude, and inhumanity from you, and that is why I
prophesied that the Supreme Being would punish you.   I
repeat that if you do not send me the 600 francs you owe
me I shall abandon you for life.

Greeting and Fraternity.
Femme LAMARTINIÈRE.[1]

This d'Alençon greatly perplexed the Commissioners.
The ability and skill he had exhibited in escaping on
the morning of the actual day fixed for his arrest
recalled to their minds a certain other personage—that
Baron de Batz who was also so impossible to catch, and
who always received timely warning of measures taken for
his capture. A special effort, therefore, was made to
wring information from the prisoner on this subject.
She admitted "that the thing so much desired by
d'Alençon was an authorisation from the Committee of
Public Safety to stay in Paris for a fortnight, which
authorisation she had asked for and obtained. Latterly
she had been again engaged in begging, on his behalf,

<hr>

[1] National Archives, W, 389.

for an extension of the time allowed him, when she heard of his flight. Further, he had written her a letter without giving her any address, saying that he was sometimes in one place, sometimes in another. It might perhaps be possible to discover his retreat at the moment by applying to a person called Briel, a *ci-devant* priest, who lived at Auteuil." [1]

The interrogatory ended there. The public prosecutor, without delay, informed the Committee of General Security of this fresh incident. Admiral and his mistress were lodged in the Conciergerie, and on the same evening the police began their search for the Abbé d'Alençon.

There was a connection, then, if a slight and indirect one, between Admiral's attempted crime and the Batz Conspiracy : for there was no doubt in anyone's mind that d'Alençon and de Batz were one and the same person. The next thing to do was to find the link, which no doubt existed, between the conspiracy and the action of Cécile Renault. On this point the inquiry yielded no information. A draper's apprentice came to report that on the morning of the 3rd Prairial, he had seen Cécile slip out of her father's house and confer " secretly with a citizen in nankin breeches with rosettes at the sides, white silk stockings, a round hat, and kid shoes ; " [2] but this tale was not taken seriously. It also transpired that a man called Admiral came fairly often to the house of the widow Joyawal, who kept a grocer's shop next door to the Renaults ; and Cécile remembered having seen this man Admiral five or six times, but had never spoken to him. On futher inquiry it appeared that this was merely a case of similarity of names, and the track was abandoned.

[1] Examination of Mme. Lamartinière.—National Archives.
[2] Deposition of Million, draper's apprentice, aged 14.—National Archives, W, 389.

A GASCON ROYALIST

Père Renault had a sister in religion, who might have imbued her niece with counter-revolutionary views. This venerable woman, therefore, was arrested in her retreat in the Rue de Babylone, but the interrogatory furnished no new information. None the less she was imprisoned with the rest. A close investigation of the Renaults' house produced no better result. There were found there, it is true, portraits of the "tyrant and his wife," and in Cécile's room, above the bed, "a sort of banner covered with fleurs-de-lys and crosses in silver paper."[1] But this innocent piece of bric-a-brac, if it might be taken as an indication of *fanaticism*, could not reasonably serve as a proof that Cécile had acted at the instigation of the Baron de Batz. In a word, the motive of her action remained—and remains to this day—unexplained.

For ourselves we think that the reason is to be sought in the Revolution itself. Cécile Renault, we believe, acted under the the influence of what is called, by modern neurologists, the *contagion of crowds*. For more than a year this child had seen, passing nearly under her windows, the daily "batch" of unhappy beings who were sent in herds to the scaffold. Her imagination, whether she would or no, was haunted by the guillotine and by the prison of the Conciergerie, which was quite near to where she lived. Every day she saw streaming thither the supply of human cattle that was required by the justice of Fouquier-Tinville. An impulse came to her to throw herself beneath the knife, "to do as others did." The case was not unique, after all. How many women cried: *Vive le roi*! in the open street, with no other object than to put an end to themselves!

This girl of twenty years had heroic qualities. Her coolness, her candour, her simplicity disconcerted the

[1] National Archives, W, 389.

department should be represented in the "batch" by its head, Étienne Jardin.[1]

While Élie Lacoste was employed in perfecting this strange collection he received a letter denouncing a man called Cardinal, on the ground that he had expressed himself flippantly on the subject of Robespierre : and the municipality of Choisy-le-Roi also sent him a medical student named Saintenac, who was attached to the military hospital in that town, and had been guilty of the same crime.[2]

These, however, were very insignificant folk : the public might well be surprised to find that the terrible conspiracy of which they had heard so much could boast of no more important confederates. A few names of distinction were an indispensable ingredient in the mixture ; and there was a large choice, since the prisons were overflowing with nobles. The first name that was considered was that of the Prince de Rohan-Rochefort, who has already figured in our story. The name of the Prince de Saint-Mauris had been heard on the lips of Roussel, and that was enough : Élie Lacoste made a note of it. He added the old Marquis

---

[1] Another Jardin was inadvertently arrested in his place, a mere waggoner, who appealed in time, and was released.

[2] For the case of Cardinal see the end of Élie Lacoste's report. The letter that denounced Saintenac is worth preserving. It is as follows :

"5th Prairial, 2.

"DEATH TO TYRANTS !

"Citizens, we have the pleasure of informing you that we have discovered in our commune a counter-revolutionary and *ci-devant* monk who is suspected of being implicated in the assassination of Citizen Collot d'Herbois. You will find all the authentic documents enclosed, and will see that there are rascals outside Paris, and that they find their way even into the hospitals, to assassinate our brave defenders.

"Choisy, 5th Prairial."

(National Archives, W, 389.)

de Sombreuil and his son, Mme. d'Eprémesnil, the Duc de Montmorency, the Vicomte de Pons, and the Comtes du Hardaz d'Hauteville, de Baussancourt, and de Marsan. These added greatly to the distinction of the "batch." The next requirement was a banker, and Jauge was chosen. A priest, too, was a necessity ; and no one could be more suitable than the Abbé Briel, whom Madame Lamartinière had mentioned as a friend of the evasive and mysterious d'Alençon. I have been unable to discover on what grounds the Amalgam included Viart, who had served in the army ; Madame Grivois, the landlady of Citoyenne Grandmaison ; Lécuyer the musician ; the merchants Paumier, Deshayes, and Comte ; Egrée the brewer ; Karadec, and Ménil-Simon.[1] I have purposely omitted a few of the victims selected for the slaughter : we shall return to them presently.

Élie Lacoste, having drawn up this list, proceeded to devise a plan on which to work. It was an arduous task, for nothing definite was known. Moreover, there was little time to spare ; for the Committees of General Security and Public Safety had decided that the report was to be read in the Convention on the 26th Prairial, and that the prisoners were to be handed over to Fouquier-Tinville on the following day, to go through the formality of a trial. This procedure, it was hoped, would strike the public imagination very forcibly, and would prove the strength and decision of those who sent the conspirators to their death only a few hours after their names had been published in the assembly. The foundation of this whole scheme, however, was weak ; and we can picture Lacoste hurrying to and fro between the Committee of General Security and the Committee of Public Safety, taking

[1] The charges brought against these wretched people in Elie Lacoste's report cannot be taken seriously.

counsel with his colleagues, and threatening every moment to throw up the whole affair unless de Batz were found. The Committee of Public Safety hoped to succeed where so many others had failed ; they took an extreme measure, and resigned themselves to offering his life to any man among the doomed confederates who should deliver to them the undiscoverable conspirator. Devaux was fixed upon as the subject of this severe test, and on the 25th Prairial Fouquier received the following letter :

CITIZEN,

The Committee of Public Safety beg you to make a fresh examination of Devaux, who was secretary to de Batz on the Austrian Committee ; and in fact it has lately been proved to us that Devaux was, with Batz, one of the four who passed behind the ranks armed with swords, when Capet was on his way to the scaffold, and cried : " *À nous*, those who wish to save the King ! "

Chatelet [1] recognised Devaux yesterday evening among the prisoners at the Conciergerie, as the one of them to whom he had spoken. You are authorised to offer pardon to Devaux if he will reveal the hiding-place of Batz : you will send the interrogatory at once to the Committee, and you will come this evening.

Greeting and fraternity.

COLLOT D'HERBOIS, BILLAUD-VARENNES.

It was a clever choice. Of all the agents of the conspiracy Devaux was the best informed ; he had only been arrested on the 13th Floréal,[2] and had certainly been in communication with de Batz until that date ; he knew his hiding-place. Moreover, he was only twenty-nine years of

---

[1] One of the jurymen of the Tribunal.
[2] Register of the Prefecture of Police.

age, was married to a woman he loved, and was the sole support of his father, a blind old man without resources. All these reasons for clinging to life would have to be taken into account in considering the terrible bargain that the Committees wished to drive with him ; and I know nothing more dramatic than this interrogatory, which we give *in extenso.* Every question is a temptation : every answer is an act of suicide.

" Devaux, do you persist in denying that you knew of the Austrian Committee that was held at Batz's house, when you were his secretary ? "

" I persist in declaring that if an Austrian Committee did exist in Batz's house, I knew nothing of it."

" Do you know Cortey, captain of the Lepéletier Section ? "

" Yes."

" Were you one of those who, with the infamous Batz, had arranged to mount guard at the Temple ; and with what design ? "

" I did not belong to the Section Péletier, and could not have gone with Cortey ; if Batz had designs I know nothing of them."

" Were you not on the boulevard when Louis Capet passed by on his way to suffer the just punishment of his crimes ? "

" Yes."

" Where were you ? "

" At the post that had been assigned to me."

" Do you deny that Citizen Chatelet saw you and spoke to you behind the ranks, when you were armed with a sword and not with a pike ? "

" I was going to my post."

" Were you not with Batz ? "

" I met him."

" You crossed the boulevards with him, in defiance of the orders to the contrary ? "

" I did not know of the orders."

" Be careful to speak the truth. You cried : ' *À nous*, those who wish to save their king,' and Chatelet heard you ? "

" It was not I, but Batz."

" Who was with him ? "

" I recognised no one but la Guiche."[1]

" Tell the truth, tell us where Batz is hidden, and you will be pardoned."

" I am innocent, and I do not know where Batz is."

This answer was the death-warrant of Devaux : he knew this, yet he did not hesitate. I maintain, without fear of being accused of exaggeration, that the nobles whom Élie Lacoste's report would soon deliver into the hands of the executioner—Rohan, Montmorency, Sombreuil—might well claim this man Devaux as one of their order, and salute him as the noblest of them all. The man who, with the choice before him, prefers his honour to his life, is a hero, and his action is all the more glorious if he be aware that posterity will accord him only indifference and oblivion.

This sublime devotion, however, discontented the Committees and clipped the wings of Élie Lacoste's eloquence. But it was imperative to publish the famous report that had been awaited for six months, and on the 26th Prairial Lacoste read it in the Convention.

---

[1] Eckard said that Devaux, when he mentioned this name, thought he was only compromising a man who had escaped ; for it was commonly believed that la Guiche had left France. It would have been easy for Devaux to make this mistake, for la Guiche had not been put with the other confederates in Sainte-Pélagie. According to the registers of the Prefecture of Police he was lodged in La Force at first, and afterwards at the Carmes. His friends, seeing that he was not with them, might well imagine him to have escaped.

He dealt with this difficult situation very skilfully. De Batz was missing from the "batch"; but none the less he was artfully put forward as the principal personage, the pivot of the whole intrigue. After enumerating all the attacks endured by the Republic during little less than two years, after recalling the actions of the various parties, the sorrows that overwhelmed the country, the proscriptions and the massacres, Lacoste exclaimed :

" All the levers that were intended to overthrow the Republic were moved by a single man, who prompted all the allied tyrants.

" This man, this audacious intriguer, had intermediary agents in every section in Paris, in the country, in the municipality, in the official departments, in the very prisons ; in the seaports, too, and the frontier towns. Being in the direct confidence of the brothers of the late tyrant, and in that of the foreign tyrants, this mercenary conspirator had at his disposal immense sums, with which he bought accomplices and paid for assassinations, poison, fire, and famine.

. . . .

" Batz, *ci-devant* baron and ex-deputy of the Constituent Assembly, is the atrocious brigand who was chosen to direct the blackest crimes of kings against humanity.

. . . .

" You have heard of the Foreign Conspiracy several times, when it was necessary to describe to you the attempts of a similar kind made by other factions. And indeed, your Committees, being persuaded that these branches of conspiracy all issued from a single trunk, acted upon a denunciation that they received on the 20th Germinal, and traced the plot step by step with so much resolution and energy that they at last

discovered it to date from the end of July, 1793—the
time when, with a bold hand, you crushed Federalism
and raised the fabric of the Constitution, which left no
hope for tyrants.

. . . .

"The principal objects of this scheme were to carry off
the widow Capet, to dissolve the National Convention,
and finally, to effect a counter-revolution.

. . . . . .

"A country-house called the Hermitage, connected with
the *ci-devant* Château de Bagnolet and situated at
Charonne, was the spot where they held their secret
councils. It was there that they meditated at leisure
upon the execution of their dark deeds. It was thence
that the correspondence of these scoundrels was despatched to their distant agents; and to evade the
vigilance of the authorities they hid their perfidy under
a patriotic veneer. The details of their plots were
communicated to their friends in invisible writing,
between the lines of the journals that were then in
favour. The recipients held these sheets to the fire, and
the orders of their leaders came into sight under their
eyes: here they read the thermometer of the conspiracy—
its rise and fall.

"Batz and his accomplices collected about twenty millions
and then consulted together as to its iniquitous use.
They had, moreover, many guineas accumulated by Pitt,
and a great number of assignats of the Monarchy, which
they tried to substitute for the paper-money of the
Republic, in order to injure the financial condition of the
country by forgeries. They bought gold at an exorbi-
tant price, with a view to reducing the quantity by hand-
ing it over to our enemies, or burying it."

. . . .

A GASCON ROYALIST

The speaker, continuing in this strain of bombastic and pretentious eloquence, next introduced all the reports of spies, all the denunciations, all the tales that had been told. Since Lacoste had no definite knowledge he spared no pains in presenting the merest hypotheses as real facts, and racked his brains in his efforts to blend the component parts of this strange Amalgam into a single whole, which, according to him, had no secrets for him. The nature of his logic appears in arguments like this: "Roussel must have been intimate with de Batz, because he was on very familiar terms with the parricide Admiral!" The following accusation of the dead shows his independence of evidence: "Chabot, Danton, and Lacroix were in league with de Batz. They ate together four times a week! There, while France was suffering from the famine that their fury had produced, they sat round a luxurious table, and in drunkenness and debauchery traded with the liberty of France, and plotted the overthrow of the Republic!"

Not a man in the Assembly rose to ask for proofs. Not a man pointed out that the report was a confused jumble, in which the innocent were indiscriminately confounded with a few who were guilty. Not one had the courage and honesty to call attention to the fact that, in the effort to injure the pitiless enemy who had declared implacable war against the Republic, fifty men and women were being sent to their death on grounds that were mere assumptions. In applauding the periods of Élie Lacoste, and in passing the Decree to which they led up, the Assembly once more connived at an appalling massacre.

The Convention would have been absolutely within its rights in putting the Baron de Batz and his accomplices to death, since such was the law of that period. But in diverting the punishment from the heads of the real

202

offenders because they could not be discovered, in making innocent people bear the consequences of its own incapacity, the Committee of General Security was guilty of a crime ; and in that crime all the representatives of the nation were implicated.

The report was greeted with acclamation, and the Decree passed with enthusiasm. The whole was despatched to Fouquier-Tinville, who summoned his jury and made his arrangements with the executioner.

For the hearing of the case, the examinations, and the sentence were no more than a mere formality. If the reader doubts the truth of this, let him meditate upon the following memoranda, which the Committee of Public Safety sent to the public prosecutor :

"28th Prairial.

" The Committee expects the Prosecutor to insist strongly upon the object of the many meetings that were held by the ex-Baron de Batz; namely, the escape of the Capet family from the Temple and of Antoinette from the Conciergerie : facts that have been absolutely proved.

"To suppress the details of the great plot that Simon overthrew : according to which Batz and his accomplices were to be included by Captain Cortey in his company on the day he was on duty at the Temple, and were to be posted by him round the tower and on the staircase : to omit these details lest they should suggest similar methods to the public : to state the fact without the details.

"To include in the charge Marino, Froidure, and Soulès, all of the police department, who connived with Michonis to deliver the Temple to Batz for money.

"Not to refer to the gardener at Charonne, in whom Batz confides.

"Not to bring the ex-Marquis de la Guiche to trial as yet, though he was mentioned in the Decree of the day before yesterday, the 26th ; but to include in the charge Rohan-Rochefort, Saint-Maurice, Laval-Montmorency, Sombreuil and his son, the ex-Vicomte de Pons, and Noël, secretary of legation, *to be condemned to-morrow.* Above all, to have them dressed in red, as murderers of the people's representatives." [1]

The Committee, as we see, had not quite lost all hope of including de Batz among the condemned : the warning *not to mention the gardener in whom he confided*, shows that an attempt was being made, on the very eve of the trial, to track him down. On that same day, the 28th Prairial, at ten o'clock in the morning, Admiral underwent a fresh examination, entirely bearing on his relations with the Abbé d'Alençon.

Admiral admitted that he knew him, and had confided to him his intention of killing a representative of the people.[2] It was evident that d'Alençon and de Batz were one and the same person. Throughout the day and night of the 28th the police were employed in seeking him in the outskirts of the town. Auteuil, Passy, and Boulogne were ransacked, but the Abbé d'Alençon was nowhere known.[3] In the face of this new defeat the Committee decided to abandon the search, and gave orders to Fouquier-Tinville to complete his work.

[1] National Archives, W, 389.
[2] Ibid.
[3] Ibid.

VII

THE RED MASS [1]

WE purposely omitted, from our account of Élie Lacoste's report, the names of the four individuals whom he declared to be the most active agents of the Baron de Batz: Mme. de Sainte-Amaranthe, her daughter Émilie, her son Louis, and her son-in-law Sartines. The link between the conspiracy and these new characters in our story was so slight that we may place them in the first rank of the innocent persons who were sacrificed to the vengeance of the Committees. When, however, they appeared before the Tribunal, the unexpected sight interested the public so absorbingly that they at once became the principal actors of the drama in which they had previously taken no part. Moreover, the part they played was due to incidents so romantic and obscure that historians have confused the facts with the strangest theories. We—in spite of all the statements of Élie Lacoste—say again that we believe the lives of these unfortunate victims to have been in no way associated with that of the Baron de Batz. It was their death alone that connected them with our subject, but it did so in such a dramatic way that we must dwell upon it for a little time.

[1] The Red Mass was the Mass celebrated in the presence of the Parlement when it first met after the' vacation. The members wore red robes on the occasion. (*Translator's Note.*)

A GASCON ROYALIST

Mme. Desmier de Sainte-Amaranthe[1] belonged to a noble and ancient family : she was the daughter of Étienne Louis Desmier d'Archiac, Marquis de Saint-Simon and Governor of the town of Besançon.[2] In her sixteenth year she fell violently in love with a brilliant cavalry officer, and her passion was so promptly and completely returned that the Marquis de Saint-Simon at once consented to their marriage, although M. de Sainte-Amaranthe, a mere lieutenant of indifferent morals and undistinguished lineage,[3] was by no means the kind of son-in-law he had a right to expect. The young couple settled in Paris, where they were so prodigal of their love and their money that at the end of a few years they were left without either.

[1] The name was really Saint-Amarand, and was so written by the whole family ; but we have adopted the form that has received the sanction of all the legal documents and of tradition. When studying Mme. de Sainte-Amaranthe's genealogy we were surprised and interested to find that the Desmier d'Archiacs were directly descended from Jean V. Desmier, founder of the families of Desmier de Chenon, Desmier de Grosbout, de Bravois, Desmier d'Olbreuse, etc. To this family of Desmier d'Olbreuse belonged Éléanore Desmier, who married, in 1665, George William, Duke of Brunswick-Lunebourg, from whom the English Royal Family are descended.

[2] From May 10, 1759, to Sept. 1, 1775. Archives of the Ministry of War.

[3] Davasse de Saint-Amarand (François Louis Barthélemy) was the son of a farmer-general and Mlle. Lallemand de Levignen. As he showed no taste for business he was put into the army. There is little relating to him in the Archives of the Ministry of War. He was a musketeer in the 1st company of the Royal Navarre Cavalry till 1765, when he became *capitaine-commandant* ; on the 5th May, 1772, he was promoted to the rank of *capitaine titulaire* ; and he sent in his resignation in 1773. He went to Besançon, where his father was living, and there he met Mlle. d'Archiac, whom he resolved to marry. " The family of d'Archiac was of very ancient nobility, the young lady was very pretty ; ordinarily, therefore, the captain's suit would have had every chance of being rejected ; but a short time previously Mlle. d'Archiac had been somewhat compromised in a love affair ; the officer was therefore accepted and the marriage took place."—*La vie privée des financiers au XVIII*^e *siècle*, by H. Thirion.

MADAME DE SARTINES.

(*Née* Émilie de Saint-Amaranthe.)

THE RED MASS

The husband went off to Spain, where his destitution was such that he was forced to save himself from starvation by driving coaches for hire. Mme. de Sainte-Amaranthe decided to retire into the country with her two children; but her coquetry, her love of pleasing, her smile, her entrancing figure, her keen and pointed wit seemed so unsuitable to a life of seclusion that her numerous friends of fashion in Parisian society implored her not to renounce the world. It is said that the Prince de Conti became so eloquent on this occasion, and employed such flattering arguments, that Mme. de Sainte-Amaranthe could no longer resist, and abandoned her intention.

The life that was before her was by no means austere. To picture it we must carry our minds back to the years that immediately preceded the Revolution. "Those who have not seen those days," said Talleyrand in his old age, "have never known the joy of living." French society at that time was at the zenith of its grace and polish: it was also at the zenith of its scepticism and immorality; and one would be tempted to deal severely with the gallant gentlemen who dismissed, as mere prejudices, all the traditions of ancient France, did one not bear in mind the terrible expiation that awaited them.

Mme. de Sainte-Amaranthe allowed herself to be easily intoxicated by the breath of liberty that turned so many heads. Her comfort was assured by the liberality of the Prince de Conti, and afterwards by a certain generous and affectionate *maître des comptes*, M. Aucane, who had an immense property in Martinique. He was an ever faithful friend, and his motto, it was maliciously said, should have been : *Quand même*; for the charming object of his devotion was always surrounded by a veritable court of adorers. Among the most assiduous were the Vicomte de Pons, a very model of elegance ; Monville, who was the creator of that delightful spot Le Désert, in the Forest of Marly, the scene of fêtes that entranced every lover of nature; Fayan of the fair and graceful head and the pale and charming face, a true hero of romance;[1] Miromesnil, a member of the *grande noblesse*—ugly, witty, and malicious; Saint-Fargeau, who was called the Alcibiades of Paris, and was a very personable man with a passion for distinction in dress. In addition to these there were Tilly, Champcenetz, Rivarol, Lajard de Cherval—and how many others!

Mme de Sainte-Amaranthe, always escorted by this guard of honour, divided her time between Paris and Lucy-en-Brie, where she owned a country-house. She had a box at the Italiens, a box at the Opera, a box at the Comédie: in her rooms at the Rue Vivienne she daily received ten or twelve persons, never more: they laughed, and talked, and listened to music while they drank tea and ate ices, and sat down to supper at a table that was renowned for its dainty dishes. Like a queen she had her *grand lever*, and admitted her intimate friends to a sumptuous dressing-room, where they had the honour of seeing her hair dressed. She had a good heart, no arrogance, and considerable wit; and, if one may believe Tilly's statement, she possessed "the rare talent of making friendship survive love."

At the beginning of the Revolution her daughter Émilie[2] was sixteen years of age. The Vicomte de Pons bore for this child an affection that was quite paternal, and it was said he had every right to do so. Mlle. de

---

[1] M. de Fayan afterwards married Mlle. de Lawœstine, sister of Mme. de Genlis' son-in-law.

[2] She is usually called Amélie; but we adopt the form that is used in the legal documents. She appeared before the Tribunal under the Christian names of Charlotte Rose *Émilie*.

THE RED MASS

Sainte-Amaranthe was dazzlingly beautiful : on this point all her contemporaries are agreed : both men and women—and this is rare—admit that the charm and attraction of her face were indescribable. "Never," says Mme Amandine Roland, "in the course of my long career, have I met so perfect a creature. Her figure was admirable and exquisitely proportioned : she was of medium height, and her bearing and her every attitude combined gentleness and charm with grace and dignity. There was a touch of archness in her smile that made it enchanting, and when it was accompanied by a certain movement of her head one's emotion was even greater than one's admiration. Her taste in dress was quite exquisite." [1]

She was, adds the Comte de Tilly, "more universally famous for her beauty alone than anyone else in France ; she was the most beautiful woman of her day ; she was beautiful in every respect ; I have never, in any country, seen beauty that could be compared with hers, beauty so absolutely perfect." [2]

It is said that when she and her mother were one day visiting the royal menagerie in London they came to the cage of a lion that had lately arrived and, being unused to captivity, was in a state of fury. All the spectators had instinctively withdrawn to some distance from the cage. Émilie approached it alone. Her emotion made her so beautiful that an English millionaire, in a transport of admiration, rushed up to Mme. de Sainte-Amaranthe and said, pointing to the wild beast : "Madame, will you allow me to give him to her ? " This mad suggestion, of all the compliments that Mme. de Sainte-Amaranthe received, was no doubt the most delicate and the most enthusiastic.

[1] *La famille de Sainte-Amaranthe*, by A. R.
[2] Tilly's Memoirs.

P

The first measures passed by the Constituent Assembly had considerably reduced Aucane's income; and he thought it wise to realise some of his capital and invest it in the gambling-house of the Arcades, which was, in 1790, the most popular in the Palais Royal. He thus became the principal shareholder, and under his management the house was so prosperous that the proprietors of No. 50, another gambling-house hard by, proposed that he should take over the management of their establishment also. Aucane, who was nicknamed the Bayard of the Green Cloth, accepted the offer, and quickly brought the famous No. 50 to a pitch of splendour previously unknown to the frequenters of the Palais Royal. It was the rule here, as in a club or private house, that no one should be admitted without an introduction: the fact that a man had money to lose was not considered enough: he must also be perfectly dressed, and the players behaved as in the most formal drawing-room of the Chaussée-d'Antin. To make the illusion complete a deputation of the share-holders came one day to offer Mme. de Sainte-Amaranthe " fabulous terms, if she would consent to appear every evening at No. 50 with her daughter, to do the honours of the salon and preside at the supper that followed the games." The amiable creature had never been able to deny her friends anything: she yielded to their wish.

A gambling-house was a curious sphere for a girl of seventeen as entirely beautiful and as closely surrounded by admirers as was Émilie de Sainte-Amaranthe. Her mother showed a strange degree of levity when she made her daughter's beauty one of the elements of success in a resort of this kind, however decorous and even refined it may have been. It was playing with fire, and it was not long before the flames broke out. Whether Tilly, or another, caused the conflagration matters little. It

is certain that Émilie did not long remain insensible
to the marks of admiration that were lavished upon
her by the most attractive and distinguished men in
France.

The first brief weakness of this poor child's heart was
succeeded by a violent and lasting passion. The whole
of Paris at that time was infatuated with a comic opera
in one act, called *Philippe et Georgette*,[1] which was being
played at the Théâtre Favart with the singer Elleviou
in the principal rôle. The success of this popular artist
was not entirely due to his gallant bearing and pleasing
face : it was well known that he came of a distinguished
family, which was seldom the case with the actors of a
hundred years ago. His father was a celebrated physician ;
his mother was a Kervalan. This gave him the charm of
novelty, and the whole house was enraptured when he sang
in his tender voice :

> *O ma Georgette*
> *Toi seule embellis ce séjour.*

One evening, as Elleviou advanced across the stage to
the footlights, while the orchestra played the air of this
song to the expectant house, his glance fell upon Mme.
de Sainte-Amaranthe's box. At the sight of Émilie the
artist stood suddenly transfixed, and missed the moment
to begin his song : then, quickly recovering himself, he
laid his hands upon his heart and, with his eyes upon
the girl, sang with more than his usual emotion and
fervour :

> *O ma Georgette !*

This was the beginning of Elleviou's passion for Mlle.
de Sainte-Amaranthe, which was soon returned. The
artist at first showed his love very discreetly ; every day

---

[1] This musical comedy was by Citizen Monvel.

he announced *Philippe et Georgette*, in order to have an opportunity of singing, with his eyes on Émilie:

Toi seule embellis ce séjour;

and every evening Émilie kept this tryst that was made upon a playbill. But their love was not merely lyric: an artless indiscretion on the part of Émilie's young brother, Lili, informed Mme. de Sainte-Amaranthe of the intrigue. In anger and tears she resolved, for the second time, to hide her shame and seek oblivion in the depths of the country.

A week later, having chosen a fairly pleasant desert, she actually set off to Rouen, accompanied by her daughter; and lest they should sink under their loneliness, the ladies took with them the eight or ten admirers who never left them.

Mme. de Sainte-Amaranthe was relentless. She informed Émilie of her fixed determination to spend the entire winter at Rouen, unless her daughter made up her mind to choose a husband from among her adorers. Confronted by this terrible threat the vanquished Émilie meditated upon the two alternatives that were open to her: to die of the provinces, or to obey her mother. She resigned herself to the second course. Three sons of ex-ministers aspired to her hand: MM. de Miromesnil, de Maupeou, and de Sartines. Her choice fell upon Sartines, who promptly trilled:

O jour d'ivresse, ô dieux propices!

This was tantamount to a formal acceptation, for in all crises Sartines expressed himself exclusively in quotations from opera, and he had suitable ones for every circumstance of life. The marriage was celebrated at Rouen, and very soon the party set out to Paris with all possible speed: for Sartines was longing for the opera, Mme. de Sainte-

THE RED MASS

Amaranthe for her beloved No. 50, and her daughter for the inconsolable Elleviou.

It would be unfair to pass judgment on such incidents as this without taking into consideration the kind of irresponsibility that prevailed at the end of the eighteenth century, an irresponsibility so genuine that it was apparent even on the scaffold. And in studying the morals of this strange epoch we must make allowance for the conditions that existed at the time—the beginning of 1793. The stately fabric that was the work of centuries of faith, having been undermined by violent hands, had crumbled into fragments, crushing beneath its ruins every tradition and belief : not a remnant was left standing of all that had constituted the strength and honour of ancient France. When a new boulevard is made through the old streets of Paris the ancient houses, with their dignified colonnades and coats of arms, crumble beneath the blows of the pickaxe and fall gradually into fragments ; and for a few days, before they are replaced by new buildings, their site is a mere formless mass of plaster and stones. Such was France in 1793, and we must not forget it. We waited so long for the new edifice promised by the Revolution, and it is still so open to criticism, that we have no right to be too severe upon our fathers, who were left beside their ruined dwelling without a roof over their heads, exposed to every angry wind that can blow upon humanity.

Elleviou had, for a long time, had a *liaison* with a young ballet-girl called Clothilde. She had made many sacrifices for the sake of the handsome singer, whom she passionately loved, and it was not long before her jealousy was roused. Suspecting the existence of a rival she took advantage one day of Elleviou's absence to break open the lock of his desk—the *sans-culottes* had brought revolutionary methods into fashion—and there she found four notes signed *Georgette*.

She did not doubt for a moment that Georgette was Émilie de Sainte-Amaranthe, and in her fury the lyric Clothilde swore, in imitation of operatic heroines, to take signal revenge upon her rival.

Time had passed : the spring of 1794 had come. The course of events had robbed the famous No. 50 of its aristocratic clients : their place had been taken by patriots, whose presence could not be resented without imprudence. Mme. de Sainte-Amaranthe grew daily less interested in the place. Since she did not care to associate with the men of the Revolution, and was well aware that she had made determined enemies of those to whom she had closed her doors, such as Desfieux, Trial the actor, Proly, and others, she retired at the end of the winter to her property at Sucy-en-Brie, where she hoped to remain undisturbed till the troubles were over. Naturally, she was accompanied by her daughter and son-in-law, and their departure had a singular result : thenceforward the Théâtre Favart seldom announced *Philippe et Georgette*. Elleviou spent his time upon the roads. Having borrowed a peasant's outfit from the properties of the theatre he went, thus disguised, to wait in the open country for a certain signal, by which he was acquainted of the propitious moment to slip through a little door into the park that surrounded his Émilie's home. The signal consisted of certain combinations of lights, alternately placed in the windows and taken away.

These telegraphic communications, this man whose graceful figure betrayed him through his disguise, this secret door that opened in the night, were more than sufficient, in 1794, to rouse the suspicions of the patriots. One evening, when Sartines and Aucane had just begun their game of backgammon, and Lili was reading aloud to his mother, and Émilie had gone upstairs, they heard a patrol halt outside their gate, and in a moment the municipal officers of Sucy were at the drawing-room door. They came to make a domiciliary visit, having been informed of the presence of a *suspect* upon the property. Instantly all the rooms in the house were invaded. Émilie hastened from her room, and stood upon the threshold, wreathed in smiles, with her hands full of tri-coloured ribbons, which she graciously distributed to the municipal officials. Such was the bewilderment produced by her beauty that they neglected to search her dressing-room. Had they done so the Théâtre Favart would have lost its brightest ornament.

The commissioners retired rather sheepishly, taking with them, in accordance with the custom of the time, all the kitchen utensils, to be melted and made into guns wherewith to destroy the enemies of the Republic !

Thanks to Émilie's coolness and presence of mind Elleviou escaped the danger that had threatened him. He did not, however, profit by the lesson. Every evening he visited the house at Sucy, and Aucane, who was unaware of the fact, could not understand why his peaceful retreat should be supposed to shelter a cabal of aristocrats. Throughout the past year—ever since Émilie, on her return from Rouen, had renewed her relations with Elleviou—the Sainte-Amaranthes had been perpetually denounced to the Committee ot General Security.[1]

---

[1] We will quote one of these denunciations, as it refers to several of the characters in our story :

"*Committee of General Security.* 13*th Frimaire, year* 2. Pierre Chrétien, delegate of the National Convention to the Îles du Vent, now residing in the Grande Maison Vauban, Rue de la Loi, appeared before the Committee, and deposed to the following facts :

" That for a long time Mme. de Sainte-Amaranthe held meetings for

Clothilde was taking her revenge. Here is one of the letters in question :

" At Sucy, at the house of the S-A's, there are meetings held, either for card-playing or for some other purpose : to go thither it is not necessary to have a passport, and this gives great facilities to the gamblers, or to the conspiracy." [1] After receiving a number of letters of this kind, and being repeatedly informed that a disguised man visited the grounds every night, the Committee, who were obsessed by their desire to discover de Batz, became persuaded that the disguised man at Sucy was he. Even

games of chance, and that her house, No. 50 in the Palais Royal, was the resort of all the most designing revolutionaries and sharpers.

"That some time after the formation of the Legislative Assembly, when Citizen Chabot, one of its members, had won a reputation for patriotism, Desfieux, who was one of the chief supporters of the Ste. Amaranthe Bank, made friends with him in order to strengthen the schemes that were concerted in that house. That at this time Chabot began to be intimate with Desfieux, spent evenings at his house and often dined with him.

"The Ste. Amaranthes have very often been denounced to the Committee of General Security. But Chabot, who was a member of it, warned them to put a stop to the gambling for 2 or 3 days.

"Mme. de Ste. Amaranthe had spies in her pay, and this was reported by Desfieux.

"Sartines is one of the supporters of his mother-in-law's gambling-house. Desfieux received him at his house every evening with Proli, Pereyra, and Dubuisson.

"Augasse (*sic*) was the intermediary between the Ste. Amaranthes and Desfieux. Augasse is a lawyer in the financial court, and has lived with the Ste. Amaranthe for several years past."

Another denunciation, signed by a man called Lormeaux and dated 16th March, 1793, was as follows :

"Especially the Ste. Amaranthe, to whose house the *chevaliers du poignard* resorted. She disgusted the patriots and kept them away by her impertinence and haughty manners : but on the other hand she petted and cajoled all the little *chevaliers du poignard*. The conversation at dinner and supper never consisted of anything but the most disgusting sarcasms, directed against the national assembly."—National Archives, W, 389, and F⁷, 4725².

[1] National Archives, F⁷, 4775².

supposing this were not the case, Sartines, it was said—probably quite falsely—had had a *liaison* with Citoyenne Grandmaison, who might very possibly have acted as a link between the Baron de Batz and Émilie's husband. In any case there was enough to compromise them in the eyes of the Committee, who were more concerned to hit hard than to hit the nail on the head.

In our opinion the mere mention of the Sainte-Amaranthes was all that was needed for their undoing. Whole-hearted democrats have a horror of superiority, as such. To breathe Émilie's name was to doom her to die : her beauty was in itself a mark of superiority.

And indeed the historians have attributed to her beauty the unpardonable crime of Émilie's fate. Some have declared that Robespierre for a moment lost his self-control in her presence, and bitterly regretted it ;[1] and others have described the fury of Saint-Just at being repulsed by her.[2] These theories are doubtless without foundation : but none the less, as we shall see, there are certain circumstances in the drama that are still rather mysterious.

On the 12th Germinal Mme. de Sainte-Amaranthe rose, at about mid-day, and came downstairs with a very doleful and dejected air. In the salon she found her children, Sartines, and Aucane, who inquired the reason of her sadness.

" You will laugh at me," she said, trying to smile ; " but I had a terrible nightmare last night : I dreamt I was the mother of three bats ! "[3]

---

[1] If we may believe the *Mémoires de Fleury*, edited by Lafitte, the Ste. Amaranthes received, two hours before their arrest, an anonymous letter advising them to fly ; and this letter was in Robespierre's handwriting.

[2] This incident was once made the theme of a so-called historical novel, named *Le dernier Amour de Saint-Just*.

[3] Mme. Amandine Rolland, who happened to be at Sucy that day, testified that this detail was not pure invention.

They tried to comfort her, but in spite of glorious weather the day passed sadly. At the very moment that the poor woman was making this singular revelation Saint-Just, from the rostrum of the Convention, was thundering forth the report that sent Danton to the scaffold. In it the orator contrived to refer to "the infamous Sainte-Amaranthe" and her son-in-law, Sartines; he upbraided them for their association with the confederates, and for their dinners at a hundred crowns per head. That same evening some commissioners from the Committee of General Security proceeded to Sucy, and arrested Émilie, her mother, Lili, and Sartines. At one o'clock in the morning they took the road to Paris in charge of a patrol, leaving behind them the desolate Aucane, whose cries of despair they could hear long after they had left the village. All the four were imprisoned that day.[1]

On the morrow at dawn one of Émilie's friends hastened to the Rue de Marivaux in search of Elleviou. She found him weeping between two pretty women, and put him in possession of the dramatic incidents of the arrest. She implored him to ask for an interview with the members of the Committee, and to confess to them that he was the mysterious individual whose visits to Sucy had roused the suspicions of the police. Elleviou was broken down by grief, and was in no fit state to take action in the matter; and moreover the measure was very repugnant to him, especially as he believed it would be useless. He still hoped that a thorough inquiry would bring to light the innocence of the prisoners; or, perhaps, that they might lie forgotten in their prison, like so many others, till the day, which must surely be at hand, when the ending of the revolutionary troubles should restore them to liberty.

[1] Archives of the Prefecture of Police.

THE RED MASS

His judgment was not greatly at fault : the Sainte-Amaranthe ladies were, as a matter of fact, forgotten.

So far was the Committee from believing them to be connected with the Batz Conspiracy that, when orders were issued, on the 13th Floréal, to gather into the prison of Sainte-Pélagie all who were known or believed to be in league with the baron, in the hope that they might make some imprudent revelation, these ladies were not included in the list. They remained in the prison of the Anglaises-Lourcine,[1] where they had been lodged after a few days of confinement at Sainte-Pélagie, and there seemed to be great hopes that they would be left there undisturbed.

Who was it who thought of them at the decisive moment ? Who was it who mentioned their names when Élie Lacoste was trying to swell the list in his report ? We do not know ; but it is evident that this report on the Batz Conspiracy served as an outlet for a great deal of personal revenge and spite. It was well known that, to be rid of an enemy, all that was needed was to denounce him at an opportune moment. " When a person's name is slipped into a big list," said Héron, " events move by themselves ; he is guillotined. The names are called over, the heads fall, and pouf, pouf, the thing is done ! "[2] Since the authorities could not catch the chief conspirators, methods of this kind were useful in filling the empty spaces in Élie Lacoste's report. " Everyone," says Sénar, " sent victims to their death " ; and though Sénar is not a trustworthy authority, having frequently proved himself a liar, he is telling the truth on this occasion. This is proved by the fact that, on the very eve of the trial of the baron's alleged accomplices, the public prosecutor had as

---

[1] They were removed thither, and Sartines with them, on the 27th Germinal, year II.—Archives of the Prefecture of Police.

[2] *Mémoires de Sénar.*

yet made no inquiry into the cases of many of the accused : he did not even know in which prison they were likely to be. The authentic documents are here so tragically eloquent that we must quote them in full.

On the 28th Prairial, when Fouquier-Tinville was occupied in gathering into the Conciergerie the unhappy victims named in the report of the 26th—*to condemn them on the morrow*, in accordance with the orders he had received—he found to his amazement that some of them were missing. Among them were Sartines and the Sainte-Amaranthes. He therefore despatched one of the ushers of the Tribunal to knock on the doors of the twenty prisons in the capital, and bring back the required *supply of game*.

This man executed his mission with zeal. He first went to the Luxembourg, where the head-jailer certified to him in the following terms, that the prison contained none of the *suspects* of whom he was in search :

" About a month ago sainte Amaranthe was transferred to the Anglaises on account of illness, with regard to the persons named dupont, égré, boissancourt, marsant, dauteville, comte and dehaies, St. amarante, mother and daughter, they are unknown at the Luxembourg.

"28th Prairial. CARON, head-jailer."[1]

A similiar disappointment was in store for the messenger at the Abbaye Prison :

" I certify that the persons named Dupont, Lafosse, Egrée, Boissancourt, Marsan, d'Hauteville, Comte, Deshaies, St. Armande, mother, daughter, and son, are not, any of them lodged in the Abbaye.

" This 28th Prairial, year 2 of the republic.

LAVAQUERIE FILS."[2]

[1] National Archives, W, 389. [2] *Ibid.*, 389.

THE RED MASS

At the refectory of the *ci-devant* monastery of Saint-Germain-des-Prés, which had been converted into a prison a few months earlier, Fouquier-Tinville's envoy was no more successful :

" *Les ci deçu nomme ne sont pas à la mai sont daret du refectoir delba beye.*

(The above named are not at the House of Detention of the Abbey Refectory.)

" NICK, head-jailer." [1]

The purveyor to the guillotine next visited the Carmes, where he found one of the prisoners he was seeking.

" I the undersigned certify that the person named Sylvain la fosse is in the House of Detention called the Carmes ; as for Dupond, égrée etc, Ste. Amarande, mother, daughter, and son, they are quite unknown to us.

" This 28th Prairial. ROBLATOR, head-jailer." [2]

In the women's prison of the Section de l'Unité [3] there was no sign of the Sainte-Amaranthes. They were also unknown in the annexe of the same building. [4] The public prosecutor's messenger was becoming discouraged, when he happened to pass the *ci-devant* Convent of the Anglaises, and entered it. It was here that he found the Sainte-Amaranthes. They were awakened and brought downstairs, their removal was entered in the register, and they were quickly despatched in a carriage to the Conciergerie, where they spent the remainder of their last night.

No inquiry was made into their case ; they were never examined, nor were there any preliminary proceedings

[1] National Archives, W, 389.

[2] *Ibid.*, 389.

[3] Attestation of the head-jailer (signature illegible, same *dossier*).

[4] Attestation of Léopod Læmin, warder of the Supplement (*sic*).—National Archives, W, 389.

221

of any kind. It is this that gives some plausibility to the theory that their trial was brought about by an act of personal revenge. To bring to trial—and what manner of trial we shall see—prisoners who were so entirely forgotten that their prison was unknown, was so completely a violation of judicial procedure that we may be excused for any theory we can put forward.

On the 29th Prairial, at a quarter past ten in the morning, the howling mob, which awaited the beginning of the performance in the public enclosure of the revolutionary Tribunal, uttered a terrific *ah!* on the opening of the little door that led from the registrar's office to the immense tiers of benches on which the accused were to be seated. Admiral appeared first. The gendarme who accompanied him placed him on the stool—ironically called the arm-chair—on which it was the custom to seat, in full view of everyone, the prisoner who was regarded as the principal member of the "batch." After him appeared, one by one, the forty-eight others, each accompanied by a gendarme. This sensational entrance was by no means quietly effected : many of the prisoners were calm and silent ; but some of them, with scarlet cheeks and sparkling eyes, talked at the top of their voices and gesticulated violently. The spectators hooted, shouted, hissed, and sang, and enjoyed themselves enormously. When Émilie entered they pushed and hustled one another in their eagerness to see her. When the prisoners, alternated with gendarmes, were all seated, the Court entered. Dumas, the president, came first, followed by Bravet and Garnier-Launay, the judges : Fouquier-Tinville took his place at the table, with his deputy Lieudon near him : [1] Wolff filled the post of registrar.

[1] Dumas and Garnier-Launay were guillotined after the 9th Thermidor. Bravet and Lieudon took flight.

THE RED MASS

The usher commanded silence, and Dumas, with the tricoloured ribbon round his neck and the black-plumed hat upon his head, rose, and amid all the uproar read the following words :

"Since the preliminary inquiry shows that Marino, Froidure, Soulès, Dangé, and Rossay are suspected of complicity with the rest of the accused, the Public Prosecutor requires, and the Tribunal ordains, that they shall be numbered with the other prisoners." Marino, Froidure, Soulès, and Dangé were, all four of them, police officials. They had been removed from their posts and placed in custody some time before, and when they were brought to the Tribunal, imagined they were to appear as witnesses. They were waiting in the registrar's office for the summons. As for Rossay, he was the Comte de Rossay-Fleury. On the previous day he had written to Fouquier-Tinville from the prison of the Luxembourg, demanding *the right to ascend the scaffold with all honest people*.

"Since this merry fellow is in a hurry," said Fouquier, "I will send for him."

The five new prisoners took their places on the platform ; the registrar hurriedly added their names to the indictment,[1] and the reading of that document opened the trial.

Dumas then began the examination of the prisoners. "Admiral," he asked, "did you make an attempt upon the lives of Robespierre and Collot d'Herbois, representatives of the people ?"

"I have but one regret," answered the prisoner, "and that is that I missed that scoundrel Collot."

Dumas asked the same question fifty-four times.

[1] In the original document these names are obviously written in great haste, whereas the list of the accused is transcribed very carefully.

Nearly all the accused simply answered : *No.*

Cécile Renault added :

"I never intended to kill Robespierre : I merely regarded him as one of the principal oppressors of my country."

The Comte de Saint-Maurice imagined he was in a court of justice :

"Citizens," he said, "I was arrested as an *émigré*. Well, here are four certificates——"

He unfolded his papers and prepared to hand them to the president ; but Dumas cut him short :

"That is not the question," he said. "I am asking you if you were implicated in the attempted murder of Robespierre and Collot d'Herbois."

"No, citizen," answered Saint-Maurice, and sat down resignedly.[1]

Michonis had prepared a written defence which he counted on being allowed to read. In it he declared he had never known de Batz, and if he knew some of the confederates it was because he had been in prison with them. This paper, on which the poor wretch had fixed his last hope, is in the *dossier*, and still bears the marks made by his hand as he mechanically crushed it during the examination of the others. He even, in his anxiety to forget nothing, added a few words while the trial was in progress. The pencil marks are hardly visible now.

Michonis, like the rest, was forced to confine himself to answering the question—always the same question—that Dumas put to the fifty-four prisoners.

"No ! " he answered.

He sat down again, in despair. Dumas, in a monotonous voice, was already questioning another prisoner.

[1] Désessarts, *Procès fameux.*

"No!" murmured Mme. de Sainte-Amaranthe.

"No!" said Émilie's sweet voice.

"No!" answered poor Lili bravely. His seventeen years [1] had not moved the Committees to pity.

They all answered thus. In less than half an hour Dumas had finished the examination. He had put fifty-five [2] questions to fifty-four prisoners.

"There are no witnesses for the prosecution," he said as he sat down. He then called upon the public prosecutor to speak.

Fouquier was not prodigal of his eloquence. Here is his charge in full:

"Citizens of the jury, you have heard the answers of the accused; it is for you to draw correct deductions from them; I merely beg you to remember that we are dealing with the most important case that has yet come before this Tribunal, and I therefore depend upon your patriotism and your usual sagacity." [3]

The president considered that this was somewhat brief: he thought it best to add a few words:

"Citizens of the jury," he said, "the prisoners you see before you are agents of the Foreign Conspiracy. The National Convention has sent them before the Tribunal in order that you may decide their fate. Their denials will not deceive you: I need not remind you that the people demand to be revenged upon the monsters who thought to deprive them of two of their most valued representatives. You will fulfil their expectations, in your verdict on the questions that I am about to submit to you."

[1] He was not yet seventeen. At the time of his arrest, the 10th Germinal, his mother declared that he was sixteen-and-a-half. National Archives, F[7], 4775[2].

[2] Two being addressed to Saint-Maurice, as we have seen.

[3] Désessarts, *Procès fameux.*

He read the question, and the jury retired. Dumas then addressed the gendarmes.

"Remove the prisoners," he said.

A murmur rose from the fifty-four unfortunate creatures crowded upon the benches. They were stupefied. In their ignorance of the summary procedure decreed by the law of the 22nd Prairial they thought the trial had hardly begun : they were expecting to be questioned, and to answer in their own defence, and to hear a discussion on the counts of the indictment. Many of them wished to speak, and appealed to the president ; but he remained unmoved, and repeated the orders.

"Gendarmes, remove the prisoners ! "

They were already being hustled towards the little door, through which they disappeared one after the other. The public, behind the barriers, were discussing the appearance of the prisoners and their probable state of mind, while the judges were conversing on the floor of the court.

This interlude lasted for half an hour. The jury returned to their seats and the fifty-four were again brought in. Each of them, on entering, glanced quickly at Dumas, as though to read upon his face the sentence he was about to pronounce.

When they were all in their places the president, taking from the table the sheet of paper that had been placed there by the chief juryman, pronounced these words amid profound silence :

"The verdict of the jury is in the affirmative on all the questions concerning all the prisoners : consequently——"

The rest was unheard. From the three tiers of the prisoner's platform there rose a storm of anger and despair.[1]

[1] Désessarts, *Procès fameux.*

226

THE RED MASS

"We have not been tried! You are murderers!" Fists were shaken in the air, and sobs were mingled with outbursts of forced laughter, and insults, and curses.

Dumas, coldly, went on reading the sentence of death: then he made a sign and left the court quickly, followed by his assistants. The gendarmes pushed out the troops of victims, while the ignoble crowd applauded. But already the hall was emptying; for the sight-seers were hurrying off to the court of the building to secure places on the steps of the main entrance, whence they were soon to see a more attractive spectacle than the trial.

It was a little before mid-day when the condemned prisoners came down the staircase that connected the offices of the Tribunal with the Conciergerie. They did not return to the prison itself, but were taken through a passage to the registrar's office, where they were to await their departure to the scaffold.

This office consisted of two rooms, of which one was fairly large and was used by Richard, the head-jailer. Usually one of these rooms sufficed to hold the condemned prisoners while they were preparing for death; but on this occasion the numbers were so large that both the rooms were crowded.

We know little, for certain, of what passed during the four hours that they remained in this horrible place. It was a terrible moment, this halt upon the road to death: the victims, while they were being made ready. nearly always fell into a demoralised state, which took the form, in some cases, of profound depression, and in others, of feverish excitement. In the Tribunal the poor wretches were not entirely without hope: in the tumbril, with the eyes of the people upon them, they wore a bold front from bravado or vanity. But here!— these slow preparations, these last farewells, this first

227 Q 2

sight of the executioners, this basket with its load of hair, dark, fair, and grey together, these cords laid ready on the bench, only half cleansed from the blood of the previous day—all these terrors were, for creatures full of life, the most horrible agony imaginable.

Of the scenes that took place here on this 29th Prairial a few isolated details are all that we know. Sanson, warned by Fouquier in the morning, had mobilised his whole staff. He had, on great occasions, eleven assistants at his disposal, but only four of these were the habitual attendants to whom he could entrust the delicate task of preparing the prisoners for the scaffold. He never assisted in the preparations himself: he contented himself with glancing at each of the victims that were ready for death, to see that the cords were properly tied, and the hair correctly arranged, and the garments cut low at the neck.

It is said that Émilie de Sainte-Amaranthe remained perfectly calm. When her turn came to sit upon the stool she took the scissors into her own hand and, twisting her marvellous hair, cut it off boldly close to the neck. Then, giving it to Richard, she said: "Take it, monsieur: I am robbing the executioner, but this is the only legacy I can leave to our friends. They will hear of it, and perhaps some day they will come to claim this souvenir of us. I rely on your honesty to keep it for them."[1]

She was thinking of Elleviou; and as a matter of fact he did indeed hear a rumour of the commission with which his friend had entrusted the jailer, and came, it is said, a few days later, to claim the treasure that was waiting for him.

It is said that Fouquier sent a message to Émilie that he would save her if she declared herself to be

---

[1] *Mémoires de Fleury*, edited by Lafitte.

enceinte; but either because the poor woman did not care
to survive all her relations, or because she foresaw that
Fouquier would demand payment for his clemency, she
disdainfully rejected the suggestion.

When the executioner's assistants were in the act
of uncovering Émilie's shoulders a cry of anguish rose
from the midst of the crowded prisoners: Mme. de Sainte-
Amaranthe had reached the limit of her endurance and
had fallen down in a faint. Sartines, foaming at the
mouth with fury, was struggling to break the cords that
bound him, that he might fling himself upon the
executioners. Lili was standing ready with his hands
tied behind him, and was sobbing aloud.[1]

From without came the loud murmur of the crowd that
thronged the courts and all the precincts of the building.
A host of people battered on the gate in the Rue de la
Barillerie. Under the hot June sky the bright garments
of the women and their gaily coloured parasols gave
a festal air to this surging mob. They exclaimed at the
number of the tumbrils: there were eight of them waiting
in a row, all ready to start, along the north wing of the
Cour du Mai. In front of the *ci-devant* church of
St. Bartholomew a squadron of mounted police was
making ready to escort the procession. Everywhere there
was joking and laughing, and merriment and gaiety: for
this was the eternal Parisian crowd, which is always the
same—always intoxicated with sunshine, and dust, and
noise.

All was ready at last in the tragic room. Richard
signed the paper testifying to the prisoners' removal: the
doors were opened widely, and the victims heard the
clamorous voice of the immense mob: "Here they
are!"

[1] *La famille de Sainte-Amaranthe*, by Mme. E. L., 1827.

Sanson gave the signal for departure : the women first !
Roughly aided by their executioners they summoned the
little strength that remained to them, and rose from the
bench on which they were huddled together. Suddenly
the order was countermanded. In the narrow courtyard
of the registrar's office a discussion was evidently going on,
and oaths were overheard. The doors closed again
abruptly : the start was postponed : the disappointed mob
howled with impatience.

Surely at this moment the hearts of the prisoners must
have leapt with one last mad hope of pardon, or of
counter-revolution. The few among them who were really
accomplices of the Baron de Batz imagined, no doubt,
that he was working on their behalf ; that he had come to
save them ; that he might, perhaps, succeed.

Such was not the case, however. The cause of the
delay was merely that Fouquier had suddenly remembered
the order of the Committees : *above all, see that they are
dressed in red, as murderers of the people's representatives* ;
and the ushers of the Tribunal were ransacking all the
shops of the neighbourhood for the materials that were
required to redeem the executioner's forgetfulness.[1] A
whole hour passed while fifty-four red shawls were hurriedly
contrived ; an hour of agony for the victims, an hour of
such cruel suspense that one marvels that human beings—
some of them women, some hardly more than children—
could endure such unspeakable mental torture.

And while these scenes were being enacted in the
Courts that had once been Courts of Justice the Conven-
tion was being regaled with a long discourse by Roger
Ducos on philanthropy ![2]

At last, as the clock struck four, they set off. In the

[1] Campardon, *Histoire du Tribunal révolutionnaire*.
[2] *Moniteur*, sitting of the 29th Prairial.

230

first tumbril were six women, among whom were Cécile Renault and her aunt, the actress Grandmaison, and Citoyenne Lamartinière. The people hustled one another in their anxiety to see them : the mistresses of de Batz and Admiral were eagerly pointed out, but the special object of interest was the little Renault girl, who had lost none of her calm, phlegmatic resignation.[1] She was summoning all her courage, no doubt, for her last momentary glimpse of the house in the Rue de la Lanterne where she had spent such happy hours. The second tumbril was being loaded : there were five more women in it, among them Émilie, fairer than ever in the red drapery that barely covered her shoulders. It is said that, when her mother was on the point of fainting for the second time, Émilie tried to infect her with her own heroism, and to divert her thoughts said with a smile :

"Look, *maman*, how pretty all the red cloaks are! We look just like cardinals."[2]

Mme. de Sainte-Amaranthe was deaf to every sound. She gazed silently, with tragic eyes, now at her daughter, now at Lili, who had been allowed, as a favour, in consideration of his age, to remain with the women.

It seems to be a well-attested fact that Fouquier, whose curiosity had led him to a window in Richard's rooms that overlooked the yard of the Law Courts, was betrayed into admiring, in his own fashion, the courage shown by Émilie. He turned to those who were with him, and said with a laugh :

"*Morbleu*! I must see if that jade does not show signs of weakness before the end! I must see her head cut off, if I miss my dinner for it!"

"Let us be quick," said Voulland, who was there ; "come

---

[1] Désessarts, *Procès fameux.*
[2] *Mémoires de Fleury*, edited by Lafitte.

along to the foot of the High Altar, to see the celebration of the Red Mass." [1]

Sanson had arranged his prisoners according to age : the third cart contained the old man—Sombreuil, Père Renault, the Abbé Briel, Deshayes, and the rest. The young men were put together in another cart ; and when all was ready the gates of the Law Courts were flung open, and the procession set off.

In the course of the past five years Paris had seen many moving, grotesque, and sinister sights, and might well have been hardened into indifference ; but the vision of these eight tumbrils, with the fifty-four red figures " swaying above the countless heads," produced a movement of acute eagerness among the crowd. The women especially drew all eyes. Émilie, erect and superb, was trying, in spite of her bound arms, to support her mother, " who was all the time on the point of collapsing." Citoyenne Grandmaison, too, attracted much attention ; and it was considered that little Nicole, who was not yet seventeen, was really rather young to die. Cécile Renault remained unmoved.

The tumbrils, preceded by a squadron of cavalry, passed slowly along the Rue de la Vieille-Draperie, and turned into the Rue de la Lanterne towards the Pont Notre-Dame. In the neighbourhood of the Renaults' house all the inhabitants of the district had gathered, and were watching the proceedings with great interest. Cécile must have recognised many familiar faces in the crowd : but not a soul dared show a sign of pity.[2]

[1] These words have been accepted by all the historians. Sénar, who records them, says they were spoken by Voulland as the procession passed the corner of the Rue de la Loi and the Rue Saint-Honoré. This is an obvious mistake, for the tumbrils approached the Place du Trône by quite a different route.

[2] Désessarts, *Procès fameux.*

THE RED MASS

The bridge was crossed in the burning sunshine : the quays and all the windows and parapets were crowded with people : the sound of many voices rose towards the cloudless sky. The throng marvelled at the youth and beauty of the women ; at Émilie, who was trying to comfort her brother with brave words ; at the old men, who were all quite calm, and talking quietly together ; at the occupants of the last tumbrils, who were gay and "making merry."[1] One, and one only, of the victims was overcome with uncontrollable grief : Portebœuf was shedding torrents of tears. And there was one moment, it is said, when Émilie de Sainte-Amaranthe, for all her heroism, failed to master her emotion : when she saw Elleviou, with distorted features and wild, distracted eyes, trying to force his way through the mob to the side of the tumbril. Mutely and solemnly she sent him a last farewell ; then closed her eyes, for she felt that her strength was failing her. When, a little later, she looked up, she turned her head away with an instinctive movement of horror ; for quite close to her, between the bars of the

[1] Désessarts, *Procès fameux.* The gaiety of the condemned prisoners on their way to the scaffold is a well-attested fact, but as it may appear incredible I give two police reports that record it authentically :

" 13th Nivôse.

" To-day five persons condemned by the revolutionary Tribunal were taking their places in the executioner's cart. There was a very tall woman who looked liked a foreigner. When the executioner held out his hand to help her she pressed it close to her and began to laugh. Three of the others talked and laughed together when the people cried : *To the guillotine.*"

" 19th Nivôse, year II.

" When I was in a café in the Rue Saint-Honoré four persons, of whom two were women, were in the cart, and were laughing among themselves at the warder and the people who stood round. The spectators said : 'They look just like traitors and *ci-devant* nobles. If we were to show any signs of weakness they would laugh at us.'— 'Look,' said one citizen, ' how they are mocking at our laws. They are going to the scaffold laughing.' And this was true."

—National Archives, F[7], 3688.

233

cart, appeared the sinister, triumphant face of Clothilde, who had come to exult over her rival's fate.[1]

De Batz himself was there, we may be sure. There is no documentary proof of the fact, but it is impossible that the relentless conspirator should have remained in hiding while the whole of Paris was watching the last scene of the drama in which he had played the principal part. What risk of recognition could there be amid this vast crowd? Moreover, he must surely have hoped that some popular impulse, some sudden movement of pity or disgust, would rouse the mob and prevent this wholesale slaughter. What were the man's thoughts, one wonders. These innocent men and women were, after all, his victims. Did he feel no remorse? Was it not borne in upon him that his work was accursed, and that all the blood that was about to flow would make him a byword in the years to come? For my part I do not believe that he was concerned with this aspect of the matter. Whether he saw the melancholy procession of his confederates, or not, I do not think he was greatly moved. On the day that he pitted himself against the Revolution, in that terrible game in which the stakes were his own head and the heads of his accomplices, he had put away from him all human sentiment; he had entered upon a pitiless war, and no war is waged without lists of the dead; his heart had grown callous, and he had long aimed at keeping it closed to every feeling but hatred; in order to face his enemies on equal terms he had freed himself, by sheer force of will, from every kind of emotion. For him, victory was everything; and if, as the tumbrils passed that day, he heard the comments of the mob, he assured himself, no doubt, that the blow that had been aimed at him would strike the Revolution and pierce it to the heart.

[1] *La famille de Sainte-Amaranthe*, by A. R.

THE RED MASS

"What!" muttered the crowd. "So many victims to avenge Robespierre! What more could they do *if he were king?*" A general feeling of suppressed pity, a stifling atmosphere of malediction, a cry that fear made mute, but that tore at the very heart-strings : "Ah! cursed be that man and this day!"[1]—such were the things to which de Batz in his triumph could have testified.

The man against whom the indignation of the people was roused by the sight of these women and children on their way to death was not de Batz, but Robespierre. He it was who had originated the iniquitous law of the 22nd Prairial, the law that had sent these people to the scaffold without a trial ; it was to his safety that they were sacrificed ; and indeed it was said that he had insisted on the death of the whole family of Sainte-Amaranthe because on one occasion, at their house, he had betrayed some important secrets in his cups ! The fall of Robespierre was not brought about by the events of the 9th Thermidor, which was merely a carefully arranged scene devised for parliamentary purposes, but was the result of the appalling massacre of the 29th Prairial, for which, rightly or wrongly, he was held responsible. As was said unjustly of another politician of a later date, *his foot slipped in blood*—and the blood was that of the accomplices of the Baron de Batz.[2]

It was not till seven o'clock in the evening that the carts drew up round the foot of the scaffold that stood in the Place du Trône. The victims alighted, and were ranged in a row before the wooden benches that had been set up, in view of the recent large " batches," round the guillotine.

[1] Michelet's *Histoire de la Révolution.*
[2] This is so undeniable that all the historians, Michelet, Louis Blanc, and *all*, have regarded the execution of the fifty-four as a device of the Committees to rid themselves of Robespierre.

A GASCON ROYALIST

What words can describe the horror of these moments of waiting, the tears and mutual farewells, " the heart-rending cries that were exchanged ? " What strange chance was it that seated the Vicomte de Pons between Mme. de Sainte-Amaranthe and Émilie? What words passed at this supreme moment between these wretched creatures who, in life, had been united by such close ties ? It is recorded that Sartines—his ruling passion strong in death—went up to his wife and smilingly quoted to her, for the last time, some lines from an opera :

La mort même est une faveur,
Puisque le tombeau nous rassemble.

Cécile Renault was already on the steps of the scaffold. For a moment she stood erect; then suddenly dropped upon the plank. The knife fell. Mme. de Sainte-Amaranthe, half mad with horror, shrieked aloud, imploring to be allowed to die before her children. The executioners took Lili, and the knife fell again.

His mother swooned, and saw no more. Then Émilie appeared upon the platform ; and when the red veil was torn from her shoulders her statuesque beauty was so transcendent that the devotees of the guillotine, who were paid to applaud, were struck dumb with admiration, and stood open-mouthed, with hands arrested. The executioners pushed her roughly upon the blood-drenched machine, and the third stroke fell. Then the inert form of Mme. de Sainte-Amaranthe was dragged upon the scaffold : she was already dead when her head fell. And the heap of headless corpses grew gradually larger, and the scaffold streamed with blood. The scene continued for twenty-eight minutes. Admiral was the last to die.

Michelet records an appalling detail. A certain man of great strength and hardness—one of those athletic people

who are all muscle and have no nerves—wagered that he
would watch the execution at close quarters without
flinching. Whether he stood with the executioner, or not,
I do not know. For a long time he bore it, unmoved;
but when little Nicole came upon the scaffold, and
arranged herself upon the plank, and said gently to the
executioner: " Monsieur, shall I be all right like that ? "
his head swam and his sight failed him, his immense
strength gave way, and he fell to the ground. For a
moment he was thought to be dead, and he was carried
home.

The Parisians took it upon themselves, as their manner
is, to avenge these murdered women. By the 30th
Prairial fashion had assumed the functions of Nemesis,
and every woman of any pretensions wore, in memory
of Émilie de Sainte-Amaranthe,[1] a red scarf flung

---

[1] The following is an interesting passage from the *Mémoires de
Thiébault:* " I again saw at the Vauxhall Ball, among other women
famous for their charms—at that time known as *demi-castors*, or *half-
beavers*—that young Mlle. de Sainte-Amaranthe who was one of the
most accomplished and exquisite beauties imaginable. . . . We were
never tired of admiring this creature, who seemed more beautiful than
ever and appeared to us to be more than human. . . . This angelic
person soon afterwards married the son of M. de Sartines. . . . But the
most remarkable thing was the heroism shown at her death by this
young and beautiful woman, who had been accustomed since her birth
to all the luxuries of wealth, position, and self-indulgence. All her
companions were crushed : she alone was imperturbable, and tried to
give courage to those she loved by her firmness and even by her jests.
Among the latter were the words she said smilingly in the fatal cart, in
connection with the red garments that had been wrapped round her
and her alleged accomplices : ' Does it not look as if we were a
procession in the Carnival ? ' " (Thiébault, vol. I., p. 165). This strange
name of *demi-castors* was given to the ladies of indifferent morals who
reigned supreme in the Palais Royal, and frequented the low-ceiled
entresols whose windows formed the top of the arcades, which gave
them the appearance of arched beaver-lodges. For this reason the
ladies in these galleries were known as *beavers*, while the name of *half-
beavers* was given to the less fortunate ones who occupied the half

coquettishly round her shoulders. This made the Jacobins furious.

of one of these little spaces, which were usually divided by a partition.

The portrait we give of Émilie de Sainte-Amaranthe is one of the famous *physionotype* portraits that have been so greatly exercising all inquiring minds for the last hundred years. The memoranda connected with this art inform us that Émilie's portrait was in the collection. Unhappily there were nearly two hundred anonymous portraits to choose from : but by dint of minutely examining the proofs and the marks they bear, and comparing dates and artists' addresses, we have arrived by a process of elimination at the conviction that the profile here reproduced is that of Mlle. de Sainte-Amaranthe. But we have no absolute proof of the fact.

After the Revolution Clothilde married the composer Boïeldieu, who had no reason to congratulate himself on his union with Émilie's tempestuous rival.

VIII

VENDÉMIAIRE

FROM Prairial to Thermidor the orgy of blood continued unchecked. The Tribunal, in a sort of hysterical frenzy, emptied the prisons to feed the guillotine. The execution of the *Red Shirts* had shown that the Parisian populace, whether from indifference or terror, would allow things to take their course; and of this apathy full advantage was taken. Every day was seen afresh the terrible sight of eight tumbrils passing on their way to the Place du Trône with their load of victims: the scene had become an integral part of the manners and customs of the Parisians: death was the order of the day.

Amid these daily hecatombs we must call attention to four names that have often appeared in the course of this narrative. A week after the day of the Red Shirts died the Marquis de la Guiche. He was known to be on intimate terms with the Baron de Batz, and was expected, if not actually to denounce his friend, at least to make some indiscreet statement. As he persisted in keeping silence it seemed hardly worth while to continue the struggle, and he was executed. Poor Aucane, who had been left at Sucy out of consideration for his state of health—he had just been through an operation for stone— was carried to the Tribunal, and thence to the scaffold.

239

He died on the 9th Thermidor.   A few days earlier Paul and Sylvestre de Lézardière had perished : the reader will perhaps remember the part they played in the first attempts of the Baron de Batz.   When closely confined in the Conciergerie they refused to reveal their father's hiding-place, and were executed on the 7th July, 1794.   A few hours before they died upon the scaffold, bravely crying :   *Vive le roi!*   they wrote upon the same scrap of paper, which is still preserved as a relic by the family of Lézardière, the following mysterious and touching letters of farewell.   Through the efforts of a faithful servant the paper reached their father's hands :

"To CITIZEN DANJOU, Hôtel Danjou, Place Saint-Michel :

"The *petites fillettes* and Mimi have just received the last and most precious consolations.   During their illness they made the sacrifice of everything ; even their tender attachment to the feelings that were inspired in them by their parents in their infancy, and by their new and valued friend.[1]   They go to meet their mother and brother in peace and resignation.   The good Henriette was replaced in a way that was quite satisfactory to them.   A word of farewell to the good Danjou and the good friends."

19th Messidor, 9 o'clock in the morning.[2]

"What can I add except that the little *fillettes* and Mimi have no regrets nor sorrow save on your account : their confidence and peace are the only supports on which two young people can lean.

"I recommend to you my poor Danjou, who took the most marvellous care of me.

[1] The Abbé de Fénelon, who was imprisoned and executed with them.

[2] The first part of the letter is in Sylvestre's handwriting ; the second in that of Paul.

VENDÉMIAIRE

"Farewell, I am going to my mother and brother. I rely upon the same great and uplifting thoughts as are raising us now above ourselves, to sustain us.

"I pray to Him before whom I am about to appear for the happiness of all of you, and of Joseph and Charles.

"Farewell again!

"I embrace my dear Danjou. I beg him to make every possible effort to enable our relations and friends to read our little message."

When one thinks of this family of the Lézardières, of which the eldest son died for his faith, and the mother died of grief at her king's death—she whom the death of her first-born could not kill!—and the two other sons died to save their father, all victims of their fidelity to a lost cause, their story seems like some tragic epic of wider issues than the ordinary course of human life, some legend full of horror, such as the poets of old so well knew how to create.

We are very busy in these days, setting up pedestals for the men of the Revolution and raising statues to them. So be it! But might we not perhaps find heroes in the other camp as well, where they are seldom sought?

The day came at last when France was surfeited with blood, and was fain to rid herself of Robespierre. That the Incorruptible desired to arrest the Terror, as his admirers have striven desperately to prove, is possibly true. He felt himself drowning in the torrents of blood that he had set flowing, and he wished to close the flood-gates: the good impulse must be attributed to his self-love rather than to his humanity.

The prisons opened their doors: Paris breathed again, and the decimated Convention having lost all of its mem-

241   R

bers who were strong enough to force themselves upon the country, fell into a state of exhaustion. The death of Nero was quickly followed by the reign of Augustulus. Louis Blanc has well said: "After the 9th Thermidor politics became merely an interchange of lies; the era of base compromises had begun"; the Terror had killed the Revolution.

The Baron de Batz could justly claim to have largely contributed to this result. The huge machine that he had set in motion had done its work as he foresaw. Through the long night of the Terror, the night that he peopled with the phantoms of conspiracy, "that night of blood in which faces were only seen when the lightning flashed," the Convention had struck out at random at both friends and foes, and had harmed friends oftener than foes, "because the former were nearer to it."[1] And now it lay wounded and despised, amazed to find itself alive, and expecting every moment to be swept off the face of the earth. To the whole of Europe it seemed that France was in a state of disorder and confusion that could only be cured by the restoration of the Monarchy.

The great mass of the people desired this consummation, or rather, desired nothing but leave to live; and for nearly a year the country was like a convalescent, slowly recovering strength after a terrible and crushing illness. A few of the younger men tried to throw off this state of torpor, and amused themselves, amid the loud plaudits of the public, with putting an end to the surviving Jacobins— maltreating what was known as *Robespierre's tail*; but this was a game of no significance, a return to the brutal methods brought into fashion by the Revolution, a feeble attempt on the part of the terrorised to revenge themselves upon the terrorists. The movement did not become

[1] Louis Blanc: *Conclusion historique.*

general. The Parisians lay still under the oppression of their recent nightmare, and resigned themselves to dying of hunger in silence; for terror had been succeeded by want: cruel, devastating want, patiently endured. It appeared a small matter, after all that had gone before.

The Baron de Batz, however, did not succumb to the prevailing inertia. The convulsion of Thermidor, which he had awaited, and worked for, and foreseen, in no way modified his schemes. He saw that the moment was at hand when the crippled Assembly, bereft of its leaders, would be too weak to fight. When that moment came the people would soon put an end to it: it would topple over at a touch. Its hour had not yet come, however: the final blow must necessarily be dealt by the people, and they were still too weary to be roused to wrath. A little patience was required.

It was at this juncture that de Batz, prompted by his ceaseless craving for action, bethought him of wiling away the time by writing the story of his conspiracy. But he soon recognised that this was a useless undertaking, and therefore contented himself with pleading the cause of his alleged accomplices at the bar of posterity, defending the fifty-four victims who had been slaughtered instead of him, and thus adding, by his revelations, to the horror inspired by the memory of Robespierre's crimes. May he not have been impelled by some vague feeling of remorse when he undertook the defence of those whom he had involuntarily sent to their death? There are moments when one is tempted to think so. But more probably his only aim was to vindicate himself, to allay any suspicions of which he might still be the object, and thus to pave the way for the unchecked pursuit of his desires.

Whatever his motive may have been, the brochure, which he boldly named *La Conjuration de Batz ou la*

Journée des Soixante, is well worth reading. Very few copies of it were printed, and it was soon so rare that in 1816, when de Batz himself wished to re-read it, he could not procure it. The National Library does not possess it, and indeed there are only two copies known to be in existence.[1] This interesting production, therefore, has all the charm of an unpublished document.

And first, we must observe that de Batz describes himself as a man in love with peace and quietness, a good citizen, with no interest in politics, and no desire but one : "the desire for rest and obscurity." Being of a very timid and prudent nature, and "guided by motives of extreme discretion," he left, on the 10th August, 1792, the lodgings that he had long occupied, and took refuge first with Roussel and afterwards with Cortey. He spent the whole of the Terror in " a state of inactivity that was almost stupid."[2] In his anxiety to leave Paris he had already secured a passport, when he heard of the arrest of his alleged accomplices. He could not make up his mind to desert them, but dared not risk his life in their service. He therefore hid himself in the house of friends whom he does not name.

" And it was at this very time, when my cruel uncertainty as to the fate of my friends had reduced me to a state of stupor, that my enemies represented me as a modern Proteus, assuming one form after another, eluding the vigilance of all the authorities, and exhibiting the most amazing activity.[3] It is impossible to describe the astonishment that all these lies that turned me into a conspirator

---

[1] One belongs to M. Victorien Sardou, the other to M. Foulon de Vaulx, who kindly allowed us to copy it. We take this opportunity of thanking him. This copy, which is valuable on many grounds, contains various notes in the handwriting of the Baron de Batz.

[2] We quote the exact words of the brochure.

[3] *La Conjuration de Batz ou la Journée des Soixante*, p. 66, note.

aroused in my good and worthy hosts, who saw me spending my lonely days in ways very different from those that were depicted. I went out sometimes, however, even in full daylight, and I never disguised myself. All my alleged cleverness, therefore, could only be invention or temerity. To tell the truth, the warnings that I sometimes received might well be regarded as the exaggerations of friendship. To judge from them my arrest had become, by order of the two Committees, the most absorbing object of all the Sections of Paris ; . . . the Decree that banished all the nobles was passed with the sole aim of depriving me of shelter ! I certainly could not believe myself to be of such importance that the fate of the French Republic depended upon me alone : so far, I had good reason to be incredulous. . . . But one day a man, who was much surprised at being addressed by my name, was arrested quite close to me in full daylight. The clamour, and transports of joy of the cannibals who thought they had arrested me, put an end to all my illusions. My concealment became more solitary, though not more absolute than before. But whenever I was anxious about my friends, or had heard no news of them, I went everywhere in full daylight. I was unaware of their fate for some time after they were dead. . . . Pity was watching over me, and deceiving me, but could not allay my terrible anxiety : whither did it lead me one day !

"If I escaped my would-be assassins and their thousand tools, ah ! never let it be imputed to my prudence, nor to my own will ! "

It is needless to point out the surprising contradictions in these confessions. This contempt for all prudence is very different from the *extreme discretion* of which we heard a moment ago. The profession of faith that follows is still stranger :

"I affirm that I took no part in any of the events, nor in any of the conspiracies, whose causes or effects have been attributed to me. I will go further : I affirm, for the edification of those who do not know me, that it would have been impossible for me to be ostensibly a citizen of the Republic while I was secretly conspiring against it ; that to ask the help and protection of its laws while I was attacking it under their shelter would have seemed to me very base and cowardly. I affirm then, that while in France I carried on no kind of correspondence nor had any relations whatever, direct or indirect, with the kings, princes, generals, and ministers whose chief agent it pleased the Committees to constitute me : nor even with any foreigner or *émigré* whatever : and to any man who can give me the lie I grant full permission to expose me. Had I played so prominent a part in Europe I should certainly seek some consolation in the glory of such important undertakings. I should at least abstain from senseless denials and disclaimers of actions that, after all my troubles, would entitle me to rewards which—to be quite frank—all the treasures and favours of all the kings of the earth could never pay." [1]

Certainly this solemn declaration, this gauntlet flung upon the ground by a gentleman like de Batz, ought to be taken into consideration ; and we should be forced to bow before so definite a protestation of innocence if it were not that the baron himself plainly contradicted his own statements at a later date. When writing to thank Eckard [2] for his *Histoire de Louis XVII* he said :

"I was in Paris (at the time that the odious law of the 22nd Prairial was passed) and was entrusted with a mission so important that it was imperative to devote my whole

---

[1] *La Conjuration de Batz ou la Journée des Soixante*, p. 64.
[2] Unpublished letter in the collection of M. Foulon de Vaulx.

life to it. This mission was expressed in these exact words, among others: *Being convinced of the important services that may be expected of the fidelity of the Baron de Batz and his attachment to the King and royal family we beg him to return to France, with a view to seeking and adopting every possible means for the rescue of the King, the Queen, and their family, etc., etc. 2nd January, 1793.*

" What I and three others attempted on the 21st January when the fatal carriage passed by, and my further attempts to rescue the royal family from the Temple and the Queen from the Conciergerie (attempts that were on the point of being successful), and other facts which it was to the interest of the infamous Assembly to conceal from the public, and which would now provide the clue to many important events, are recorded in what is left of the archives of the two Committees. . . . I had in my possession some important papers relating to the great crimes and secret movements of the two Committees. But I lost a large portion of them irretrievably on two occasions when I should infallibly have lost my life if the papers had been found, and the only way to avoid this danger was to destroy a large number of them, or to have them destroyed. A very accurate journal, written in shorthand for my own use only, fell into the hands of the police. If I could retrieve it (it is believed to be still in the collection deposited at the Prefecture of Paris or of the Police) it would supply you with a great deal of valuable information." [1]

And later on he wrote thus :

[1] It is certain, then, that the Baron de Batz wrote a daily account of his doings, the secret history of the Revolution. His journal was either in the Prefecture of the Seine or in the Archives of the Police as late as 1816, and no doubt remained there, hidden and forgotten, till 1871. Both these stores of archives were burnt by the Commune, and consequently the baron's journal is irretrievably lost.

"It is well known that I was the victim whose death was especially desired, and that the law of the 22nd Prairial was passed on my account. I was rash enough to show myself *because it was important for me to watch the course of events and to set an example of boldness.* I actually entered the den of the Conventionists (on the day when the law was discussed). It is true that I was in a group of men among whom I was easily hidden, but none the less Robespierre's eye found me out. Our eyes met, and his told me that he was surprised, but was not deceived. My retreat was prompt but not hurried. Robespierre lost no time in pointing me out to his myrmidons, with the intention of sending me to the scaffold. . . . My escape was due more to good luck than to good management. I was young, and swift-footed, and full of life, and I played with danger." [1]

In a man capable of such acts of bravado as this it is difficult to recognise the frightened, lonely outlaw, who passed his days in a state of *stupid inactivity*! There is a striking contrast, truly, between these two sketches of the same individual. In the one we find "extreme discretion"; in the other a degree of audacity that amazes himself! What must we then conclude? That the Baron de Batz was a liar? Why, certainly : he had accepted his rôle of conspirator with all its consequences, and was so well made up and disguised that even now he is hard to identify, even now he successfully eludes those who would fain inquire into his strange personality.

The *Journée des Soixante*, then, must be read with caution : de Batz by no means tells the truth in it. He divides the victims of the 29th Prairial into two groups. Those whose alliance with him was a matter of personal devotion, such as Citoyenne Grandmaison, Roussel, Devaux, Biret-Tissot and la Guiche, he exonerates com-

[1] Unpublished letter in the collection of M. Foulon de Vaulx.

pletely. They took no interest in political events, he maintains, and their execution was sheer murder. But the others, those whom he bought with money, Burlandeux, Lafosse, and their like, he in no way spares; he declares he was victimised by their greed, and he exposes their low intrigues.

He does not steer his way very skilfully amid these reservations. It is always a delicate matter to deal in half-truths: the man who attempts it will sooner or later be brought up short by some obstructing contradiction, or will trip over some awkward piece of evidence. So it is with the Baron de Batz, who does not deny having been acquainted with Chabot—"that miserable cut-purse," Bazire, Julien of Toulouse, Delaunay of Angers, and Lhuillier, the *procureur-syndic* of the department: a dangerous circle of friends for a person so deeply enamoured of *solitude and obscurity*. He does not hide the risks he ran, and confesses that more than once the Committees were on the point of seizing him.

"The horrible man," he says, "who one day set spies upon my track to take me by surprise, owed me all his comfort and some money that I lent him at a time of pressing need. Moreover, he had in his possession a considerable amount of my furniture and other movables of all kinds—the monster!

It was he who denounced and betrayed the people who were associated with me and died in consequence."[1]

There is one passage in which the Baron de Batz is palpably sincere: and that is his account of the execution of his alleged accomplices. That this is the account of an eye-witness is evident. Up to this point he tells his story in cold and formal terms: but here he is so obviously in the grip of a sudden emotion, so plainly obsessed by the memory of the horrible sight, or even torn, it may be,

[1] *La Conjuration de Batz*, p. 86, note.

by remorse, that in the reader's mind the conviction is formed : " He was there : he saw them die."

" When the infamous carts," he says, " had paraded the sufferers at great length through the immense crowd, amid all the insults that were paid for by the tyrants, they arrived at last at the place of execution, and the executioners helped the victims to alight. . . . The sufferers were ranged in front of the scaffold, standing ; and the chain they formed was as long as their numbers extended in single file. Their backs were turned to the scaffold, but the scaffold was low, and they could not make the least movement without seeing the horrible execution. In the fearful silence that reigned in the presence of death every fatal stroke made their hearts tremble. They could hear ! . . . Sometimes the blood sprinkled those who were standing nearest ; soon it spread over the scaffold, and drenched the ground, and flowed beneath their feet . . . each of them went up in turn and presented the hideous spectacle that he had already witnessed. It is a quick death, they say, for each of the victims ; but when there are sixty, though the first endures but one death, the last dies sixty times. And then the baskets . . . the heaps of dead. . . . the horrible, impious mingling of ages and sexes, of crime and innocence . . . the sacrilegious blending of impure blood with blood—Ah! my task is over, I have done. It was thus they died—those whom I have no strength left to name." [1]

While the Baron de Batz was writing the *Journée des Soixante*, and before the brochure was even printed, the royalist reaction had gained so much ground that it felt strong enough to carry the government by assault, and to triumph finally over the Revolution.

[1] *La Conjuration de Batz*, pp. 93, 94,

VENDÉMIAIRE

The recent insurrection of Prairial (May, 1795) had pointed the way. On that day Paris had witnessed the astonishing sight of the whole populace taking the government by the throat and demanding an end to their sufferings. The rising of Prairial was the rising of hunger, and the Convention had heard the threatening and significant cry: *Give us a King or give us Bread!*—a faint echo of another occasion, when in October, 1789, the mob had rushed upon Versailles to seek *the baker, the baker's wife, and the little baker's boy.*

Since the 9th Thermidor, and especially since the rumour of the dauphin's death in the Temple had enabled the Comte de Provence to proclaim himself King of France, the royalist party had been active. In Paris numbers of agents were employed to distribute large sums of money, their orders being "to spare no efforts to win over the constituted authorities to the King's cause; to tempt the representatives of the people with alluring promises; and to pardon in advance all regicides who were willing to uphold the monarchy."

A whole book might be written—an entirely new and deeply romantic book—dealing with the actions of the monarchical party during the year that preceded the establishment of the Directory. Will anyone ever penetrate behind the scenes of that period of intrigue, and plotting, and treason? Will anyone ever give us a picture of Parisian society in that amazing year of 1795, when conspiracy was carried on, so to speak, under the open sky? The government, having neither money, nor credit, nor morals, no longer attempted to defend itself: every day there appeared some fresh brochure in which the Convention was pilloried. There had never been so many foreigners in Paris: the hotels of the Faubourg Saint-Germain, which had been empty six months earlier, could scarcely contain the crowd of Chouans, and *émigrés*, and refractory priests, and divorced women, and rich young men belonging *to the transport department* who were drawn to the capital by the prospect of a complete renovation of ideas and conditions. The royalists had borrowed the costume of the Chouans: grey coat with lapels, and black or green collar. As for their meeting-places, they frequented the café Garchy, at the corner of the Rue de la Loi, the theatre of the Rue Feydeau, the Boulevard des Italiens, and especially the Palais Égalité.[1]

Among the agents of Louis XVIII were the Abbé Brottier, Duverne de Praile, the Chevalier Despomelles, a mysterious individual named Formalaguez, who suddenly emerges from obscurity and disappears again without giving any hint as to his rôle, and a certain Lemaître with the cognomen of Boissy—or possibly a certain Boissy with the cognomen of Lemaître—who had been working in the cause of the Bourbons for a long time, as appears from the following testimonial, written by the Comte de Provence himself:

"The Sieurs Despomelles, Brottier, and Lemaître remained in France by the orders and for the sake of the late King our brother, whom they constantly served with every mark of the purest devotion and most ardent zeal, and after the King's melancholy end it was only by our express orders and with a view to serving their king that they continued to dwell in a guilty land. We therefore, by these presents, formally bear witness to the courage, fidelity, and devotion of which the Sieurs Despomelles, Brottier, and Lemaître have given, and are still giving, constant proofs, at great risk to themselves.

"Louis Stanislas Xavier."[2]

---

[1] Louis Blanc: *Histoire de la Révolution*.

[2] This document, which is quoted by Louis Blanc, is dated 9th July, 1794, when the Terror was at its height.

VENDÉMIAIRE

It was true enough that these secret agents were wasting no time: the whole of France was in a fair way to become one huge Vendée: the insurrection was being organised quite openly. Already uniforms were being despatched to England to clothe an army of thirty-thousand men: " red coat buttoned over the chest, white scarf across the breast, pale green waistcoat, round hat adorned with the brush of a white fox and a white plume." Everything had been thought of: the design of the colours—fleurs-de-lys on a white ground ; the names of the regiments ; even the pattern of the belt-buckles !

And public opinion—either because it was cleverly influenced, or because disgust and misery had really done their work—went docilely in the desired direction: to everyone it appeared that the restoration of the Monarchy was merely a matter of days, and this belief was openly expressed. Among the National Archives are a host of documents that bear witness to the unanimity of this desire, this desperate appeal of a famished nation to its former masters. We are told, for instance, of a certain Taillardat saying openly in the street: " Louis XVI, in the whole course of his reign, did less harm than the Convention in one day "; and of a hairdresser, Claude Perrin, exclaiming : " If I die for it I want Louis XVII ! " The cry of Prairial had become the cry of the nation : " *Give us a King or give us bread !* " for the whole nation was starving, and from every mouth rose the piteous lament of the hungry.

" It is three days since my dog had anything to eat," said one.

" It is awful to have nothing but a quarter of a pound of bread in the day ! " added another.

" Oh for the days when wine was eight sous a bottle ! " sighed a third.[1]

[1] National Archives, W [2].

And these complaints, which were carefully collected and recorded by the detectives of the Committees, swelled the hymn of misery that was chanted in heart-rending unison by the disillusioned and repentant people.

The Baron de Batz, as he watched this growing ferment, saw that the hour had come to act. It was now the end of September, 1795 : the Assembly was discussing the Constitution of the year III, which gave birth to the Directory. The Convention, being aware that it was abhorred by the army even more than it was despised by the people, had taken a curious step : it had deprived itself of the power to summon troops to Paris.

Now Paris, as we know, was divided into forty-eight sections, governed by as many Committees : each of these Committees exercised sovereign authority over its own district : they were therefore so many governments, whose local decrees had the force of law. The inconvenience of this usurpation of power was little felt as long as the forty-eight sections were of contradictory opinions ; but if by chance a measure were brought forward in regard to which the forty-eight Committees were unanimous, the very fact of their combination instantly created a power as strong as the Convention—stronger, indeed, in virtue of the revolutionary maxim : " The functions of any constitutional body cease in the presence of the assembled people."

The deputies, at this time, were so entirely discredited that anyone who should bring forward a measure in direct opposition to them was certain of unanimous support.

What should the measure be ? Here the Baron de Batz—for it was he who organised the whole intrigue, as he tells us himself in a little unpublished memoir that is now before me [1]—gave evidence of sound and truly politic

---

[1] This interesting fragment is called : *De la journée appelée des Sections de Paris ou des 12 et 13 vendémiaire, an IV, octobre* 1795. It belongs to M. Foulon de Vaulx, who has kindly allowed us to use it.

judgment. He knew that the whole Parisian populace regretted the vanished General Council of the Commune, —dissolved after the 9th Thermidor—and deplored the loss of their autonomy : and it occurred to him to bring forward through the Lepéletier Section, where, as we know, he had many friends, a measure for the establishment of a Central Committee, which should sit in the Town Hall. The other sections were then invited to express their approbation of the measure.

The Convention, seeing the danger, decreed that any citizen who should consent to sit on this Central Committee should be considered guilty of an assault upon the sovereignty of the people.

The opposition of the Assembly to a sectional decree was quite enough, however, to secure its adoption by a majority of the *sectionnaires*, on the strength of their sovereign power. The plan succeeded perfectly. On the 2nd October, at the very hour when the Comte d'Artois was landing at the Île d'Yeu, the Lepéletier Section, having secured the support of all the others, called upon the people to rise, on the ground that they had been " deceived, betrayed, and murdered by those to whom they had entrusted their interests, and that they must therefore save themselves." Of the forty-eight sections thirty-two greeted this suggestion with enthusiasm. The Assembly, therefore, had only two alternatives : either to summon troops to Paris, an illegal measure which would give the sections the right to enter upon a civil war in the name of the law ; or to submit—which would mean the end of the Republic.

For, had the Convention given up the struggle, the Central Commiteee would instantly have replaced it. Then, before the joyous and triumphant populace had even taken in what was going forward, this body of carefully picked men would have opened the doors of the Temple, would have led forth Louis XVI.'s unhappy daughter, who was the object of universal sympathy, would have fraternised with La Vendée and summoned the princes—and in four days the restoration would have been achieved.

If all this had taken place the royalists would have been using revolutionary weapons against the Revolution, and adopting the same measures in the cause of the Bourbons as the Jacobins had once adopted in the cause of Robespierre.

Such was the scheme of the Baron de Batz. He had foreseen everything except the incredible ; and it was the incredible that God had in store for France.

The Convention did not hesitate. It broke the law, and summoned to its aid the troops that were encamped round Paris. The Committee of the Lepéletier Section retaliated by constituting itself an Insurrectionary Committee, and inciting the other sections to arm themselves and call out their national guards.

The 4th October (12th Vendémiaire) was an ominous day. The Convention, at bay, distributed muskets to all who came to defend it : determined Jacobins, and inconsolable followers of Robespierre, and *Septembriseurs* all hastened to offer their devoted services, and in its pressing need it dared not repulse them, though it feared them more than the anger of its enemies. The walls were placarded with a notice informing the people that " the motion brought forward by the Péletier Section was sent from London to the traitor who proposed it ; and for the last two months it had been expected by the Committee of Public Safety, who were prepared for the event, and had taken measures to ensure for the Convention the glory of saving the country."

VENDÉMIAIRE

De Batz, his friend de Redon [1] (who had been a member of the Constituent Assembly), a young man called de Lallot, and a dozen others, were holding a permanent sitting in the ex-convent of the Filles-Saint-Thomas, the headquarters of the Lepéletier Section. De Lallot, whose zeal was intense, was, so to speak, the *piper* of the conspiracy: his fiery speech, his energetic gestures, his satirical eloquence had the power of inspiring the mob. Every hour he mounted his horse and rode quickly through the neighbouring districts, spreading enthusiasm and kindling valour, and then returned to the Filles-Saint-Thomas to be at the disposal of his leaders.

By the evening the whole town was under arms. At the street-corners the call of the sentries was heard, as though Paris were besieged; messengers dashed hither and thither distractedly, declaring that the sacking of the city was about to begin; there were placards on the walls saying that the Convention had flung itself into the arms of bloodthirsty assassins; the streets were full of patrols; the shops were closed; and through torrents of rain came the muffled sound of the drums beating to arms.

It was the Convention that opened hostilities, by ordering General Menou to go, with ten thousand men, to invest and take by assault the Convent of the Filles-Saint-Thomas, the headquarters of the insurgents. Menou divided his men into three columns, and set off. At about ten o'clock the centre column arrived by way of the Rue Vivienne, the right column by the Rue Notre Dame des Victoires, and the left by the Rue des Filles-Saint-Thomas. The Lepéletier Section was thus completely

---

[1] As a reward for his services to the royal cause, the government of the Restoration appointed M. de Redon first president of the court of Riom.

surrounded. But we must give the words of the Baron de Batz himself, who was an eye-witness of the strange incident he describes :—

"The ten thousand soldiers under Menou's orders, accompanied by three Commissioners, members of the Convention, arrived at Lepéletier.[1] Panic preceded them ; one saw nothing but men flying in all directions. But young de Lallot, who was not troubled by fears, went to meet them at the outer door of the Section. One of the Conventionists said to him : 'Go and tell the Péletier Assembly that they may have ten minutes to adjourn and leave the place empty : after ten minutes have elapsed any man who is still here will be regarded as an enemy of the State.' De Lallot answered more or less in these words : 'Who dares to use such language? Who has the audacity to forget that the Péletier Section is at this moment invested with sovereign power, and therefore gives orders here, but does not take them? What is the meaning of these weapons and all these warlike preparations? Are you Austrians? Is the Péletier Section a battle-field?'

"As he spoke, one of the Conventionists came in and cried in a fury : 'Here, men, seize this traitor !' Far from retreating, Lallot stepped forward, saying : 'Stop, men ! The thought of committing such a crime as the violation of these precincts should make you tremble. Let me tell you that the law forbids you to pass the threshold, and you will not pass it save over our dead bodies ; that Paris is amazed at your presence, and the whole town at this moment is rising in arms ; that it would wreak the most prompt and terrible vengeance upon you, and that your

[1] We are quoting the words of the baron's unpublished account, but here and there we have altered incorrect or obscure expressions, which make the story less vivid.

name would be for ever hated, for ever doomed to infamy. Soldiers, your country's eyes are upon you : your country will judge you. In the name of the law I command you to retire.'

" The soldiers were filled with astonishment and hesitated. The disconcerted Conventionists approached Lallot, and from the inside of the building came several individuals to support him, among them being the man who is writing these reminiscences at this moment, with the same hand that he had the strongest reasons, just then, for using to hide his face.

" There then followed the most surpassing debate between, on the one hand, several members of the Government and a general with ten thousand men behind him ; and on the other hand a very young man, who, by the sheer force of his words, restrained the rage of the Conventionists, and prevailed upon the general to order his troops to retire ! "

It must not be imagined that this is mere exaggeration. The facts, as narrated by de Batz, are true in every detail : an army of ten thousand men retreated—vanquished by the words of a single obscure individual. Such were the defenders that remained to the Convention. Menou and his three columns marched back to the Tuileries. An hour later he was cashiered ; and the Baron de Batz, with an exultant heart, went back to his post at the headquarters of the Lepéletier Section. He was confident now of victory on the morrow.

He was mistaken, however. He had not observed, while de Lallot was addressing the troops, that there was standing near him a thin, pale young man, wearing a long threadbare riding-coat and a hat that was too large for him. His chest was hollow, his complexion livid, his whole appearance poverty-stricken. He had just left the Théâtre

Feydeau, where he had been spending the evening, and was returning to the Rue des Fossés-Montmartre, where he was staying at the sign of *La Liberté*, an unattractive hostelry. This young man, seeing the troops and hearing a noise, had drawn near, and with no motive but curiosity had gradually made his way through the crowd that surrounded the door of the Filles-Saint-Thomas. He had therefore witnessed Lallot's oratorical triumph and Menou's retreat.

When the troops were gone this shabby individual stood for a moment wrapped in thought. Then he walked away towards the Rue du Mail, but suddenly retraced his steps and followed the troops.

He reached the Tuileries at the same time as they ; he entered the palace, and went to one of the public galleries of the Convention, which was holding a nocturnal sitting. He saw the agitation of the Assembly at the news of Menou's failure, and heard the deputies hailing Barras as the general in command of the troops. He was on his way back to his inn when, as he passed the offices of the Committee of Public Safety, he saw that they were crowded with people, some of whom were expressing their views on the situation, while others were mere idlers, greedy for news.

He entered. Everyone was speaking at the same time, but none the less he succeeded in making himself heard. He had witnessed the scene in front of the Lepéletier Section : he described it, discussed the incident, gave his opinion, and put himself at the disposal of the Committee should they be willing to accept his services. Finally he gave his name. He was called Napoleon Buonaparte.[1]

---

[1] Louis Blanc throws doubt on the accuracy of the *Mémorial de Sainte Hélène*. "Napoleon," he says "spent the evening in the Théâtre Feydeau and only left it to go to the Convention : it is

VENDÉMIAIRE

This was the obscure individual whom the Baron de Batz on the following day, the 13th Vendémiaire, found blocking his way.

The part that Napoleon played on the 13th Vendémiaire is too well known to be described here. Since we have no new light to throw upon the opening of a career that is, and must always be, "the greatest prodigy of history," we will confine ourselves to our subject, and will simply give the details of this day's events as recorded in the fragmentary *Mémoires inédits* of the Baron de Batz, a document of the greatest interest. Barras, Réal, and the Emperor himself have described the insurrection from the point of view of the victorious party. The account we are about to read will give us, so to speak, the reverse side of their story; for it shows us the insurrection from the point of view of one of its leaders :—

" There was nothing to be done but to march, without a moment's delay, upon the Tuileries : there was nothing to prevent us from hemming in the Convention, which was entirely without defenders. But, by some fatality, the Central Committee gave the command of the Parisian army to a certain M. Danican, of whom perhaps the kindest thing one can say is that he was inept. Instead of taking advantage of the prevailing enthusiasm, he seemed to make a special point of quenching it. He postponed the attack on the Convention till the morning. . . . This serious blunder gave the Assembly time to breathe, and send out agents into every part of Paris, and spread false

therefore hard to understand how he can have witnessed the incident in the Rue Vivienne, which took place between 10 o'clock and midnight." It is easily explained. Napoleon *could not avoid* passing the Rue des Filles-Saint-Thomas on his way from the theatre to his hotel. The play ended, as was the custom of the day, at 10 o'clock *at latest*. We cannot refuse to believe, then, that Buonaparte witnessed the scene at the door of the Lepéletier Section.

reports, and bring the most violent terrorists from their prisons, and arm them, and give them Buonaparte for their leader.

" Though victory was postponed, however, it seemed none the less certain. At four o'clock in the afternoon (of the 13th Vendémiaire) more than sixty thousand *sectionnaires* were under arms and awaiting the order to march. But all Danican's arrangements were senseless. He despatched twenty thousand men to the Tuileries by way of the little Rue du Dauphin, and ordered the remainder (at least forty thousand men) to cross the Pont Neuf and return to the Tuileries by the Pont Royal !

" Thus, having at his disposal a force numbering at least forty to one, he chose, for his points of attack, a bridge and a defile.

" Indeed such was the confusion that reigned in this general's head that he had omitted to put anyone in command of the Péletier column, though the others were to follow it ! M. de Batz, having observed a young officer, M. Chartier, who was disposing his men admirably and seemed to have the gift of encouraging them in words very much to the point, said to him : ' Young man, take command of the whole column resolutely, and they will all obey you.' Who does not know that in revolutionary movements of this kind the place of authority always belongs to the man who can take it ? Chartier took command, and was obeyed. At the sound of his voice the Péletier column advanced, and crossed the Pont Neuf to the quays on the further bank of the Seine, in accordance with Danican's orders.

" As this column advanced it was reinforced by the troops of the other sections, who marched in its rear.

" The head of the column had reached the Rue des Saints-Pères, when General Danican appeared at last, followed by a numerous staff. He rode full trot to the Pont Royal, the end of which was defended by two hundred brigands, with a single piece of ordnance loaded with grape-shot.

" After a parley of no more than a minute the general and his suite retraced their steps, and somewhat precipitately entered the Rue de Beaune. At the same instant, as though at a given signal, the gun was fired upon the column. Chartier gallantly turned round and said: ' Forward, friends—do not fire—the gun is ours.'

" Before these few words had left his lips not a soul was left to hear or follow him. The men of the two first ranks had fired, but such was their anxiety to be gone that they fired in the air without taking time to aim; after which they and the entire army disappeared in as many directions as there were streets abutting on these quays. In a word, of the forty thousand men only four individuals remained! It was not the destruction dealt by the gun, however, that produced this panic, for it had been aimed in the wrong direction, and had scattered the grape-shot over the paving-stones, which were glittering with it. That was all the damage that was done, except that one shot had ricochetted and had detached the sheath of M. de Batz's sword from his sword-belt.[1]

[1] The story of this encounter should be read in the *Mémoires* of Barras, who is completely in accord with the Baron de Batz :—

"I had sent Buonaparte to the Pont Neuf; he returned in great haste to tell me that immense columns of National Guards were emerging from all the streets between the Quai Voltaire and the Pont Royal. I had one twelve-ton gun, under the walls of the Hôtel de Nesle, near the Rue de Beaune. I gave orders to fire, and the first charge of grape-shot threw down some of the foremost National Guards. The whole of the column wavered, and its retrograde movement showed me that it could not hold out long. I at once ordered my men to continue firing, but to fire in the air, as it seemed to me the noise would suffice to disperse the enemy's ranks."

Mémoires de Barras, Vol. I, p. 257.

" While MM. Chartier and de Batz were exchanging a few words of surprise and horror, a group of National Guards reappeared at the end of the Rue des Saints-Pères. M. Chartier hurried towards them, in the hope of rallying them and bringing them back. But they all vanished again at the sound of the gun firing for the second time, and of some other guns, charged with powder, that were fired on the other side of the Seine. M. de Batz had hoped that at least the troops would rally at the centre of the Lepéletier Section. He therefore proceeded thither, but found no one except M. de Lallot, a few members of the Committee, and M. Chartier, who thought M. de Batz had been killed by the second shot, and was saying so at the moment when M. de Batz appeared.

" As for the column that had advanced by the Rue du Dauphin, a few shots had sufficed to stop it. If, instead of the *sectionnaires*, some simple Vendean peasants had been there, even in much fewer numbers and only armed with sticks, they would have darted across the short space occupied by that little street, have overwhelmed the handful of brigands that Buonaparte commanded, and surrounded the Conventionists in their lair.[1]

" The *sectionnaires*, less inured to war and ill-commanded, had confined themselves to taking up their position at the Church of Saint-Roch, of which one corner faces the Rue du Dauphin. Others had posted themselves in the Rue Saint-Honoré, at the two corners of the Rue du Dauphin :

---

[1] " I was opposite Saint-Roch, which was the position on which the *sectionnaires* founded their hopes of victory. There is no doubt that if they had boldly descended that fictitious mountain (the steps of the church) they could have made a rush at the battery itself, which was the sole obstacle before them. At the sacrifice of a few of their men they could have taken our guns and turned them against us."

Mémoires de Barras, Vol. I, p. 254.

they charged their muskets under shelter, and only exposed themselves while they were firing at the brigands, who discharged their muskets and guns quite at random. It was, so to speak, a battle between noise and terror.

" On both sides, however, there were dead and wounded. But as soon as the incident on the quays became known at Saint-Roch the *sectionnaires* were discouraged, and gave up their feeble struggle : they dispersed and disappeared.

" To prolong the intimidation Buonaparte had some guns dragged about the streets of Paris in the night, charged with powder only, and the town was soon as empty as the most silent desert. It was thus that a little smoke and noise put an end to the most immense hopes, at a time when nothing but a miracle could have prevented their realisation. . . . Paris, and all France, relapsed beneath the yoke of the revolutionaries ; Buonaparte, their deliverer, became their hero ; this incident was the starting-point of his destiny. . . . "

And indeed on the following day, the 14th Vendémiaire, Buonaparte was promoted to the rank of lieutenant-general ; on the 18th his name was mentioned for the first time in the Convention ;[1] it forthwith appeared in the papers, and emerged for ever from obscurity. A fortnight later he was appointed general in command of the Army of the Interior, and was installed in the fine official residence in the Rue des Capucines.

Though the Convention was prudent enough to reward a man of whom the Republic might again have need, it was not strong enough to punish those who had attempted to destroy it. It is true that three courts-martial were held by its orders, to try the originators of the *Crime of Vendémiaire*, but they only lasted for ten days, and were but a feeble imitation of the Revolutionary Tribunal.

[1] By Fréron.

The proceedings were conducted with systematic carelessness. No doubt the restoration of the Monarchy seemed
to be merely postponed, and measures of excessive
severity against the royalists may have been judged
inopportune. A certain number of *sectionnaires*, who were
especially compromised, were taken to the Tuileries and
packed into the cellars of the Committee of Public Safety ; [1]
but as they were very uncomfortable there, they were
lodged in the *ci-devant* college of the Quatre Nations. Of
all the military leaders Lafond, who had led a column of
the insurgents, was the only one executed : he died on the
21st Vendémiaire ; De Lallot and Redon, who were
condemned to death for default, hid themselves successfully
and escaped the scaffold. As for de Batz, his fame as a
conspirator was such, his reputation as an incorrigible
abettor of sedition was so well established, that he was
perhaps the only one of them all who was sought with any
real energy.

He was then living in furnished rooms in the Hôtel de
Beauvais, No. 31 Rue de Vieux Augustins, on the first
floor above the entresol ; and on the 16th Vendémiaire, at
the request of the Committee of General Security, the
police-commissioner of the Section du Mail repaired thither
at six o'clock in the evening to arrest him.

Naturally de Batz was not at home. Citoyenne Mernier,
the manageress, stated that he had spent the night in his
room, and had not gone out till nearly three o'clock in the
afternoon. The commissioner and his registrar requested
to be taken to the room. They knocked at the door, and
as it was locked they affixed seals to it. [2]

This caused no inconvenience to de Batz, who had
secured shelter for himself elsewhere ; and he went to and

[1] National Archives ; *Affaire de Vendémiaire.*
[2] National Archives, F[7], 4588.

fro in the streets of Paris, and boldly appeared in the most frequented quarters. Lest one of his numerous domiciles should be searched, however, he carried about with him the various documents connected with the unsuccessful conspiracy. If he were arrested with these papers on him it would mean certain death for him ; but, at all events, he alone would be compromised.

In the afternoon of the 19th Vendémiaire, as the Baron de Batz was crossing the Rue de Choiseul, he observed a man named Klotz, who had been one of his agents during the Terror, and had even for some weeks given shelter to the Marquis de la Guiche.

De Batz went up to his former friend, and taking him by the hand expressed his pleasure at seeing him, and asked where they could meet. Klotz held the baron's hands, and turned to some disreputable-looking men who were at some distance from him :

" Arrest this man," he cried ; it is the Baron de Batz."

The indignant baron flung himself at the villain's throat, threw him in the gutter, and kicked him in the face. The bewildered police stood stock-still in their amazement.

M. de Batz soon recovered his equanimity, and saw the extreme and urgent danger he was in. He walked rapidly towards the boulevard, while Klotz, without rising, cried : *Murder ! Stop the murderer !* as did also his assistants.

This reiterated cry brought all the people to their doors and windows : they saw one man lying in the mud and another running away, and they all joined in the cry : *Stop the murderer !*

M. de Batz, being swifter of foot than his pursuers, was escaping from them, when unluckily a patrol of dragoons who were passing along the boulevard closed the end of the

Rue de Choiseul and surrounded the fugitive, who was led off to the Police Committee of the Convention. . . . He had upon his person papers that must infallibly prove his death-warrant : of this fact the reader will have no doubt when he learns that M. de Batz, during the preceding days, had drawn up some manifestoes which painted the Convention in its true colours : he had also sketched the design of the Central Committee, and even the messages that were to be sent to the Vendeans, entrusting them with the prompt recall of the Bourbons. Now, all these fatal papers were on him, and in accordance with custom the first order to be given would be : " *Search this citizen.*" [1]

So at last de Batz fell into the hands of the Committee that had been his implacable enemy for two years ! This elusive man, who had slipped through the fingers of Robespierre's cleverest agents, and had successfully baffled detectives such as Héron and Rousseville, had now, so to speak, delivered himself up.

The exultant Klotz accompanied his captive to the Tuileries. He wished to reserve for himself all the profits of his treacherous action—for he knew that a very high price had been at one time set upon the baron's head— and he therefore left the detectives at the door, and went on alone with his prisoner into the ante-room of the Committee. There, in his haste to report the good news to the commissioners, who were sitting in permanence, he left his prisoner in charge of a few gendarmes.

De Batz, still trembling with rage, threw himself upon a seat. The gendarmes, who were unaware of the prisoner's importance, walked about the room and paid no attention to him. None the less it was impossible to escape : if he had made the slightest movement in the direction of the door he would have been thrown to the ground, and

[1] Unpublished narrative of de Batz.

seized, and bound. After sitting in an armchair for a few moments and looking about him with eyes that darted fire, he rose and walked angrily to and fro with his arms crossed upon his breast, awaiting the moment when he should be summoned before the Committee.

The door opened: Gauthier (of l'Ain) appeared, followed by Klotz. Gauthier was one of the commissioners of the Convention, and had formerly been a member of the Constituent Assembly, in which the Baron de Batz was his colleague. He therefore recognised him at once.

"So we have got you at last!" he cried. "Let us see what papers you have."

"I have no papers on me," answered de Batz steadily.[1]

Gauthier turned to the gendarmes:

"Search him!" he ordered.

The Baron de Batz submitted with a good grace to the gendarmes' investigations. They thrust their hands into the pockets of his cloak and of his coat, and found—nothing!

They unbuttoned his jacket and waistcoat and felt all over his shirt: they searched him from head to foot, and found—nothing!

It was plain that there were no papers of any description upon de Batz.

We will not conceal from the reader that the prisoner had taken advantage of the brief absence of Klotz to slip the compromising papers that he had upon his person beneath the cushion of the arm-chair into which he had thrown himself. The fatal packet might have been found at any moment, but, by a miracle of good fortune, no one discovered his expedient. De Batz—who only tells as much as he chooses—declares that he never knew " to what good soul or chance he owed this extraordinary circumstance."

After a short examination he was taken to the prison

[1] Unpublished narrative of de Batz.

of the Orties, which was quite close to the Committee Room. There he was closely confined. A few days later he was transferred to the Plessis.[1] In this celebrated house of detention the regulations had never been very strict, even at the height of the Terror : the prisoners were allowed to receive visitors and lived in comparative freedom. De Batz took advantage of these conditions to keep himself posted in the course of events. He learnt, through trustworthy friends, that his trial was being postponed in order to make his execution more impressive : that the Conventionists desired before their dissolution to punish him, with due solemnity, as the representative of all the conspiracies to which they attributed their past discords and their present humiliation.

A few days later he was informed that a reaction was taking place : the majority asked for nothing but reconciliation and peace. For no one knew of the part played by de Batz in the insurrection of Vendémiaire, and it was considered useless to revive worn-out passions by bringing this man to trial—this man who, after all, had been Robespierre's opponent. Would it not be better to let him lie forgotten in his prison?

De Batz thought otherwise : he demanded to be tried or set at liberty. He made no secret of the fact that he wished to have an opportunity at last of refuting all the accusations that had been brought against him during the past two years. He promised to reveal the truth with regard to his alleged crimes, and to show how many impostures and murderous atrocities had sheltered themselves behind the name of the Foreign Conspiracy.

The Convention would have none of his revelations at any price. It was afraid of this enemy, who still defied and threatened it from his prison-cell.

[1] Archives of the Prefecture of Police.

VENDÉMIAIRE

As soon as de Batz was quite convinced that the Committees dared not face the exposure of a public debate his demands for a trial before the Tribunal became incessant. As his appeals received no answer he despatched an usher—yes, actually an usher!—to the Convention, to lay before that body his formal demand for a trial, and to call its attention to the law on which he founded his demand.

This audacious challenge was entirely successful. The Committee summoned de Batz and examined him. But the terrible man had an answer for everything : he made so brave a fight, and showed such a profound knowledge of his subject, that his questioners longed to be rid of him. He was therefore set at liberty, though for the sake of appearances he was placed in charge of a gendarme, on whom discretion was especially enjoined. It was a futile precaution : de Batz employed such convincing arguments that, on that very evening, the gendarme was relieved of his duties.

But, indeed, the political barometer was indicating *set fair*. It was at this time that the Comte de Castellane, who had been sentenced to death for default, remained in Paris none the less, and was even rash enough to appear in public. Being met one evening by a patrol, he answered their cry of *Qui vive ? :*

" *Parbleau !* it is I, Castellane, defaulter ! "

" Pass, friend," was the reply.

On the 4th Brumaire (26th October) the Convention held its last sitting. The Decree that it passed that day is perhaps, of all its innumerable Decrees, the only one that is still in force to-day. Prompted by some feeling of remorse, it decided that the *Place de la Révolution*—the spot that it had inundated with blood—should for the future be known as the *Place de la Concorde*.

Then, amid profound silence, Génissieux, the president, rose, and in a solemn voice pronounced these words:

"The National Convention declares that its mission is fulfilled, and that its session is at an end."

The hour was half past two. The terrible Assembly had sat, without a single day's intermission, for three years and four months. One man, and only one, had opposed it from first to last: one man, and only one, was engaged in a hand-to-hand fight with it to the very end, without ever losing courage or relaxing in his efforts—the man whose story we have tried to tell. At last he saw the complete and final defeat of the portentous power that he had so often attacked: of the many who had entered the arena of the Revolution, he was one of the few survivors: he had seen all his fellow-conspirators and all his enemies fall dead at his side; and he stood there unharmed, almost triumphant, indeed, since he could almost dream that he had been victorious in his duel with the all-powerful Assembly. And now he had seen its miserable end; and by a strange irony of fate, the final struggle had produced the man who was destined to profit by all the bloodshed and suffering of the past years.

De Batz had dedicated his life to the destruction of the Convention and the restoration of the Monarchy. His end was attained: the Convention was destroyed and Monarchy was about to be restored. It was to be restored, however, in the person of the thin, fragile young man who had entered the lists as though by chance. And if this story have a moral it is this: the boldest heroes are after all mere tools in the hands of a mysterious force, which does with them what it will: all their actions, though they do not know it, are but acts of obedience. This is a thought that may well humble the pride of man—the blind and ignorant pygmy who struggles in the guiding hand of God.

APPENDIX

With the events of Vendémiaire the Revolution may be said to end. The period of the Directory was merely an interlude that gave Napoleon time to grow : as soon as he came upon the scene he occupied the whole stage. But we need not, therefore, believe that the Baron de Batz gave up conspiring : that would have been contrary to his nature. It is at all events certain that, until 1804, when the execution of the Duc d'Enghien destroyed the last hopes of the royalists, Louis XVIII continued to employ secret agents in France, in the belief that Buonaparte had a vocation for the rôle of Monk. When the establishment of the Empire robbed the partisans of the legitimate Monarchy of their last illusions the Baron de Batz retired from the field. Whether he remained in France or went abroad we do not know ; for after the events of Vendémiaire we lose sight of him entirely.

In order, however, that we may follow him to the end of his eventful career, we will give, in chronological order, all the facts we can glean from the Archives of the War Office relating to his life during the Restoration.

On the return of the King in 1814 he was made a Knight of Saint Louis (on the 17th September). At this time a Commission of émigrés and retired officers of the army was appointed to hear, classify, and investigate the grievances of such of the Bourbons' faithful followers as had been ruined by the Revolution. This Commission drew up a short report on each person who asked for a post. Under the name of the Baron de Batz there is a fairly long note, recalling his eminent services and ending thus : "The Commission thinks it right to do more than merely establish the claim of M. de Batz to the rank of field-marshal ; and begs his Excellency the Minister of War to call his Majesty's attention to the services of this field-officer, who deserves some special mark of distinction for his devotion, zeal, and great qualities, of which he has given abundant proof."

The Marshal de Viomesnil added a postscript to the effect that the Commission, being restricted in its powers, regretted that it was unable to state plainly that the distinction it asked for was the Order of St. Louis.

Consequently the Baron de Batz, whose services in Condé's army had come to an end on the 31st December, 1800, was promoted by order of the King on the 18th March, 1815, to the rank of field-marshal, to date from the 20th March, 1797.

Two days later Napoleon returned to the Tuileries, and Louis XVIII was again in exile.

De Batz probably followed the King to Ghent, for we see that, when the Minister of War asked the Commission of Émigrés for a list of the officers of every rank who could be most suitably employed against the usurper, the name of the Baron de Batz headed the list. No doubt he made himself useful, for on the 2nd November, 1815 his promotion to the rank of field-marshal was confirmed. He at once asked to be employed in that capacity, and on the 9th March, 1816, was given the command of the Department of the Cantal, to date from March 29th, 1812. In the course of these events he had married.

On the 17th May, 1816, the general in command of the XIXth military division wrote to the Minister of War : "I have heard a great deal said, I must confess, against the vacillating character of M. le Baron de Batz, who appears to be of the nature of a weather-cock. It is for your Excellency's wisdom to decide whether, circumstances being what they are, it would not be advisable to have really trustworthy authorities in the Cantal, since they are a long way from my own eye."

De Batz, it must be said, though promoted on the 9th March, as we have seen, had remained in Paris (he was living at 21, Rue de la Michodière), and on the 1st August had not yet taken up his duties. The Minister of War ordered him rather curtly to do so or to resign his commission. He set off at once, and arrived at Aurillac on the 4th August.

In April, 1817, he returned to Paris, on the pretext of an important lawsuit. He remained there—without permission—till the 13th November. On that date he was removed from his post and put on half-pay. The authorities did not know where to find him to inform him of this decision ; they were obliged to enlist the services of the police, who found him at last in the Rue de la Chaussée d'Antin, at No. 34. On the 30th December, 1818, his name was placed on the retired list : in 1820 he begged in vain

APPENDIX

that it should be restored to the active list, in consideration of the great services he had rendered to the royal cause.

He then retired to his estate at Chadieu, in Puy-de-Dôme—the estate that he bought under an assumed name when the Terror was at its height.

He died there on the 10th January, 1822—of apoplexy, says Eckard.

Is this true? It is still believed at Authezat, where the Château de Chadieu is situated, that the death of the Baron de Batz was less natural and more in harmony with his eventful life. We have had the privilege of questioning those who lived for many years in the company of Mme. la Baronne de Batz, who only died in 1855. To tell the truth, local tradition is not complimentary to our hero. He is described as a brutal, unscrupulous, impecunious adventurer, who oppressed the peasantry, and was named by them, in revenge, *the robber*.

We were even assured that he was actually guilty of forgery; but with regard to this point we have no means of ascertaining the truth. It is said that, early in January, 1822, Louis XVIII sent a messenger to Chadieu to inform de Batz that the King was aware of his disgraceful conduct, and was determined not to interfere with the course of justice in the matter of the forgery; but that, in order to save the honour of one of the most devoted servants of the Monarchy, the baron would be allowed twenty-four hours, in case he wished to escape arrest by taking his own life. On the following day, says the story, he was found dead in a summer-house in the park of Chadieu. He was not buried in the consecrated ground of the cemetery, but at the roadside. The peasants who were at the funeral did not hesitate to say, with a laugh, that the baron had certainly crossed the frontier, and that there was nothing in the coffin but stones and sand. But when the coffin was dug up, thirty years later, to be removed to the cemetery, it was seen that this tale was an invention.

We need hardly add that we only give these stories for what they are worth. There is no historical document to support the tradition; and the rural population with whom it originated regarded the Restoration with disfavour, and, owing to the baron's brutal ways, was not inclined to treat him with indulgence.

INDEX

277

INDEX

INDEX

279

INDEX

Chevaliers du Poignard, 145 *and note* 4, 215 *note* 1.
Choisy, village of, 2–3.
Chouans, 252.
Chrétien, 23 *note* 1, 61, 215 *note* 1.
Children, natural, Chabot's speech, 54.
Cis-revolutionaries, 155.
Clément, 79,
Clootz, Anacharsis, 121, 155.
Clothilde, 213–14, 216, 233–34, 237 *note* 1.
Coblenz, 14,
Coburg, Marshal von, 24–25, 54, 148.
Coigny, Duc de, 13, 132.
Comédie, the, 208.
Commandeur, Le, postillion, 132.
Commission of Émigrés 274.
Committee of General Security, 48, 51, 58, 59, 91, 105, 127, 132, 138, 139, 149, 152, 165, 172, 182, 196, 266 ; confederates of de Batz among, 59, 80 ; Chabot's proposal to, 124–26 ; search of Charonne, 134–35 ; news of the conspiracy, 143–50 ; denuncia- of the Sainte-Amaranthes, 215, *and note* 1–17.
Committee of Public Safety—
20, 39, 53, 83, 124, 139, 148, 175, 196, 197, 266 ; memoranda sent to Fouquier-Tinville, 203.
Committees, Revolutionary, elec- tion of, 58.
Committees, United, of Public Safety and General Security, 153.
Commune, the, 110, 255—
Arrangements for Louis' death, 7 ; and Simon, 23–24 ; destruc- tion of archives, 247 *and note* 1.
Compiègne, 173.
Comte, merchant, 196, 220.
Conciergerie, the, 179, 183, 191, 192 197, 203, 220, 221, 227, 247.
Condé, army of, 274.
Constand, gendarme, 128–30, 168, 193.
Constituent Assembly, the, 14, 111, 257, 269.
Conti, Prince de, 207.
Convention, the, 4, 12, 30, 41, 51, 56, 225, 230, 268, 270.
Intentions regarding the Royal

Family, 24 ; designs of de Batz concerning, 59, 89, 152–53 ; Chabot's speech, 55 ; confeder- ates of de Batz in, 80–81 ; the commission on the India Company's bill, 95 ; the speech of Philippeaux, 112–13 ; Chabot's reply, 113–15 ; submission to Dufourny, 117–18 ; deputations from the Commune of Franciade, 117, 118 ; the deputation of the Gravilliers 118 ; the conspiracy to destroy, 143–150 ; reception of Amar's report, 153–54 ; Robespierre's change of policy, 241 ; and the Lepéletier Section, 254–56 ; the events of Vendé- miaire, 256–272 ; dissolution, 272.
Cordeliers, the, 147.
Cornet, Commissioner, 129.
Cortel, Citizen, 44.
Cortey, Captain, 11, 18, 21–24, 61–63, 71–74, 165, 166, 168, 193, 198, 203, 244.
Caste, his restaurant, 136.
Courtille, La, Barracks of, 133.
Couthon, 186.

Dangé, 223.
Danican, M, 261.
Danjou, Citizen, 240–41.
Danton—
The India Company, 90 ; rela- tions with Fabre, 99, 100 ; policy, 152, death, 155 ; trial of the Dantonists, 160–65 ; *men- tioned*, 28, 36, 37, 52, 81 *and note* 2, 82, 110, 114, 139, 146, 160, 202, 218.
Dauphin, the, 251.
David, 91, 139, 162.
Debrouse, Hospice, 65.
Declaration of the Rights of Man, 118.
Deforgues, 39.
Delaboge, Marie, 12 *note* 3.
Delaporte, Rev., *cited*, 17 *note* 1.
Delaunay—
Relations with de Batz, 27–28, 30, 31 *note* 1, 45, 81 *and note* 2 ; interview with Chabot, 50–54 ; his speech against the India

280

INDEX

Company, 88, 93–95, 105; arrest, 127; imprisonment, 140, 141; and Fabre, 149; *mentioned*, 125, 154, 160, 161, 249.

Delcher, 172.

Delessert, 90 *note* 1.

Delorme, 134.

Dématin, Citoyenne, 180.

Demi-Castors, 237 *note* 1.

Denis, St., relics of, 117–18.

Deresmont, Catiche, 97 *and note* 1, 100 *note* 1.

Desardier. *See* Lézardière, Robert de la.

Desardy, Citizen, 72.

Désessarts, *quoted*, 29 *note* 1, 30 *note* 1.

Desfieux, 36, 214, 215 *note* 1.

Desforges, 66.

Deshayes, merchant, 196, 220, 232.

Desjardins, 38.

Desmier, Eléanore, 206 *note* 1.

Desmoulins, Camille, 100, 126 *note* 1, 147, 152, 155, 160, 163, 164.

Despomelles, Chevalier, 252.

Devaux, gendarme, the escape of Biret, 78–80, 80 *note* 2.

Devaux, Jean L. M.—
Loyalty, 6–7, 8 *note* 1, 18; letter by, 85 *and note* 1; the offer from the Committee of Public Safety, 197; the interrogatory, 198–99; *mentioned*, 168, 194, 248.

Didier, deposition of, 182.

Diederichsen, advocate, 160–62.

Dillon, 84.

Directory, the, 251, 254, 273.

Dominicans, the, 59 *note* 1.

Dubiez (Houdart), 169.

Dubocage, *La Borgnesse*, 96.

Dubuisson, 215 *note* 1.

Ducange, 169–71.

Duchatelle, 158 *note* 2.

Duchesne, 171.

Ducos, Roger, 230.

Dufils, 175, 179 *note* 1.

Dufourny—
Attack on Bazire and Chabot, 54, 56, 115–17, 121–22, 159 *note* 1; the Jacobin deputation, 119–20.

Duluc, 60 *note* 1.

Dumas, President, 222–25, 226, 227.

Dumouriez—
His pledge, 6; flight of, 24; *mentioned*, 84.

Duplay, 125, 174, 182.

Duplay, Eléonore, 182.

Dupont, 220.

Duverne, de Praile, 252.

ECKARD, correspondence with de Batz, 8 *note* 1, 246.

Églantine, Fabre d'—
His reply to Delaunay's speech, 95; career of, 96–99; children of, 98 *note* 2; friendship with Danton, 99; work, 99; the affair of the India Company, 101–5; the bribe, 123–25; arrest, 149; the charge against, 161–62; *mentioned*, 37, 38, 52, 82, 96, 139, 147, 154, 160.

Egrée, brewer, 196, 220.

Elizabeth, Mme., 152.

Elleviou, Singer, 211, 213–14, 218, 228, 233–34.

Émigrés, the, 14, 16, 252.

Enghien, Duc d', 273.

Épée Royale, the, 77.

Epinal, Roussel d', 100 *note* 1.

Espagnac, Abbe d', 45 *and note* 2, 160, 161.

Esprémesnil, Mme. d', 168, 196.

Estampes, Cabinet des, 64 *note* 1.

FABREFONT (Fabre-Fons), 98, 162.

Favart, Théâtre, 177 *and note* 1, 211, 214.

Fayan, de, 208 *and note* 1.

Fénelon, Abbe de, 240 *note* 1.

Feroussac, Citoyenne, 72.

Feuillants, the, 33, 145 *note* 3.

Feydeau, Théâtre, 259–60, 260 *note* 1.

Figaro, 96.

Filles-Saint-Thomas, section of, loyalty of, 58–59, 59 *notes* 1–2; convent of, 179; events of Vendémiaire, 257–72.

Firmont, Abbé Edgeworth de, 1–4.

INDEX

Flamarens, Comte de, 13 *note* 1.
Fleury, Édouard, "Histoire" *cited*, 12.
Flichy, 119.
Floral Games of Toulouse, 96.
Fons, Jeanne Marie, 98 *note* 2.
Force, La, prison of, 74, 76, 99, 199 *note* 1.
Foreign Conspiracy, the, 151, 160, 186, 200, 225, 270.
Forest, 157.
Formalaguez, 252.
Fouquier-Tinville—
    Reports, 8 *note* 1; letter to, 24 *note* 2; letter from the Committee, 165-66; his plans to catch de Batz, 167; trial of the Sainte-Amaranthes, 220, 222, 223, 225, 228-29, 231-32; the red shirts, 230; *mentioned*, 152, 155, 185, 192, 203, 204.
Fouré, Nicolas, 135.
Franciade, Commune of, deputation to the Convention, 117-18.
François, 135.
Frey, Emmanuel, 33, 35-48, 50-54, 121, 132, 137, 160, 161.
Frey, Junius—
    and Chabot, 32, 33, 50-54, 80; profession of, 34-35; a portrait, 34 *note* 1; removal of the seals, 87; denunciation, 91 *and note* 1; Dufourny's attack on, 121; arrest, 132, 137; *mentioned*, 160, 161.
Frey, Léopoldine—
    "Chabot's Austrian," 57; story of, 91-92; *mentioned*, 43, 87, 104, 106, 116 *note* 1, 120, 121, 137.
Froidure, 203, 223.
Frotté, Comte de, 17 *note* 1.

Gachard, 100 *note* 1.
Garchy, café, 252.
Garnier, coachman, 132.
Garnier-Launay, 222 *and note* 1.
Gauthier, 269.
Génissieux, 272.
Genlis, Mme. de, 208 *note* 1.
Gentilhomme, Citoyenne, 184, 185.

Geoffroy, locksmith, 178.
German soldiers in Paris, 148.
Gervoise, Café, 175.
Ghent, 274.
Girondists, the, 36, 37, 110, 114, 120.
Glandy, 41, 42, 104.
Gobel, 27.
Godin, Marie, Nicolle, 98 *note* 1.
Gonnaz, 76.
Goupilleau, 147.
Goutz, 12 and *note* 2.
Grammont, 78.
Grandmaison, Citoyenne—
    Visit of the patriots to Charonne, 68-74; imprisonment, 74; search of bedrooms, 134-35; release, 156 *and note* 1; death, 231-32; *mentioned*, 15-16, 31, 61, 77, 128, 129, 168, 170, 171, 193, 196, 248.
Grangeneuve, 30.
Gravilliers, section of the, deputation to the Convention, 118.
Grivois, Citoyenne, 61, 170, 171, 196.
Guffroy, 135 *note* 2.
Guiche, Marquis de la—
    Loyalty, 6-7, 18; imprisonment, 74, 76; Devaux's evidence, 199 *and note* 1, 203-4; death, 239; *mentioned*, 61, 71-72, 248, 267.
Gusman, 161, 162.

Hamburg, 33.
Hardaz d'Hauteville, Comte de, 196.
Hébert, 36, 81, 116, 122 *note* 1, 139, 142, 144, 147, 152, 155, 160.
Henriette, 240.
Herbois, Collot d'—
    Attempted assassination, 173-79, 187-88, 223; *mentioned*, 98, 147, 197.
Héron, 268.
    Search of Roussell's rooms, 169-71; arrest of the Renaults, 184 *and note* 1; *quoted* 219.
Hermitage, the, 65-66, 67, 134-35, 201.
Hoffman, merchant, 49.
"Honest Innkeeper," the, 133.
Hospice de l'Évêché, 160.

INDEX

INDEX

INDEX

National Assembly, terms to Louis, 4.
National Debt, 94.
National Gendarmerie, the, 8.
National Guard, the, 8, 18, 169 ; events of the 13th Vendémiaire, 263–72.
National Library, 49 *note* 1, 244.
National Record Office, 11.
National Treasury, 6.
Naury, Medical Officer, 160.
Neuville, Baron Hyde de— *cited*, 4 *note* 1, 5 *note* 1, 8 *note* 1, 18 *note* 1 ; his account of Cortey's attempt to save the Queen, 21–23.
Nice, 172.
Nicolas, 147.
Nick, jailer, 221.
Noailles, Duchesse de, 152.
Noël, 204.
Nôtre Dame de Bonne Nouvelle, 10.

Opera, the, 208.
Orgeville, deputation to the Assembly, 119.
Orléans, Duc d', 163 ; the Château de Bagnolet, 65, 66, 67.
Orties, prison of the, 270.
Ozanne, magistrate, 194.

Palais Égalité, 252.
Palais Royal, 36, 76, 187, 210, 237 *note* 1.
Papillon, Marie, 72 *and note* 3, 73, 74 *note* 1.
Papin, Mlle., 180, 183–84.
Parc de Monceaux, 164.
Paris—
Rising of June 20th, 1792, 14 ; quarries surrounding, 67 ; news of the conspiracy, 143–50 ; Vendémiaire, 239–72 ; famine, 243, 253 ; a picture of the year 1795, 251–52 ; insurrection of Prairial, 251–53.
Passy, 204.
Paumier, merchant, 196.
Payen, Café, 182.
Payot, 132–33.
Pelé, 185.
Péletier, 17 *note* 2, 23 *note* 1.

Pelletier, J. B., 177–78, 179 *note* 1.
Père Duchesne, the, 51.
Péron, 62.
Perrin, Claude, 253.
Petit Luxembourg, the, 144.
Petits-Pères, battalion of, 59 *note* 2.
Peyre, 157.
Philippe et Georgette, 211.
Philippeaux, 147, 160, 162 ; his speech in the Convention, 112–13.
Piédecoq, 132.
Piprel, mayor, 63, 68.
Pitt, 54 ; "Pitt's guineas," 82–84, 110, 201.
Place de la Concorde, 271.
Plessis Prison, the, 60, 270 *and note* 1.
Police, charges against the, 194.
Pomerel, François, 64 *note* 1.
Pons (of Verdun), arrest, 148–49.
Pons, Vicomte de, 196, 204, 207, 208 ; death, 236.
Pont Notre-Dame, 232.
Portebœuf, 194, 233.
Pottier de Lille, 18–19, 61–62, 168, 194.
Prévot, Suzanne, 176 *and note* 1, 179 *note* 1, 185.
Proly, "son of the Austrian Minister," 36, 122, 133, 155, 214, 215 *note* 1.
Provençe, Comte de, 251, 252 *and note* 2.
Public Charity Office, Archives *cited*, 66.

Quarries around Paris, 67.
Quatre Nations, College of, 266.
Queen's Regiment, the, 13–14.

Ramel, 52, 95, 105.
Raulot, 174.
Réal, 261.
Récollets, Prison of, 132.
Red Mass, the, 205–38.
Red Shirts, the, 239.
Redon, constituency of, 60.
Redon, de, loyalty of, 257 *and note* 1, 266.
Regency, the, 31, 65.

285

INDEX

Renaudin, 116.

Rénault, Antoine, 179, 180, 183, 184, 194, 232.

Rénault, Cécile—
Story of, 179–185 ; reason for her action, 186–87, 191–94 ; trial and death, 224, 231, 232, 236.

Renault, Jacques, 179, 181, 183, 184, 194.

Rénault, Mme., 194.

République, Théâtre de la, 99.

Revolutionary Committee of Surveillance, 59, 74, 80.

Revolutionary Tribunal, the 57, 61, 155.
Formula used, 153, 155 ; summary procedure, 222–28, increase of executions, 239–40.

Richard, jailer, 38, 227, 228, 229, 231.

Riding School of the Tuileries, the, 145 *and note* 3.

Rine, Citoyenne, 189.

Riotter, 185.

Rivarol, 208.

Robert, name adopted by Lézardière, 3.

Roblator, jailer, 221.

Robespierre—
his papers 34 *note* 1 ; the India Company, 95 ; Chabot's interview with, 122 *and note* 1–25, 138–39 ; his opinion of the Conspiracy, 150–55 ; the " Foreign Conspiracy," 162, 186 ; speech after the trial of the Dantonists, 165 ; the supposed attempt on his life, 173, 179, 182, 185, 223–24 ; and the Sainte-Amaranthes, 217 *and note* 1 ; fall of, 235 *and note* 2 ; change of policy, 241 ; recognition of de Batz, 248 ; *mentioned*, 28, 36, 44, 90, 110, 114, 270.

Robinet, Dr., *cited*, 8 *note* 1, 100 *note* 1.

Roblot, Claude, 71 *and note* 1, 73, 74 *note* 1.

Roche, Arry La, 85.

Rochefort, village of, 133.

Rodez, School of, 31.

Rohan-Rochefort, Prince de, 133 *and note* 2, 168, 195, 199, 204.

Roland Mme., *cited*, 54, 209, 217, *note* 3.

Rollet, cook, 71 *and note* 2, 74, 74 *note* 1.

Romainville, 135.

Romme, 112.

Ronsin, 155.

Rossay, Comte de Rossay-Fleury, 223.

Rossignol, 147.

Rouarre, 132.

Rouen, 212–13.

Rougeville, attempts to save Marie Antoinette, 46–47 ; flight, 67.

Roussel—
Arrest and examination, 71–76 ; 80 *note* 3 ; fabrication of false assignats, 85–86 ; searching his rooms, 168–71 ; Admiral and, 187 ; *mentioned*, 19, 61, 193, 195, 202, 244, 248.

Rousseville, spy, 144, 268.

Rovère, 110.

Rue Charlot, 21–22.

Rue du Bac, 4.

Saint-Amarand, genealogy of the family, 206 *note* 1.

Sainte-Amaranthe, Émilié de—
her beauty, 205, 208–11 ; love for Elleviou, 211–12 ; Marriage with Sartines, 212 ; reception of the Municipal Officers, 215 ; arrest, 218–21 ; the red scarf 237 *and note* 1–38 ; trial, 222, 225, 228–29 ; death, 229, 231–32, 233, 236.

Sainte-Amaranthe, Lili, 205, 215, 218-21, 225 *and note* 1, 229, 231, 233, 236.

Sainte-Amaranthe, M. de, 206–7.

Sainte-Amaranthe, Mme. 36, 205–8, 212, 215—
her dream, 217 ; arrest, 218–21 ; trial, 225 ; death, 229–36.

Saint-Bartholomew, Church of, 229.

Saint-Denis, 173.

Saint-Fargeau, 59, 208.

Sainte-Germain, Comte de, 13 *note* 1.

Saint-Germain, Commune of, 80.

Saint-Germain-des-Près, 221.